MARRIAGE
and DIVORCE
in CANADA

Edited with an Introduction by
K. ISHWARAN
York University

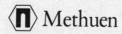 Methuen

Toronto   New York   London   Sydney   Auckland

Canadian Cataloguing in Publication Data

Main entry under title:
Marriage and divorce in Canada

ISBN 0-458-95790-9

1. Marriage - Canada.   2. Divorce - Canada.
I. Ishwaran, K.

HQ560.M37   306.8′1′0971   C82-095263-X

Printed and bound in Canada

1 2 3 4 5   83   88 87 86 85 84

Contents

Preface

I have already published two books—*Childhood and Adolescence in Canada* and *Canadian Families—Ethnic Diversity*. This is the third book in the series.

Since the publication of the first edition of my *Canadian Family* in 1971—the first book of sociological readings on the family forms and functions in Canada—an impressive amount of information, collected and analysed by experts in several subfields of family studies in Canada, has been accumulating. The time, in my view, is now ripe for serious attempts for theory-building, both in specific and generic senses. In the absence of such attempts, the future of family studies in Canada is going to generate nothing more than an unorganized pile of unconnected empirical studies. Such attempts, if they are to prove useful and interesting, must carefully avoid the presupposition that the family forms and functions in the United States and Canada are basically the same and that, therefore, it is pointless to think in terms of anything like a unique set of theories relevant to the Canadian context. The questions of similarity and difference are both conceptual and data-based. We now have enough data for thoughtful comparisons and for the required growth of awareness that conceptual issues, located in the tasks of theory-building, must begin to receive adequate attention from the scholars interested in the Canadian contexts of the family.

I am indebted to our contributors for writing new material, expressly for this volume. My indebtedness is also due to my former colleague and friend, Dr. K. Raghavendra Rao, Dharwar, India, for his thoughtful comments.

In addition, I wish to record my appreciation to the Secretarial Services Division of York University for their support in preparing this volume.

K. ISHWARAN

Part I

Introduction: Perspectives on Marriage and Divorce

K. Ishwaran

Throughout human history, one of the institutions that has persisted, in some form or other, is the family. However, sociological theorists cannot establish a universal paradigm except through a systematic examination of the data relating to specific historical and concrete experience. Yet, without a dialectical and reciprocal interplay between the universal and the historical-contingent, it would be difficult to construct meaningful theoretical structures. From the universal perspective, it seems indisputable that the family, whatever other functions it may have acquired in specific circumstances, has performed two minimal functions for most societies. The first is the social-survival function of perpetuating biologically a given society. This is the family's function of socially approved reproduction, for reproduction outside the family in virtually every society has carried social stigma and penalty. Unlike the case of non-human populations, human populations are not strictly structured and perpetuated by merely biological processes. There is always social mediation to a significant extent.

The second function that the family has performed, has been, and has continued to be the function of socializing the young into a whole set of behavioural patterns, attitudinal configurations, and value-preferences. This second function is also a reproductive function in the sense that it involves ideological stability and persistence as a central process of social life. The family has the dual function of ensuring biological and cultural survival for human beings both as individuals and as social groups.

1

If the survival and identity of a society is so clearly and significantly dependent on the family, it is no less true that the family, in its turn, takes its structure and texture from its specific social milieu. Rightly regarding the family as a key social institution, societies take elaborate care, interest, and precaution to control the structure and functioning of the family. It is not surprising, therefore, that societies generate and sustain detailed rules and norms to regulate various aspects of family life. In doing so, they may employ informal methods and devices as well as the instrumentality of formal law. Such regulatory patterns related not only to the working of the family itself, to such matters as intrafamily relationships, biological reproduction, and child-rearing, but also to other supportive and related institutions and processes like courtship and marriage.

Marriage and the family are so inextricably intertwined as social institutions that it is not meaningful to refer to one of them independently of the other. Indeed, marriage is a prelude to, and foundation for, family life, just as courtship constitutes a process culminating in marriage. The specifics of the marital process, as well as of family life, have been variable as between different societies, spatially separated, and for the same society as between different historical points. With changes in the material basis and the ideological superstructure of a society, concomitant changes emerge in the structure and functioning of the family and the marital and courtship patterns.

Since society is a somewhat general and all-encompassing category, one must reach down to the narrower and more immediately relevant contexts of the marital system and the family. Such factors as class, geography, religion, and ethnicity, either singly or, more usually, in complex, interactive arrangements, exert profound influence on the marriage system and family life.[1]

As a major focal institutional element in the society, marriage has naturally become an object of considerable innovative action by societies throughout history. For instance, to cite a recent innovation in the western industrial nations, dating has emerged as an institution designed to perform the function of promoting marital relationships structured around personal lives. As a social-institutional innovation that has surfaced since the Second World War, it has enabled young people to enter into marital relationships and family relationships, geared to the modern social values and norms of individual choice and romantic love.[2] Counter to this development, factors such as ethnicity, race, religion, and class have operated to set the parameters within which the new marital pattern finds itself. The process of establishing the suitability of marital partners is controlled by the family and eventually, of course, the wider social order. The "filter theory" accounts for the manner in which cultural determinants act as filters through which marriage partners are carefully selected. Marital eligibility is a strictly socially governed and legitimized qualification for potential marital partners.[3] The freedom exercised by modern men and women comes to be institutionalized and socially regulated by a set of cultural determinants in the interest of the stability and continuity of the social order. However, over a period of time, societies are characterized by changes in their socio-cultural patterns and institutional arrangements. A society's central institutions, such as the family or marriage, are especially subject to the impact of the contradictory needs for continuity and dynamism. In fact, the historical resilience and durability of societies depend on their capacity to contain and resolve the tensions and conflicts engendered by this impact.

Marriage and Family: The Theoretical Perspective

The Canadian data, as well as the American data, suggest that marriage is a very popular institution that plays an important role in the lives of individuals and groups. Therefore, a fundamental question in these societies, from a sociological approach, concerns the significance and functionality of marriage and the family. Three theoretical paradigms have dominated the sociological understanding of marriage and the family. The first paradigm characterizes marriage as a sacred and religious act, and thus both marriage and the family are regarded as phenomena outside conscious human choice, being divine in origin. The second paradigm, which is secular, invests marriage and the family with overriding social necessity and teleology. From this standpoint, marriage and family become socially determined structures, brought into existence by the larger social system as well as its constituent units such as the kingroup or the ethnic or the religious group in order to meet their individual and group needs, serving as an institutional resource to enable them to handle their life situations and problems. The third paradigm is an individualistic one, which views marriage and family as institutional arrangements, primarily oriented towards individual choices and predilections.

But these three are abstract and theoretical paradigms which sociology has developed to impose order on overwhelming empirical data and to identify sociologically meaningful structures. In concrete terms, none of these paradigms exists anywhere in purity and isolation. In fact, marriage and family, as empirical and concrete entities, display a wide range of structural and functional variations, combining in different proportions of quality and quantity the features and elements belonging to the three theoretical paradigms.[4]

Both individual commitment and religious sanction in respect of marital patterns and family forms have been mediated through explicit social semantics and institutionalization in all societies.[5] A further complication relating to any analysis and understanding of this institutional complex are the cross-cultural variations, as well as diachronic variations within a single historical society. This has led to considerable confusion about social and legal definitions of concerned institutions—marriage, family, and kinship. This is as much an issue of sociological theory as of social living.

Even the basic term "marriage" has been conceptualized both empirically and normatively in a number of ways. Christensen views marriage as a social institution, drawing together men and women as a prelude to family life.[6] Burgess et al. have made a conceptual distinction between marriage as a socio-cultural institution and the biological process of sexual stratification.[7] Marriage, in this view, is a socially structured and culturally legitimated heterosexual union, whether polyandrous (one wife for more than one husband) or polygamous (one husband for more than one wife). This entails clear institutional roles for husband and wife, to whom a society attaches specific duties, rights, and functions.

According to yet another definition, marriage consists of certain features, such as socially legitimated sex relationships between men and women (comprising both normative and legal aspects), a public declaration of producing and raising a family, and an interpersonal relationship with some degree of durability, based on a contractual system of mutual rights and obligations, socially and legally observed, as between spouses and between parents and children.[8] Reiss emphasizes, in his more universal perspective, the causal interrelationship between courtship, marriage, and family.[9] Following Eshleman, the constituent elements of marriage may be identified as:heterosexuality, involving at least one male and one female; socially approved and legitimated process of mating and reproduction; the public character of the marital relationship's mutuality of obligations towards, and claims on, spouses; and some degree of bindingness and continuity in relationships.[10]

The Marital Process and Its Dynamics

In a modern society, such as in Canada, no institution can survive unless it has potentialities for dynamism, creative adaptability, and flexibility. This is most true of society's central institutions such as marriage and family. Marriage, therefore, as an institutionalized process, involves an internal dynamic of its own. The key question to be raised in this context is: What are the modalities and motivational bases of marriage as a social process? Understanding the marital process as dynamic amounts to examining how and why individuals choose their marital partners. In addition, there are follow-up questions regarding the interactive behaviour of the spouses within a marital framework, and the psychological, pragmatic-instrumental, and ideological factors that support such behaviour.

The Canadian marital process and its dynamics may be meaningfully analysed in the context of the foregoing questions. Such an analysis can gain from a comparative perspective, involving particularly American data. Increasingly, and more particularly since the Second World War, the North American marriage system has been individualized, that is, shaped by a significant degree of individual initiative and free choice of marital partners. One meaningful way in which this situation can be conceptualized is to hold that marital arrangements are increasingly dominated by the ideal of romantic love—the ideal that assumes that a marital relationship should be rooted in the spontaneous emotional attraction and attachment between the marital partners. To use a non-technical vocabulary, a marriage is regarded as most desirable when it is the end-product of a romantic and emotional event referred to as "falling in love." Thus marriage and family have been increasingly defined in terms of what are called love relationships.[11] The North American institution of dating reflects this idea of mate selection in which the theme of love is dominant. But the course of love does not run smooth, and ideals, apart, the Canadian marital process is a good deal more circumscribed by considerations other than the emotion of love.

Mate Selection

The process of marriage begins logically with the process of mate selection. The modality and form of mate selection represent and reflect the same normative and empirical considerations as those involved later in the marital process. There is, thus, a close interdependence between mate selection and the marital process. The social values and behavioural patterns that characterize the married life are a structural continuation of the values and behavioural patterns that define the mate-selection process. Hence, different societies develop different patterns of mate selection.

At one end of the spectrum there are the patterns developed by the traditional societies in Africa, Asia, Latin America, and the Middle East, and at the other end there are the patterns found in modern industrialized societies in Europe and North America. In the former pattern, the kingroup and the family of the marital partners play a relatively major role in the process of mate selection. In the latter, the personal wishes of the partners play a comparatively more significant role. From this, however, it would be unreasonable to infer that the two clusters of mate selection patterns constitute conceptual and empirical polarities; and this is because neither of the patterns, traditional or modern, excludes elements, components, and features belonging to the other. The relationship between the two is not antithetical and mutually exclusive but creates a continuum.[12] To cite a striking illustration, the Canadian pattern, a predominantly modern one, manages to work out a balance between the modern norms of romantic love and individual freedom and the more traditional values of family solidarity and ethnic and/or religious identity. This is true, for instance, for such ethnic groups as the French Canadians, Italians, and Greeks.

Both socio-psychological and structural factors go into the determination of the mate-selection process. Structural factors identified in this connection have been: proximity, religion, class, race, and ethnicity. The socio-psychological factors relate to the personal need for psychological and/or physical gratification. These factors, however, operate within the limits set by the structural factors.[13] The socio-psychological aspect of mate selection centres on complementarity of needs, in the sense that each partner seeks in the other what he or she needs and does not possess, but finds or hopes to find in the other partner. But complementarity itself presupposes an initial situation of similarity between the eligibles. Thus, mating, as a psychological and social act, implies both similarity and dissimilarity between the partners. The structural factors constitute the aspect of similarity, while the socio-psychological factors refer to complementary dissimilarity. This theoretical position has come under scrutiny recently.[14]

In Canada, romantic love does not affect the mate selection process in isolation but in conjunction with other structural variables, such as religion, propinquity, ethnicity, race, and class. In 1970 as many as 84.6% of the Jewish community, 79.5% of the Catholic, and 77.3% of the Protestant contracted marriage within the community.[15] The overall demographic number for religious endogamy for the entire Canadian population during 1975 has been estimated at 61%. The statistical data for the ethnic factor is equally revealing. For the same year, with the lone exception of Scandinavians, those of the different ethnics who married within their own group ranged from 52% to 92%.[16] Next to religion and ethnicity, the most significant factor was geographical proximity, which implied not merely spatial closeness but also shared in a common socio-cultural matrix. Nonetheless, this pattern, however circumscribed by structural factors, is far removed from the traditional process of arranged marriage, in which the individual's parents or kinship community play a decisive role. The purpose of marriage in the perspective differs radically from the one postulated for marriages based on substantial personal choice. While in the arranged marriage, the purpose of marriage may be material or non-material interests of the family, the kingroup, and the wider community; in the latter it may be romantic love, companionship, need for progeny, or simple sex gratification.[17]

Ethnicity in Mate Selection

In Canada, as in the United States, multi-ethnicity influences the mate-selection process in a significant manner. It is the most powerful among the structural factors involved in the marital process. Some of the papers in this volume reveal the significant role of ethnicity in mate selection.

Using the concept of propensity for intermarriage, Kalbach works out the propensity ratios for the various ethnic groups at two points of time, 1961 and 1971. Further, he suggests that these ratios may be used to measure the decline of ethnicity and the degree of assimilation into the mainstream of Canadian society. He finds significant variations between the ethnic communities and between the provinces. For instance, native-born men from the Jewish group revealed the lowest propensity to intermarry, while those with a Scandinavian origin registered the highest propensity for intermarriage. The propensity ratio for the twelve ethnic groups that were examined showed a ranking order which remained substantially intact between the years 1961 and 1971. However, these interesting figures and findings notwithstanding, ethnicity still dominates the marital process in Canada.

Driedger, in a comparative study of a sample of University of Manitoba students belonging to seven ethnic groups (British, French, German, Ukrainian, Polish, Scandinavian, and Jewish), focussed on dating and mating behaviour. He found that the Jewish students were more oriented towards "a more closed traditional orderly replacement system," while the Scandinavian students tended more towards "the more open universal availability mode." Looking at the situation from the parental perspective, Chimbos explains that the Dutch were most favourable to interethnic marriages, while the Greeks remained the most resistant. Probing further, he argues that more than mere ethnicity is involved in the situation—factors such as educational level, rural-urban backgrounds in the home country, sex, and age at the time of immigration are important.

Dating. The end of mate selection is an intended change in the status of the individuals concerned from being "single" to being "married." When the mate selection is examined in terms of its specifics, it becomes comparable to game-playing, with its rules, targets, tactical manoeuvres, strategic designs, advances, retreats, moves, and countermoves.[18] But there may be more than one kind of game being played, one by the male and another by the female, leading to a very complicated process of games-within-games and games-against-games.[19] This accounts for the stress on dating as a crucial phase of the mate-selection process. Dating is a concomitant of the North American ideological and normative concern with individuality and free choice. It represents an institutional innovation responding to the changing nature of the family in the mate-selection process and the demand by individuals to exercise free choice.

Dating is a multi-functional process, in which at least four functions may be identified: 1) recreational, providing immediate entertainment to participants; 2) a mode of socialization in which members of different sexes imbibe the skills for handling interpersonal interaction; 3) a status game in which individual status may be enhanced by dating with persons scoring high in the peer-group system of status and prestige; and 4) courtship, leading to the gaining of a marital mate.[20] Depending upon which aspect is operative in a given situation, dating evokes appropriate behavioural responses— immediate gratification, attentive absorption and learning, serious one-upmanship (or one-upwomanship), and a serious quest for a spouse. Each aspect invokes a corresponding role.

Theoretical attempts have been made to place dating cases along a continuum, from the merely expressive to the instrumental-pragmatic.[21] The degree of seriousness and personal involvement is related to the type of role intended to be played out. Furthermore, dating takes place in the context of cross-purpose between the participants.[22] As the dating game proceeds, the serious and the committed are shifted, a process of elimination operates, and the stage is set for the serious business of marriage. At this point, the more "nitty-gritty" issues like financial resources enter into the calculation.

The Role of Sex

In understanding the marital process and its dynamics, sex attitudes and sex behaviour occupy a crucial place. The social sciences have contributed significantly to a theoretical understanding of the role of sex in the marital process. In the domain of social psychology, the most notable contributions have been interaction theory, reference group theory, and exchange theory. In sociology, structural-functionalism provides the main theoretical resource. The interaction theorists rely on a common and general principle of interactive relationships to account for all relational phenomena, including sexual relationships.[23]

They hold that, while some interpersonal relationships lead to co-operation and fulfilment, there are others leading to frustration, tension, and hostility. This paradigm extends to sexual relationships as well. These relationships, however, function within a normative and ideological framework.

Briefly, the reference group theory maintains that the behaviour of persons tends to be modelled after the norms, values, and expectations prevailing in the group or groups that they hold in great esteem. An adolescent may take as a reference group his or her playmates or schoolmates, in protest against the parental models. For the young, the peer group invariably constitutes a significant reference group. The axiological and behavioural standards of the reference group determine one's own pattern of value preferences and attitudes. If they are conservative and church-oriented, the youth tend to develop a non-permissive culture.[24]

The exchange theory is based on the assumption that all social relationships, the sexual included, partake of the nature of an exchange. A relationship involves an exchange transaction in which, in the fashion of market behaviour, each person involved acts in such a way as to maximize benefits and cut down costs. This model has been applied to the analysis of dating behaviour. On one campus, a competition existed for dating "the Campus Queen"—each competitor sought the maximum rewards which took the form of recreation and affection.[25]

The structural-functionalist theory postulates that the parts of a system are interdependent in the sense that any part of it has consequences for other parts and aspects of the system. The parts and institutions comprising the social system are conceptualized in functional terms, that is, as performing identifiable functions for the system. The behavioural norms characterizing premarital sexual activity have specific functional consequences for the family or the kingroup. The stress on virginity at the time of marriage in certain societies is functionally related to the preservation of the central role of the kinship community, especially its property system. Thus societies with an arranged marriage institution prescribe the norm of premarital chastity. In societies where mate selection is predicated on some measure of free choice, premarital sexual relations assume social acceptance.[26]

According to the functionalist view, the level of premarital sexual permissiveness increases directly in proportion to the degree of freedom from the family influence enjoyed by individuals during courtship, and it correlates positively with the wider norms of the society with regard to premarital sexual permissiveness.[27] It has also been suggested that sexual permissiveness is an outcome of an interplay between a variety of factors, such as individual predilections, reference group, personal liberty, and the perception of the level of sexual permissiveness in membership groups.[28] Further, the structural-functionalists have advanced the view that cultural norms, especially as functioning value preferences, play a significant role in determining the nature and degree of premarital sexual permissiveness. In non-permissive societies, promiscuousness produces serious negative results, because it involves behaviour in contradiction to the prevailing norm.[29]

Premarital Sex in Canada

Since research on premarital sexual relationships in Canada is confined to student samples, it suffers from a major limitation. Mann's two of the four studies on premarital sex are of relevance here.[30] The first involved 60 female students at York University and 40 female students at Western University in 1965, and the other involved 93 male students at York and 80 male students at Western in 1969. The research was designed to determine the degree of sexual intimacy among the students. For the male sample, 50% at York and 35% at Western admitted to sexual intercourse; and for the female sample as a whole, 37% had experienced sexual intercourse. Some of the causes promoting pre-marital sexual relationships identified in these studies are: age, laxity in church attendance, impact of city life, being away from home, abnormal and unhappy family backgrounds.

In a survey of 156 students, carried out during 1970-71, Perlman found that, among the students interviewed, 67% of the males and 60% of the females were involved in sexual intercourse, and, of these, 65% of the males and 53% of the females said they were in love. While 55% of male and 42% of female respondents agreed to coitus if the partners were affectionate, 20% males and 13% females accepted coitus even in the absence of any affection.[31]

In a wider-based and more representative study in 1968—a study which was also longitudinal—Hobart chose his respondents from one school in each of the provinces of Alberta, Ontario, and Quebec. In 1977, he returned to these samples to do a further study, but he then took additional samples from a technical school in each of the provinces of Nova Scotia, British Columbia, and Ontario.[32] In all, his data pertain to 1104 respondents in the 1968 round, and 2062 in the second round of interviews in 1977. Of the latter, 413 were Francophones and 1649 were Anglophones. Designed to identify the attitudes of students to premarital sexual intercourse as well as their reactions to actual instances of such intercourse, the Hobart study found that there was an increase in permissiveness among men, especially in the acceptability of a sexual relationship if engaged or in love, from 59% in 1968 to 82% in 1977. For cases without affection, the increase is relatively marginal, from 25% in 1968 to 32% in 1977. Further differences existed between men and women, and between the engaged and the non-engaged. During the period, the increase in acceptance of premarital sex by men and women was 7% and 14% respectively. Considerable difference also existed between Francophones and Anglophones, especially in regard to the fun standard. For instance, in 1968, 23% Anglophones did not accept kissing from the partner in the absence of affection, and by 1977 this had dropped to 19%. Among the Francophones, the percentage for 1968 stood at 67%, but had come down to 28% by 1977. Hobart's study shows an increase in the acceptance of the love standard on the part of men, and an overall increase in the premarital sexual relationship. The differences between Anglophones and Francophones were explicable in terms of the increasing modernization of the French Canadian society during the period 1968–77.

Perlman's overarching survey in this volume (Chapter 5) notes an increasing acceptance of premarital sex by both the general public and the students. He cites the Gallup Poll data to show that, between 1970 and 1975, there was a 16% increase among those who condoned premarital sex. He cites Hobart to point out that between 1968 and 1977, the percentage of Francophone students accepting premarital intercourse for a female in love rose from 46% to 84%, and for the Anglophones it rose from 51% to 80%. The "double standard" between males and females with regard to acceptance of premarital sex was fast eroding. His survey of the empirical and theoretical literature points to the need for an open mind, since no single factor nor the kind of factor explains the phenomenon adequately.

Marriage as an Institution:
Meaning and Significance of Marriage

Logically, the next sequential phase in the study of the marital process, after mate selection, courtship, and premarital sex, is marriage itself, its structuring, functionality, and institutional dynamics. Marriage is a socially approved and encouraged sexual union between two persons of opposite sex, based on the expectation of some permanence in relationship, mutual sharing of rights and duties in terms socio-legally defined for roles of husband and wife, and in the rearing of the offspring arising out of the marital relationship. In functional terms, marriage legitimizes a sexual relationship and the procreation of children, ensures a condition of stability for the family, and provides for the fulfilment of marital obligations and privileges.

The factors associated with the premarital phase of the marital process operate in marriage, and, hence, the typology of marriage like the typology of courtship and mate-selection patterns, should be one of a continuum, not a polarity, between the traditional and the modern forms. In the traditional system of marriage, group considerations and wider social factors are more decisive than the immediate interests and wishes of the marital partners; whereas, in the modern system, the marital partners occupy a central place in the institutional arrangement of the marriage and its functioning. But the two systems usually share a minimum set of common functions, such as legitimation of sexual relationship, procreation, and the stability of the family. The dramatic decline in the significance of the kinship factor in the marriages of modern, industrial societies does not imply that no socio-cultural considerations enter into the marital process, but it does imply that there is a relatively greater stress on the bio-psychological needs of the marital partners. Hence, the two types of family forms, corresponding to the two marriage systems, have been identified as the traditional family and the companionship family.[33] The latter, which is the norm for industrial societies, involves mutual emotional attachment, deeper interpersonal communication, and an equitable sharing of work and participation in decision-making.

This change in the marriage and family type betokens a shift from "orderly replacement" to "universal, permanent availabilities,"[34] and implies changes in the nature of sex roles and their interaction.[35] The historical shift in the marriage type from the traditional to "the universal, permanent availabilities" type represents a shift from a stability-oriented, closed system to one in which marital partners are available on a more open and universal basis. The historical change in terms of an ideological shift toward individualism has resulted from the process of industrialization. This, in its turn, has brought about changes in the definition of the role and function of the sexes. On the economic level, industrialization creates opportunities for women to participate significantly in the system of production and the labour process, and this development contributes to the redefinition of sex roles. Therefore, modern marriage has become an institution functionally integrated into the industrial society and ideologically transformed to promote individualistic values and interests.

The individualistic ideology of Canadian industrial society is reflected in its liberalized laws and morals, which provide greater opportunity for the individual to choose a lifestyle, including the choice to opt out of the marital system. Yet the trend in recent decades has been towards an increase in marriage rates.[36] The marital orientation of young Canadians, studying at two Canadian universities and a trade school in French and English Canada, showed conservatism to be dominant; yet there was a significant recognition of the existence of companionship between spouses.[37] The dominance of conservative attitudes among Canadians is confirmed by public opinion polls. According to a poll conducted in 1973, 62% male and 57% female respondents believed that gainful employment of married women undermined family life.[38] Another public poll conducted in 1975 showed that 75% of the Canadians interviewed were opposed to mothers with young children taking gainful employment outside the home. Those above 35 years, with skilled labour and public school education, were opposed consistently to the idea of working wives with children.[39]

Evidence suggests that, since the 1960's, the Canadian family has moved away significantly from the traditional pattern of authoritarian male control to one characterized by a more democratic relationship.[40] A similar trend has been noticed in French Canada, where decision-making within the family was divided—a joint process in some matters, exclusive competence of the wife in some matters, and exclusive competence of the husband in certain other matters. Though husband-wife decision-making was the most favoured, with 73% of the households supporting joint budget-making by husband and wife, in actual practice this was implemented only in 45% of them. The considerable prevalence of patriarchialism in Canadian families correlates significantly with such factors as religious ideology, ethnicity, and ecology and has been found to be associated with the existence of traditional family constraints, restrictions, and duties.[41]

The solidarity of modern industrial society is based on division of labour, and this has had its impact on the marital system and on intrafamilial relationships. In spite of all the changes wrought by industrialization, the male continues even in a modern, industrial society to be the major breadwinner, and the woman continues to be saddled with household chores. A study of an upper-class family in a metropolitan setting has shown that a clear-cut division of labour between husband and wife existed and that any joint work done by both was purely voluntary.[42] In rural households, this role-differentiation is more pronounced, with women mostly restricted to housekeeping. Yet they participate in farming operations like roundups, fencing, bookkeeping, etc., in the ranch culture of Southern Saskatchewan. The rural wife also functions as a junior partner in her husband's business. The division of labour between the spouses has, however, not prevented the possibility of interaction on a companionship basis.[43]

The husband and wife roles are functionally well differentiated, with joint activity being wholly voluntary, in the cases of the Hutterite colony in Saskatchewan and the Dutch village communities in the Holland Marsh. In these groups man is the boss and the breadwinner, yet he contributes to domestic work on a voluntary basis. The national poll of 1975 clearly established that the division of labour takes place significantly on the basis of sex in Canada.[44]

Marital Interaction

The essence of marital life is the interaction between the husband and wife, whereas family life involves the addition of children. Three types of issues are salient for marital life. These are financial, sexual, and psychological, and it is around these that marital interactions configure systematically. There is evidence that working-class husbands expect their wives to contribute to the family finances by taking up outside employment. At the same time, they are reluctant to acknowledge the extra income for what it is and downgrade it by characterizing it as inadequate. They express ambivalence towards their wives' work, but they cannot do without it. The women themselves may characterize their work as unimportant in order not to reflect on their husbands, who may even be unskilled labourers. Such a mutual underestimation often results in marital distress, tension, and divorce.[45]

Middle-class husbands and wives exemplify a situation quite the reverse of the one among working-class spouses. The middle-class husbands and wives function in concert, as a team, mutually strengthening each other, accommodating each other in terms of felt needs and special requirements, and managing to contain emerging tensions and conflicts. The middle-class husbands lose some of their status resources as a result of the employment of their wives; whereas, in contrast, the working-class husbands gain when they derive financial assistance from wives. While the middle-class wife's "self-image" becomes upgraded if she is an earner, the working-class wife suffers a substantial loss of self-image because she is gainfully employed. Thus the class factor produces contrasting consequences in similar marital situations.[46]

In 1969, Metro Toronto families, irrespective of class distinctions, were found to suffer no disruption in family stability because of two-parent careers. In fact, two-parent-career families revealed close and harmonious interpersonal relationships. But such a relationship, being centred on marital partners, tended to minimize involvement in explicitly family-control activities. Contrary to the prevailing views, the occupational component in dual working-parent families, affect not only the wage-earners but all the members of the family. This results in a more frequent blurring of boundaries between the work world and the non-work world in such families, compared with the families of single wage earners.[47]

The second major aspect of the husband-wife relationship pertains to sexual behaviour. Therefore, sexual adjustment is an issue in marital relationships. For instance, extramarital sexual relationships often lead to marital violence, culminating sometimes in homicide.[48] Some wives may show little enthusiasm in meeting the sexual demands of their husbands and yet enter into the sexual act unwillingly. However, the participation of wives in the labour process tends to lessen opportunities for extramarital relations, and, in fact, it promotes smoother marital communication and interaction in respect to sexual relationship.[49] A successful handling of sexual relationship is crucial to the marital process.

Most importantly marriage involves a systematic and intense emotional interaction between two individuals. Therefore, in the last analysis, the success of the marital process depends on the skill and ability of the partners to establish a well-adjusted psychological environment. But psychological factors are themselves affected by, and affect other socio-cultural and economic factors in the marital process. Such emotional problems arise particularly in immigrant families uprooted from their homeland culture and ethos. For instance, the Sikh immigrant families of British Columbia, hailing from a rural, patrilineal, "paternalistic-materialistic," joint-family background, faced emotional problems in their efforts to make adjustments with the Canadian environment. The resulting behavioural pattern has been a highly complex set of adjustments, some moving closer to the Canadian model, some away from it, and others representing a synthesis.[50]

These behavioural adjustments have involved enormous strain on individuals, especially women, called upon to accept role changes. The marital tensions as well as intergenerational conflicts among the Sikhs have been attributed by the Sikhs themselves to environmental changes. A similar situation of emotional tension and adjustment has been noted in the case of immigrant Lebanese Muslim families. The Canadian socio-cultural environment and the legal system have deprived the Lebanese Muslim family of its distinctive properties. The traditional institutional resources have been found inadequate to enable some of these families to resolve their emotional dilemmas.[51]

Some Canadian Indian groups under the stress of changing circumstances, have developed a new family type, the matrifocal family, though it would be difficult to predict whether this form will consolidate itself structurally or prove to be a merely transitional phenomenon. The matrifocal family is one in which the male "is absent or subdominant." This type has involved an increasing participation of women in decision-making in response to a situation where men are excluded from making decisions. Women thus may come to play a crucial role in changing the marital and family structures to enable them to make adjustments.[52]

The Dynamics of Marriage

The contributions in this volume focus on specific issues and aspects concerning the process and dynamics of marriage in Canada. Though marriage is still a very widely accepted and practised social institution in Canada, the pressures and forces that shape and sustain a modern, industrial society affect the marital forms and functions, but they also provide a context for behaviour and activity relating to ambiguous heterosexual relationships outside the marriage system. Hobart examines the phenomenon of unmarried heterosexual cohabitation as an alternative to marriage in Canada. He makes a comparative analysis of the situation between different points of time, 1967–68 and 1976–77. His data pertain to attitudes towards heterosexual relationships outside the marital frame, that is, "cohabitation." In 1967-68, only 25% of the respondents approved heterosexual relationships outside the marital frame, while 31% expressed an attitude of tolerance. Those rejecting it constituted 43%. The 1976-77 data show that the proportion of those rejecting such relationships, both for themselves and others, fell dramatically from 43% to just 12%. More detailed responses indicated that while 48% had earlier stated that it would shock them if their own sisters were involved, in 1976–77, only 15% held this view. More people, in fact twice as many, were aware of such relationships in 1976–77. More significantly, differences in attitude between men and women became substantially reduced in the period. In particular, women no longer held that cohabitation should lead to marriage. No significant variation was noted between university students and students from technical schools; but there were significant differences in terms of regional subsamples, those from Quebec giving the strongest approval to the practice of cohabitation. Hobart notes that moral resistance to cohabitation was weakening, although this did not mean that there were no practical and pragmatic hindrances to cohabitation. Cohabitation is as yet a marginal phenomenon, but the situation may alter in its favour because of macro-social shifts.

In his demographic analysis of mean age at marriage in Canada, based on the 1971 census, Basavarajappa shows that the mean age for both men and women increased until 1911, but has been declining since then. His data is in terms of the status categories of regions, urban/rural background, religious affiliation, and ethnicity. Though he does not draw any explicit theoretical conclusions, Basavarajappa's data can be effectively used to illuminate changing patterns in the Canadian marital system and family. Boyd's exploration of the relationship between marriage and mortality in Canada is also demographically framed, but, unlike Basavarajappa, she addresses herself explicitly to sociological theory. Her demographic data reveal that, in the age range of 25-64 for both men and women, during the three-year period of 1970–72, the mortality rate was higher for the unmarried than for the married. Psychological factors accounted for this situation. Married persons enjoyed a lower mortality rate than the divorced or widowed, because they were equipped to face death psychologically. Their ability to do so derived from the fact that they were relatively more integrated into the social system. This finding is consistent with the social integration theory first developed by Durkheim in his classic study of suicide, but later elaborated by Gove.[53] The latter suggests that this is not conclusive since other hypotheses are equally plausible. Hence she argues for a multi-factor theory, involving factors other than social integration, such factors as socio-economic status, health care, health culture, and life chances. These two studies emphasize the need for a demographic perspective in the study of marital process and its dynamics.

Like the Hobart paper, the contribution by Peters is concerned with behaviour that is oriented towards a non-marital frame. As Peters points out, the single female has not been much noticed in sociological research, though more recently some marginal interest has been shown. Demonstrating a discrepancy between sociological theory and popular perception in regard to the single female, Peters rejects the validity of current stereotypes of the single female, especially the media myth of her liberal lifestyle. He finds intergenerational variations in the attitude of "singles" to cohabitation, the younger ones being more tolerant. The single women studied considered loss of the opportunity to bear children one of the regrets of choosing to remain single. Some of them wanted companionship but would calculate its cost. One of the reasons for choosing to remain single was the fear of making unsuitable matches in marriage. The older single women had less income and education and were more religious in their orientation. However, the single female remained out of tune with a predominantly marrying society. She had yet to gain social approval and acceptability. Peters found considerable ambivalence in his respondents' attitude to their singleness—they were undecided about the benefits and costs of being single.

Premarital sex does not represent behaviour that is necessarily opposed to marital norms, although it might certainly influence marital patterns. Perlman offers substantial empirical evidence, supported by theoretical discussion, to suggest that the phenomenon of premarital sex requires further and greater theoretical attention in sociology, if it is to be understood in its wider socio-cultural ramifications. He shows that premarital sex cannot be isolated from a whole institutional and ideological complex generated in the course of the emergence of modern, industrial society with its sophisticated technological base.

Looker and Pineo focus on the extent and kind of participation made by married women in the labour force. They assume that this factor has profound impact on marital relationships in Canada. Their data relate to a sample of 400 male and female teenagers and their parents, located in Hamilton, Ontario—data collected in the spring of 1975. While the teenagers were interviewed, their parents were asked to fill in a questionnaire. The research design permitted a cross-generational comparison of attitudes and values, centring on the labour process. The paper recognizes the influence of two-parent careers in marital relationships, but suggests that differentiation in influence exists, in terms of the occupation chosen by the wife. They argue that the changes in Canadian marital relationships could be explained by the inflow rate of married women to the labour market and by the degree to which married women choose occupations other than those traditionally cast as "women's work." They underline the fact that the process of change is a gradual one, facing considerable resistance from traditional and conservative habits and attitudes. However, the situation is in a formative stage, and it is likely that "more complex adaptations" may emerge as the number of wives entering the less-traditional labour market reaches a critical size.

Ishwaran and Chan show that marital stability and marital commitment are related to cultural, ideological, technological, and ecological factors. They also use a developmental framework and work within a historical context. Their study of Dutch Canadians suggests that ethnicity, not directly but as mediated by economic, social, and cultural factors, contributes to the healthy functioning of the family. In particular, they emphasize the role of religion and the church, which actually control a variety of community institutions, like the school, in ensuring marital stability and commitment. But they also suggest that forces from the wider Canadian socio-economic and cultural environment, with its stress on individualism, poses a serious source of destabilization for the Dutch Canadians.

Our general survey and the brief analysis of the contributions to this volume demonstrate that marriage is a dynamic and flourishing institution in Canada, though it is increasingly beset with marginal challenges from changing attitudes, values, and behaviour that question the marital norm.

Ethnicity and Marriage

Briefly, an ethnic group is one which refers to itself, and is referred to by others as sharing distinctive, common, socio-cultural tradition and heritage, transmitted intergenerationally over time. The central aspect of ethnicity is its ability to perpetuate its unique group identity, rooted in race, religion, national origin, or some combination of such factors. The process of industrialization and urbanization tends to erode ethnicity, but the relationship between modernization and ethnicity, however, cannot be conceptualized in a unidirectional way. The continuation from generation to generation of the cultural patterns, social institutions, and normative-ideological beliefs of the ethnic group cannot be achieved without systematic socialization. The industrial and urban ethos of modern society weakens the ethnic community's socialization process because it involves institutional factors outside the family, which promote individualistic values, norms, and attitudes. Nonetheless, the ethnic community is able to establish its self-identity through a socialization process in which language has been playing an increasingly important role.

In combination with linguistic homogeneity and religious ideology, the ethnic family, that is, the family pattern dominant in the ethnic group, becomes an effective agent for socialization into the mores and values of the ethnic community. The family life and activities provide the institutional context for such socialization. Thus, the ethnic family is the chief preserver and transmitter of the ethnic community values, attitudes, and behavioural patterns.[54]

**Ethnicity and the Family Content
of the Marital Process**

The Canadian population increased from 3 700 000 in 1871 to
21 600 000 in 1971. During this period, a demographic dominance of
the British (English, Irish, Scottish, and others) is noticeable,
accounting for a decrease from 60% to 45% of the population. This
dominance continues except in Quebec and the Prairie Provinces. The
French Canadians are concentrated mainly in Quebec where they
constitute 79% of the population. The remaining population
comprises European groups (other than the British and the French), the
Asians, and others. Of the non-dominant European ethnic groups, in
1971, the Germans were the largest (6%), followed by Italians (3.4%),
Ukrainians (2.7%), Dutch (2%), Scandinavians (1.8%), Poles (1.5%)
and the Jews (1.4%).

The marital systems and processes of the ethnic groups in Canada
derive their distinctive characteristics immediately from their family
content. The form and structure of the ethnic family is determined by,
and determines, the marital process.

Among the English Canadians, though the norm is a small family
in which the marital relations are relatively less authoritarian,
decision-making more democratized, and interpersonal relationships
more egalitarian, ethnicity is emphasized through the use of kinship
networks, despite spatial diffusion of the families.[55]

The French have, over the years, evolved a distinctive family
pattern with its own unique norms and ideals. The demographic and
socio-cultural importance of the community has been translated into a
political ideology, rooted in linguistic and religious culture, and this
has been used to enhance the status of the community in the context of
multi-ethnicity. Membership in the French-Canadian community has
implied a specific and unique set of attitudes and beliefs relating to the
community's self-identity.[56]

However, there is evidence that this pattern of family and marital
life becomes modified in response to regional and local variations,
though only marginally. The French-Canadian community-identity is
found to be reinforced by kinship networks constructed across America
and Canada, and such networks have been harnessed to promote the
material and socio-cultural interests and goals of individuals and
individual families belonging to the community.[57] There is also

evidence that a subtle but discernible shift is taking place among the French Canadians towards the conjugal family type, with a strong stress on individualism, behavioural and ideological autonomy from the kinship network, and extension of women's role. This shift has led to a significant democratization of intrafamily relationships, between husbands and wives, and between parents and children. Thus, the French-Canadian family, while continuing to maintain its ethnic uniqueness, has increasingly responded to pressures from the process of modernization.[58]

The French-Canadian marital system is predominantly one in which the husband-wife relationship remains tilted in favour of male dominance. But the increasing pressures of modernization are pushing the French-Canadian marital system in a more democratic and egalitarian direction. In this process, ethnicity plays a dual role. On the one hand, it tends to emphasize traditional patterns of intrafamily relationships; on the other hand, it serves also as content for changes in this pattern.

The German Canadians have been sociologically somewhat inadequately studied. Their population is mostly located in the more rural parts of Ontario and the Prairies. The only studies available are about the Hutterites and Mennonites of German extraction. The Hutterites make a unique community. Though their kinship system is formally bilateral, it functions with a strong patriarchal bias. The marital family and kinship system of the community is characterized by patrilocality, colony exogamy, and endogamy in relation to the three historical branches into which the community is divided. Though courtship is technically free from parental control, it is obviously restricted by communal norms and limited local opportunities. Marriage is regarded primarily as an institution for promoting procreation and channelling sexual needs. Like the Hutterites, the Mennonites present a minority pocket isolated from the mainstream society. As among Hutterites, the marital pattern and the family system are designed to perpetuate a distinctive community life and culture, founded on a religious-ethnic ideology. Yet, it is found that the Mennonite parents have shown a high degree of aspiration for their children.

In view of the strong persistence of the traditional family system, the Italian marital process has tended to preserve the traditional patterns brought over from the homeland culture. The husband-wife relationship continues to be one in which male authoritarianism dominates. Ethnicity, through the socialization process within the context of the family, has reinforced this pattern. But in the process of adjustment to the new industrial-urban society, ethnicity has been used, not as a conservative factor, but as a resource enabling families to adapt themselves to the new environment. Thus, the Italian marital system is in a transitional phase.

The traditional Italian family values associated with the homeland culture are dominant in the marital and family system. The norms of family obligations and loyalties are rigidly followed, but they have been perceived as necessary for the protection of individuals facing the crisis of acculturation. Thus, paradoxically, what enables the individual members to meet the demands of the new environment also prevents them from being integrated into it on a large scale by reinforcing a narrow ethnicity. This suggests that ethnicity can both be a means of cultural isolation and of integration into the mainstream of Canadian society. However, the Italian community seems overly concerned with the former objective than with the latter.[59]

The Dutch Canadians are relatively less urbanized than the Italians. While the national average for Canada is an urban population of 75%, only 65% of Dutch Canadians are urban. Although the dominant family type is the smaller family, strong ties and networks have been systematically forged between family units scattered widely across Canada. These play an active role in maintaining the identity and solidarity of the ethnic community. Religious ideology has contributed to the strengthening of the distinctive Dutch family pattern, which is characterized by male authority, stress on the maternal and domestic role of women, rigid socialization based on role differentiation between the sexes, the recognition of the eldest child as a parental surrogate, and the structural emphasis on the role of extended kin ties in family life. The community takes an extremely conservative attitude towards intermarriage, permissive sex behaviour, contraception, and divorce. The values inherent in this conservative ideology and the role of the Dutch language and Dutch customs, have combined to reinforce the community's own concept of Dutchness and have helped it maintain a significant degree of socio-cultural continuity. A developmental study of the Holland Marsh community, carried out in the seventies, showed that the Dutch community had successfully implemented their religious and cultural values and ideology in their community life. Yet this study also drew attention to the emergence of conflicts and tensions, leading to considerable strain, especially among the younger generation, due to exposure to the external environment. This may very well develop into a source of threat to the internal coherence and cultural distinctiveness of the community.[60]

Dutch-Canadian marital life, largely because of its strong commitment to ethnic norms, values, and institutions, has continued to be a predominantly traditional one. It has been characterized by a significant degree of male dominance in decision-making as well as in resource-control. But there are indications that this pattern is now under pressure to change towards a more modern pattern because of increasing exposure, especially of the younger generation, to the mainstream Canadian environment.

According to 1971 census data, the Jewish communities are concentrated in Toronto, Montreal, and Winnipeg. Their fertility rates are among the lowest in Canada, their incomes and educational levels among the highest. Most of them pursue professional, managerial, and technical occupations. The Jewish families tend to follow the cultural patterns of the towns where they had settled earlier in Europe. This has been the focal point of the activities of the extended-kin community. It is also the institution which preserves and maintains the identity and coherence of the community.[61] On the one hand, the family serves as the institutional context for the intensification of ethnic self-consciousness, and, on the other hand, it also inculcates the norms and values of secular achievement, through its traditional stress on learning and formal education. Judaism is a strong rallying point for ethnic identity, especially among the younger generation. The Jewish marital and family system emphasizes an egalitarian ideology, superimposed on a sex-based division of labour in domestic and occupational domains, permissive and love-based childbearing practices oriented towards high achievement, and the focussing of attention on the immediate family at the cost of far-off kinship connections. Thus, we find among the Jewish community a paradoxical conjunction of emphasis on ethnicity and an orientation towards material and secular goals, as reflected in the marital process and the family system.

The Polish community, numbering around 316 425, is located

mainly in Ontario and the Prairies. Historically, the original pattern of the traditional patriarchal and extended family has evolved in the Canadian context into a predominantly conjugal pattern, characteristic of mainstream Canadian society. The modernizing forces in Canada undermined significantly the traditional aspects of marriage and family life such as unqualified male dominance, arranged marriages, the large family, repressive forms of childrearing, and solicitude for the aged. Some of the main factors in this process of change have been the absence of tradition-reinforcing infrastructures like the church, spatial dispersion, socio-cultural isolation, and educational socialization into the Canadian social ethos. The postwar immigrant Polish families in Toronto have tended to show new patterns of family interaction, new attitudes, and new beliefs. The nuclear-family norm has replaced the traditional family values, permissiveness has increased, and authoritarianism has declined. In short, Polish marriage and family and life have converged on the Anglo-Saxon model.[62]

What emerges from this brief review of extant and ongoing research in the area of ethnicity-family interaction is that the overall situation is far from clear and crystallized. Nonetheless, certain trends and directions are indicated. While ethnicity continues to significantly influence the marriage and family systems of the ethnic groups, especially the French, the Dutch, and the Jewish, the degree of this influence and its nature are changing. While there is a measure of truth in the thesis that ethnicity works as a conservative force against the assimilation of immigrants into mainstream Canadian society, and primarily through the marital and family system,[63] it is increasingly on the defensive against the process of modernization. It is also not quite accurate to hold that ethnicity is necessarily opposed to change, since it might also turn out to be a resource for individuals and individual families in their efforts to come to terms with change.

The studies on the theme of ethnicity in this volume present a very complex sociological situation about which no easy and clear-cut generalizations can be made. The paper by Kalbach (Chapter 8) on propensity for intermarriage in Canada notes that while ethnicity is declining as a barrier to assimilation, the degree to which assimilation is increasing or the degree to which ethnicity is declining as a barrier to such marriages, shows significant variation between the various ethnic groups. The French Canadians show the least degree of propensity for intermarriage, although the regional factor interposes to differentiate between the propensity of the same ethnic groups separated in different regions. Moreover, ethnicity becomes salient, not in isolation, but in alliance with other factors like religion, residential concentration, and occupational characteristics. Driedger's focus is on student dating and mating as preludes to marriage and family life. Using the theoretical notions of "orderly replacement of the ethnic tradition" and "more universal permanent availability," he argues that the first is a relatively closed model while the second is relatively more open. The first facilitates the stability and continuity of ethnic cultural identity, while the second promotes assimilation through ethnic intermarriage. Driedger found a gap between student attitudes which were favourable to ethnic intermarriage and their practice which tended to follow a closed model. Therefore, his study underlines the persistence of ethnic identity and solidarity in marriage and family life in Canada. He suggests that this persistence moderates the pace of interethnic marriage and assimilation. The Jews showed, until recently, the least inclination towards intermarriage, while the Scandinavians were more oriented towards such marriages. Therefore, ethnicity becomes salient in those groups which already have strong, ongoing, ethnic institutional structure.

In his comparative study of Dutch, Greek, and Slovak respondents, Chimbos demystifies ethnicity by suggesting that factors other than ethnicity explain ethnicity. Such factors include educational level, antecedents in the home country (urban/rural), sex, and age at the time of immigration. Therefore, he rejects simple explanations to account for the persistence or decline of ethnicity in marriage and family life.

In sum, the role of ethnicity in the marital process and dynamics in Canada is bidirectional. On the one hand, it tends to ally with the forces of stability and thus helps maintain community identity. On the other hand, it serves as an institutional resource for selective change and adaptation. In addition it is important to study ethnicity, not as an isolated phenomenon, but as one among several factors on the social scene. Therefore, there is need for increasing research on the interaction between ethnicity and the non-ethnic factors. Very often discussions of ethnicity have been misleading precisely because of failure to attend to such relational and interactive processes.

Marital Conflicts and Dissolution

When a marital relationship reaches a breaking point, it involves issues of institutional pathology and malfunctioning. Marital dissolution and divorce take place almost as a logical consequence.

In statistical terms, the divorce rate in Canada has been registering a steady increase, from 54.8 per 100 000 population in 1968 to 235.8 per 100 000 population in 1976. This steady increase in the divorce rate should be attributed, in part, to the fact that the Canadian law relating to divorce was altered in 1968 in a more liberal direction. But these figures require to be interpreted carefully. The increase in the number of divorces relates to the crude birth rate. The number of these divorces pertains to a population that has been married for a large number of years, and these marriages relate to a smaller population of marital ties in any single year. Canada has a ratio of one to four, in the crude divorce rate, in contrast to the USA where the relevant ratio is one to two. The latest available number for Canada, which is for the year 1976, is a divorce rate of 236 per 100 000 population. (The actual number of divorces for the year was 54 207.) Between 1969 and 1976 the average annual increase in divorce has been around 11%.

There are significant interprovincial variations in the divorce rate, although the overall pattern has remained consistent. According to statistical data for 1976, British Columbia recorded the highest divorce rate of 333.7 per 100 000, with Alberta coming out a close second, at 309.9. The divorce rates in these two western provinces have been widely variable in a long time perspective. Currently, it is significant that Quebec has a higher divorce rate than Ontario, 243.6 against the latter's 224.9. Quebec has been maintaining this margin of lead consistently since 1974. Prior to 1974, the Quebec divorce rate never rose above the average Canadian divorce rate. Newfoundland has now the lowest rate, only 76.0. According to the latest available statistics, those for 1978, all the provinces registered some increase over the 1975 rates, with the sole exception of Manitoba, which showed a decline of −2.51. However, it is necessary to take a long-range historical view of the Canadian divorce rates in terms of their intraprovincial and interprovincial differentials. This is particularly true of provinces showing usually and comparatively low divorce rates. The province of Prince Edward Island, for instance, had a total of 75 divorces in 1975, which rose to 116 in 1976—a dramatic increase of 41. But it would be misleading to infer that such a high rate of increase characterizes the long-range historical pattern for the province, especially because the preceding year registered a decrease.

The revision of the civil code in 1968 was the immediate cause for a jump in the divorce rate in all the provinces, with the Canadian average rate registering a phenomenal rise from 54.8 to 124.2 within a year. This trend was steadily sustained except in 1971, when there was a small decline of -2.4. It is worth noting that the period after the Second World War showed a steady and consistent rise in the divorce rate. During 1975, some 5.5% of divorce cases on record had previous divorce antecedents. Of the 197 585 marriages registered in that year, about 11.5% showed that at least one partner had been divorced. This implies that remarriage is a significant feature of the situation, and that marriage has deep roots in the cultural values of Canadian society.

The themes of marital dissolution and divorce have heavy demographic overtones and need to be set in a demographic context for an adequate interpretation. One important demographic variable has been shown to be age at marriage. There is clearly a positive relationship between the factor of early marriage and the incidence of divorce. For instance, in 1976, 24% of all the brides and 7% of all the bridegrooms were under twenty at the time of marriage. Further, 42% of all women and 13% of all men, who divorced, were married first when they were under twenty. These figures explain why such a high proportion of the divorcees are relatively young. We find that 39% of all women and 54% of all men among all the divorcees were first married in the most frequent marriageable cohort, that is, in the age range of 20–24. This represents again a slightly larger proportion for those marrying at that age. Thus, the evidence for the relationship between age at marriage and the divorce rate in Canada, is well established statistically.

This raises the sociological question of why early marriages lead generally to divorce. Inadequate experience, excessive romantic idealism unrelated to realities, and insufficient background in handling interpersonal relationships appear to be the major causes accounting for the correlation between early age at marriage and divorce. The average age of husband and wife at the point of divorcing is 38.2 and 35.3 for men and women respectively. There is now a declining trend in this regard. There are, as may be expected in such a diversified country as Canada, interprovincial variations. Alberta has the highest percentage of husbands and wives divorcing under twenty and in the age range of 20–24.[66]

The question of marital duration is an important aspect of the marital process because it relates to the crucial issues of marital stability and commitment. For Canada, average marriages which culminated in divorce usually lasted for a period of around eleven years. Cases in which divorce occurred in less than five years after marriage accounted for 16.7% among all the divorces. Marriages of less than ten years' duration represented 30% of all divorces. (All figures are for 1972–75.) The modal year of marriage duration of the divorced works out to five years, but the years between four and nine years of marital duration are reasonably comparable. The Canadian statistics for marital duration for the divorced are noticeably higher than the American. The latter had, for instance, a median duration of seven years in 1967. The usual period of separation prior to divorce in Canada is between two and three years. During 1972–74, the trend was towards a gradual decline in marital duration for divorcing. This suggests that, while marriage continues to be popular, marital stability and commitment are relatively on the decline.[67]

The process of marital dissolution and divorce in Canada stems from a variety of causes, and has produced various grounds and claims and counterclaims. In 1976, the most frequently advanced ground, representing around one percent of the causes, was a period of separation of more than three years. This number has been more or less consistent for the last five years. The second most common ground for seeking divorce was adultery, accounting for 30% of the cases. Other grounds for divorce were: mental cruelty (17.7%) and physical cruelty (14.5%). The trend is towards an increase in mental cruelty as grounds for divorce, and this is likely to continue. On the other hand, the ground of desertion for a period of more than five years is on the decline—from 6.4% in 1970 to 2.8% in 1976.[68]

But divorce is only one of the causes for marital termination. It may occur also because of death, annulment, or separation. By and large, mortality seems to be a more powerful source of marital termination than divorce. Statistics, however, are available only for the USA, where 19.3 per 1000 marriages were dissolved by death in 1970.[69] Annulment is a judicial pronouncement that the marriage did not take place within the meaning of law. Some common reasons for annulment are bigamy, force, and duress. Finally, separation implies an arrangement by which the spouses agree to leave each other alone, but are not allowed to marry other partners. It is best described as a limited divorce, since the partners live separately without divorcing. Although it does not betoken a marginal dissolution, it does indicate marital malfunctioning.

While dissolution and separation are obvious indicators of marital failure, their absence does not qualify a marriage automatically to be called a success. This is because a couple may be living together in a marital relationship, but may be acutely unhappy, spending their days in constant conflict and tension. Therefore, a more adequate list of criteria for marital success would comprise such conditions as: personal satisfaction and contentment of the spouses, quality of permanence in the marital relationship, psychological and sexual adjustment, attitude and behaviour consistent with the goals of marriage, and interpersonal integration and complementarity between the spouses.

The presentations in this volume focus on some of the central aspects of Canadian family and marriage. Boyd's paper attempts to locate divorce in its social setting. Pointing out that, in recent years, Canada has experienced a rise in divorce rate, she explains this as an essentially sociological phenomenon. Among the causes she identifies are: the effect of urbanization and industrialization, the impact of World War II, and the recent liberalization of divorce law. The variations within Canadian society in respect to divorce rate is also explicable in sociological terms—in relation to such factors as age at marriage, low-income status, female labour participation, urban residence, religious culture, broken family, or origin. Boyd's close examination of the 1971 census data on separated, divorced, and currently married couples indicates that variations in the pattern of marital dissolution correlate with education, religion, ethnicity, and language. But she also emphasizes that divorce, while being affected by social factors, generates its own impact on social processes. She notes two consequences of such an impact: female-headed families, and reduced income, especially for women. The reduced income is shown, in turn, to have significant bearing on the structure of the family and the plight of children within it.

Chan's study of wife-beating takes a theoretical and empirical note of the presence and prevalence of marital violence and cruelty. His study identifies four areas for further research: the relationship between socio-economic status and wife-battery, the socio-psychological mechanisms and processes that tend to structure intrafamily violence into a stabilized pattern, economic and socio-psychological dependency of women, and the fact of isolation of problem-ridden and violent families.

Palmer is concerned explicitly with the plight of children in the wake of a marital breakdown. Basing her study on empirical data, she finds that the current post-dissolution arrangements are heavily tilted in the interest of the parents at the cost of the children. She finds that children suffer either because of mother's marital infidelity or because of inadequate financial support from the father. Children's need for parental attention was scarcely met. For instance, parental visiting was highly unsatisfactory. She pleads for a greater attention to children's needs by both the parents and the courts.

Whitehurst, Booth, and Hanif go into the causality of cases of separation and divorce. The factors they identify as significant are changing sex-roles, sexuality, careers, children, division of household labour. They report that wives felt more than husbands that their feelings were being neglected prior to separation. Specifically, the wives felt that husbands did not help with domestic chores, were too demanding, authoritarian, and abusive. Husbands made them feel inferior. On their part, the husbands complained that they were allowed little caressing and sexual interaction. The changing sex-roles involving the wife as an earner of income led to complications. Women were asked to play the changing roles as well as the traditional ones equally well, and this was hard on them. While 44% suggested that children deterred separation and divorce, 17% suggested that children, in fact, were the cause of marital tensions. The causes for separation according to the respondents, were loneliness, lack of companionship, and social isolation. With the increase in the possibilities for women to be independent of men, the more extreme forms of husband-dominance are likely to weaken significantly in some circles.

Remarriage

A divorce may not always be followed by a remarriage, but the chances of this happening increase if a marital system encourages this. A remarriage is generally characterized by a weak mental commitment and lack of stability, and hence the divorce rate increases with successive marriages. A frequent reason for interpersonal tensions in a remarriage is the existence of children, especially tensions between step-parents and step-children, and among step-children. Children play an important role in remarriages, but in contradictory ways. They may persuade a parent to remarry and they may equally discourage such a decision. Children may suffer not only because of the divorce but also because of the remarriage of their parents. In 1973, of the total marriages that took place, 18.1% accounted for second marriages, while the comparable data for 1966 were only 12.4%. The data show that the number of men involved in a second marriage was higher than that of women. Of those remarrying, 71.3% had been divorced and 28.7% had been widowed. Those divorced, but unmarried, come, on the average, from the age range of 35–39. Similar data for the widowed show an age range of 52–58. Around more than two and a half times as many divorced Canadians marry for a second time, as do those who are widowed. The rise in the remarriage rate in Canada is related to the increase in the divorce rate. In 1973, some 70% of the remarriages involved at least one spouse who was divorced. An interesting fact is that a divorced person tends to choose a single spouse rather than another divorced person. In 50% of the remarriages, a single person marries a previously married person. Thus, in the two most frequent patterns of marital union, single persons are involved.[70]

According to Schlesinger's study conducted around 1973, in the area of Toronto, the average age at remarriage was 37 for males and 32 for females. For the divorced male, it was 36.5 and for divorced females, 33.5. The average age for a remarrying widowed male was 35, and for the female, 37. The average age of a single male marrying a formerly married female was 32, and for the female, 27. The widowed females were considerably older than either the divorced or single women, at the time of remarriage. According to Statistics Canada, the average age at the time of first marriage is 25 for males and 22 for females. Hence the singles who married the widowed or the divorced tend, usually, to be older than those choosing a single spouse for the first marriage.

Schlesinger's data show further that of those marrying for the second time, the divorced or the widowed were on the average at the time of their first marriage 24 for both widowed and divorced males,

22 for widowed males, and 21 for divorced females. These statistics underline the fact that virtually no differences existed between the widowed and the divorced in respect of their age at the time of first marriage.

The average duration of the first marriage for divorced males was eleven, and for divorced females, nine years. For the widowed male, it was seventeen years and for the widowed female, nineteen years. Understandably the duration of first marriages of the widowed was relatively longer than that of the divorced. The average time-lag between the first and second marriage was one and a half years for the divorced male, and two years for the divorced female. For the widowed male and female, it was three and seven years, respectively. It emerges from the statistics that the widowed respondents had to wait longer than the divorced between marriages.[72] For both the divorced and widowed, the waiting period between marriages was longer for the female. There is further complementary data showing that 9.8% of Canadian families had single parents, and that, of these again, 83% were fatherless and 17% motherless.

Cutting through complex demographic details, certain broad facts emerge about remarriage in Canada. The first is that remarriage takes place on a significant scale, and this is an indication of the cultural importance attached to the institution. Secondly, there is a clear correlation between divorce and remarriage.

An Overview and Evaluation

The marital process is preceded by a premarital phase and it culminates in the founding of a family. Conceptually, the premarital stage, the marital process and family life need to be distinguished without, however, ignoring their causal interconnection. A survey of the literature on the theoretical perspective and the empirical Canadian situation, with regard to the marital process, including marital dissolution, reveals certain broad features.

In the premarital stage, two issues deserve close attention and focus. They are the mate-selection process and premarital sex. The mating process in the Canadian context reveals an interplay of two sets of variables. On the one hand, the ideological enshrining of individuality, which characterizes all modernizing societies, including Canada, promotes the role of romantic love, individual free choice, and psychological needs in the process of mate selection. On the other hand, given the special aspects of Canadian society such as its multicultural population, largely immigrant, certain forces and factors are generated by the social structure, which tend to counter and limit the operations of the ideology of romantic love. The latter may be called the structural variables, and they comprise religion, propinquity, ethnicity, race, and class. The emerging pattern of mate selection is one of continuous and dynamic interaction between the ideological and structural variables. As Ramu has suggested, there is no finality to this pattern of interaction between romantic love, symbolizing the force of change, and the structural variables, symbolizing the forces of stability.[73] In fact, the social dynamics of the situation lies precisely in the tension between the process of social change and the compulsions for stability.

Once the existence and impact of the individualistic ideology, whose manifestation in this context is romantic love, are noticed, the role of dating in mate selection becomes meaningful. The permissibility of free interaction between potential marital partners leads to the issue of premarital sex. In contrast to traditional societies dominated by the system of arranged marriage, the Canadian mate-selection process allows for the possibility of premarital sex. The evidence from relevant literature suggests that premarital sex may be on the increase, although more studies are necessary to throw light on the details of the causes and consequences of premarital sex.

While the traditional marriage form is intact, by and large, it has not been insulated from the forces radiating from the wider social and cultural system and the overall impact of technology. Alternatives to marriage as a way of handling the problem of heterosexual relationships have emerged, however dimly and hesitantly. Charles Hobart, for instance, draws attention to what he calls the institution of cohabitation, which implies heterosexual relations outside marriage. John Peters examines the question of single females, which is particularly threatening to the traditional marriage, since it rejects the stereotypic image of women as almost congenitally prone to marriage. While it is difficult to estimate the future impact of these developments, there can be no question that currently they remain marginal and peripheral phenomena, scarcely able to assail significantly the marital system.

A major feature of Canadian society and population is its multiethnicity and multicultural framework. The Canadian marital process has not escaped the overriding impact of this fact. Ethnicity permeates social life in Canada in many, and often subtle ways. Ethnicity might affect the marriage system in one significant way and that would be by institutionalizing ethnic endogamy. The conflict between ethnicity and interethnic marriage has yet to be explored sociologically in greater depth. The extant literature, however, is not definitive. While the trend is in the direction of interethnic marriage under the pressures of modernization, there are considerable interethnic variations. For instance, the Jewish group seems to emphasize ethnicity relatively more strongly than others in mate selection and eventual marriage. The Scandinavians are relatively the most well-disposed towards interethnic marriages. It is also important to remember that most of the relevant literature comes from research dealing in student samples.

It is part of the marital process and its dynamics that it generates forces and encounters factors tending towards marital conflict, breakdown, and dissolution. The most crucial aspect from this point of view is the incidence of divorce. In the case of divorce, as in other aspects of marital process, there are interprovincial and interethnic variations, often in collusion. In general terms, the trend has been towards an increasing divorce rate, especially since the liberalization of divorce law in 1968. But divorce is a response to a complex array of micro- as well as macro-causes, ranging from interpersonal interactions to wider socio-economic or legal processes. Divorce creates the problem of caring for children left with one parent. The current Canadian handling of this problem is in need of change. In particular, there is a need for shifting some attention from the parents to the children themselves. Both legality and social norm are currently deficient from the child's perspective.

Thus, in 1983, we find that the Canadian marital system and process exemplify an interaction between the conflicting forces of stability and change. While the changes currently noticeable may appear marginal, their cumulative impact, from a longer historical perspective, may be more radical, involving a restructuring of the social arrangement of marriage. But this is largely speculation, and, in the final evaluation, marriage continues to be a basic social institution, with divorce leading to a significant number of remarriages and serving as an eventually reinforcing mechanism.

References

1. Malinowski, Bronislaw. "Parenthood, the Basis of Social Structure," in Calverton, V.F., and Schmalhausen, S.D., eds. *The New Generation*, New York: The Citadel Press, pp. 113-168; Bierstedt, Robert. *The Social Order*, 4th ed. New York: McGraw-Hill, 1974, p. 10.
2. Waller, Willard. "The Rating and Dating Complex." *American Sociological Review* 2 (1937), pp. 727-734.
3. Kerckhoff, A.C., and Davis, K.E. "Value Consensus and Need Complementarity in Mate Selection." *American Sociological Review* 27 (1962) pp. 295-303; and Murstein, Bernard I. "Stimulus-Value-Role: A Theory of Marital Choice." *Journal of Marriage and the Family* 32 (1970), pp. 465-481.
4. For further discussion, see Cavan, Ruth S. *The American Family*, 4th ed. New York: Thomas K. Crowell, 1969, pp. 21-40; Eshleman, J. Ross, *The Family: An Introduction*. Boston: Allyn and Bacon, Inc., 1981. pp. 7-8.
5. Murdock, G.P. *Social Structure*. New York: Macmillan, 1949.
6. Christensen, Harold T., ed. *Handbook of Marriage and the Family*, Rand McNally, Chicago, 1964, p. 3.
7. Burgess, Ernest W., Locke, Harvey J., and Thomas, Mary Margaret. *The Family*, 3rd ed. New York: American Book, 1963, p. 1.
8. Stephens, William N. *The Family in Cross-Cultural Perspective*. New York: Holt, Rinehart & Winston, 1963, p. 7.
9. Reiss, Ira L. *Family Systems in America*. Hinsdale: Dryden, 1976, p. 41.
10. Eshleman. *op. cit.*, p. 83.
11. Goode, William J. "The Theoretical Importance of Love." *American Sociological Review* 24, (1959), pp. 38-47.
12. Goode. *op.cit.*
13. Winch, Robert F. *Mate Selection*. New York: Harper, 1978, p. 89.
14. For relevant studies, see Bowerman, Charles E., and Day, Barbara R. "A Test of the Theory of Complementary Needs as Applied to Couples during Courtship." *American Sociological Review* 21 (1956), pp. 602-605; Rosow, Irving. "Issues in the Concept of Need Complementarity." *Sociometry* 20 (1957), pp. 216-233; Murstein, Bernard I. "Empirical Tests of Role, Complementary Needs, and Homogamy Theories of Marital Choice." *Journal of Marriage and the Family* 29 (1967), pp. 689-696; and Udry, J. Richard. "Personality Match and Interpersonal Perception as Predictions of Marriage." *Journal of Marriage and the Family* 29 (1967), pp. 722-724.
15. Heer, David M., and Hubay, Charles, Jr. "The Trend of Interfaith Marriages in Canada: 1922-1972," in Ishwaran, K., ed. *The Canadian Family*, Revised ed. Toronto: Holt, Rinehart & Winston, 1976, pp. 408-417.
16. Kalbach, Warren E., and McVey, Wayne W. "The Canadian Family: A Demographic Profile," in Larson, Lyle E. *The Canadian Family in Comparative Perspective*. Scarborough: Prentice-Hall, 1976, pp. 97-98.
17. See, for instance, Peters, John Fred. "Mate Selection among the Shirisma."

Practical Anthropology 18 (1971), pp. 20-21; Rosenblatt, Paul C., and Corgby, Paul C. "Courtship Patterns Associated with Freedom of Choice of Spouse." Journal of Marriage and the Family 34 (1972), pp. 689-695.

18. Waller, Willard (revised by Reuben Hill). The Family: A Dynamic Interpretation. New York: Holt, Rinehart & Winston, 1951, pp.160-164.

19. For illustrative studies, see Collins, John K. "Adolescent Dating Intimacy: Norms and Peer Expectations." Journal of Youth and Adolescence 3 (1974), pp. 317-327; and Collins, John K., and Francis, Ronald D. "Insights into a Dating Partner's Expectations of How Behaviour Should Ensue during the Courtship Process." Journal of Marriage and the Family 38 (1976), pp. 373-378.

20. Skipper, James Jr., and Nass, Gilbert. "Dating Behaviour: A Framework for Analysis and Illustration." Journal of Marriage and the Family 28 (1966), pp. 412-413.

21. Skipper and Nass. op. cit., p. 413.

22. Ehrmann, Winston, Premarital Dating Behaviour. New York: Holt, Rinehart & Winston, 1959; Clayton, Richard R. "Religiosity and Premarital Sex." Social Forces 47 (1968), pp. 469-476; and Hill, Charles T., Zick, Rubin, and Peplau, Letitia Anne. "Break-ups before Marriage: The End of 103 Affairs." Journal of Social Issues 32 (1976), p. 153.

23. Christensen, Harold T., and Gregg, Christina. "Changing Sex Norms in America and Scandinavia." Journal of Marriage and the Family 32 (1970), pp. 616-627; Hobart, Charles W. "Sexual Permissiveness in Young English and French Canadians." Journal of Marriage and the Family 32, No. 2. (1972), pp. 292-303.

24. Reiss, Ira L. The Social Context of Premarital Sexual Permissiveness. New York: Holt, Rinehart & Winston, 1967, p. 43; Clayton, Richard R. "Religiosity Premarital Sexual Permissiveness: Elaboration of the Relationship and Debate." Social Analysis 32 (1971), pp. 81-96; and Clayton, Richard R. "Premarital Sexual Intercourse: A Substantive Test of the Contingent Consistency Model." Journal of Marriage and the Family 34, (197), pp. 273-281.

25. Waller, Willard. "The Rating & Dating Complex," op. cit., pp. 727-734; McCall, Michael M. "Courtship as Social Exchange: Some Historical Comparisons," in Farber, Bernard, ed. Kinship and Family Organization. New York: John Wiley, 1960; and Edwards, John N. "Familial Behaviour as Social Exchange." Journal of Marriage and the Family 31 (1969), pp. 518-526.

26. Goode. op. cit., p. 47.

27. Reiss. op. cit., p. 167.

28. Reiss, Ira L., and Miller, Brent C. "A Theoretical Analysis of Heterosexual Permissiveness." The Minnesota Family Study Center, Minneapolis, 1974.

29. Christensen and Gegg. op. cit.

30. Mann, W.E. "Canadian Trends in Premarital Behaviour." The Council for Social Science, No. 198 (1967); Mann. "Sex at York University," in Mann, ed. The Underside of Toronto. Toronto: McClelland and Stewart, 1970. For other details, see Hobart, C.W. "The Courtship Process: Premarital Attitudes and

Behaviour." In Ramu, G.N., ed. *Courtship, Marriage and the Family in Canada.* Toronto: Macmillan of Canada, 1979, pp. 37-58.

31. Perlman, D. "The Sexual Standards of Canadian University Students," in Koulack, D., and Perlman, D., eds. *Readings in Social Psychology: Focus on Canada.* Toronto: John Wiley, 1973.

32. Hobart, Charles W. "Sexual Permissiveness in Young and French Canadians." *Journal of Marriage and the Family* 34, No. 2 (1972), pp. 292-303.

33. Burges, Locke, and Thomas. *op. cit.,* p. 4.

34. Farber, Bernard. *Family Organization and Interaction.* San Francisco: Chandler, 1964, Chapters 1 and 4.

35. Scanzoni, John H. *Sexual Bargaining: Power Politics in the American Marriage.* Englewood Cliffs: Prentice-Hall, 1972.

36. Wakil, S.P., and Wakil, F.A. "Marriage and Family in Canada: A Demographic-Cultural Profile," in Ishwaran. *op. cit.,* 1976, pp. 380-407: Kalbach, Warren E. "Canada: A Demographic Analysis," in Ramu, G.N., and Johnson, S.D., eds. *Introduction to Canadian Social Society: Sociological Analysis.* Toronto: Macmillan of Canada, 39 (1976), pp. 11-76.

37. Hobart, Charles W. "Orientations to Marriage among Young Canadians." *Journal of Comparative Family Studies* 3 (1972), pp. 171-193.

38. Cook, Gail C.A. *Opportunity for Choice: A Goal for Women in Canada.* Ottawa: Information Canada, 1976, p. 6; cited in Nett, Emily M. "Marriage and the Family: Organization and Interaction," in Ramu, ed. *Courtship, Marriage and the Family in Canada.* Toronto: Macmillan of Canada, 1967, p. 66.

39. *Women in Canada.* Decision Marketing Research Ltd., 1976, cited in Ramu. *op. cit.,* p. 66.

40. Elkin, Frederick. *The Family in Canada.* Ottawa: Vanier Institute of the Family, 1971, p. 97.

41. For instance, see Peter Kal. "The Hutterite Family," in Ishwaran, *The Canadian Family,* Revised ed. Toronto: Holt, Rinehart & Winston, 1976, pp. 289-309; Carisse, Collette. "Cultural Orientations in Marriages Between French and English Canadians," in Wakil, S.P., ed. *Marriage, Family and Society: Canadian Perspectives.* Scarborough: Butterworth, 1975, pp. 97-112; Ishwaran, K., *Family, Kinship & Community—A Study of Dutch-Canadians.* Scarborough: McGraw-Hill Ryerson, 1977.

42. Seeley, John, Sim, R.A., and Loosely, E.W. *Crestwood Heights: A Study of the Culture of Suburban Life.* New York: John Wiley, 1956.

43. Kohl, Seena B. *Working Together: Women and Family in Southwestern Saskatchewan.* Toronto: Holt, Rinehart & Winston, 1976.

44. Nett, Emily M. "Marriage and the Family," in Ramu. *op. cit.,* p. 70; and Meissner, Martin, Humphreys, Elizabeth W., Meiss, Scott M.R., and Sheu, W.J. "No Exit for Wives." *The Canadian Review of Sociology and Anthropology* 12 (1975), pp. 429-449.

45. Palmer, Sally E. "Divorcing Families: A Case Study in Southwestern Ontario,"

in Ishwaran. *op. cit.*, pp. 644-658.

46. Burke, Ronald J., and Weir, Tamara. "Relationships of Wives' Employment Status to Husband, Wives and Pair Satisfaction and Performance." *Journal of Marriage and the Family* 38 (1976), pp. 279-287.

47. Butler, Peter M. "Husbands and Wives," in Ishwaran. *op. cit.*

48. Chimbos, Peter D. "Marital violence: A Study of Husband-wife Homicide," in Ishwaran. *op. cit.*, pp. 580-599.

49. Komarovsky, Mira. *Blue-Collar Marriage*. New York: Random House, 1967, p. 111.

50. Ames, Michael M., and Inglis, Joy. "Tradition and Change in British Columbia Sikh Family Life," in Ishwaran. *op. cit.*, pp. 77-91.

51. Barclay, Harold D., "The Lebanese Muslim Family," in Ishwaran. *op. cit.*, pp. 92-104; and Sheron, Abu-Lagan. "Arab-Canadian Family Life." *Arab Studies Quarterly* 1, No. 2 (1981), pp. 135-156.

52. Cruikshank, Julie. "Matrifocal Families in the Canadian North," in Ishwaran. *op. cit.*, pp. 105-119.

53. Gove, Walter R. "Sex, Marital Status and Mortality." *American Journal of Sociology* 79 (1973), pp. 45-67.

54. Mindel, Charles H., and Habenstein, Robert W., eds. *Ethnic Families in America: Patterns and Variations*. New York: Elsevier, 1968; Ishwaran, K., ed. *Canadian Families: Ethnic Diversity*. Toronto: McGraw-Hill Ryerson, 1969.

55. Ostereich, Helgi. "Geographical Mobility and Kinship—A Canadian Example." *International Journal of Comparative Sociology* 6 (1965), pp. 131-145; Boissevain, Jerome. *Italians of Montreal*. Ottawa: Queen's Printer; Piddington, Ralph. "A Study of the French-Canadian Kinship." *International Journal of Comparative Studies* 2 (1961), pp. 3-22.

56. Garigue, Philippe. "French-Canadian Kinship and Urban Life." *American Anthropologist* 58 (1956), pp. 1090-1100.

57. Piddington. *op. cit.*

58. Tremblay, Marc-Adelard. "Authority Models in the French-Canadian Family," in Gold, Gerald, and Tremblay, Marc-Adelard, eds. *Community and Culture in French Canada*. Toronto: Holt Rinehart & Winston, 1973.

59. Boissevain, Jerome. *op. cit.*

60. Ishwaran, K. "*Family, Kinship and Community—A Study of Dutch-Canadians.*" *op. cit.*

61. Kallen, Evelyn. "Family Life Styles and Jewish Culture," in Ishwaran, ed. *The Canadian Family*, Revised ed., pp. 145-161.

62. Radecki, Henry, and Heydenkorn, Benedykt. *A Member of a Distinguished Family: The Polish Group in Canada*. Toronto: McClelland & Stewart, 1976; and Radecki, Henry. "The Polish-Canadian Family: A Study in Historical and Contemporary Perspectives," in Ishwaran, K., ed. *Canadian Families in Ethnic Variations*. Scarborough: McGraw-Hill Ryerson, 1980, pp. 41-64.

63. Ramu. *op. cit.*, p. 111.

64. Statistics Canada. *Vital Statistics*, Vol. 2, *Marriage & Divorce*, 1976.

65. _____ . *op. cit.*, pp. 25-39.

66. Peters, John F. "Divorce in Canada—a Demographic Profile." *Journal of Comparative Family Studies* 7 (1976), pp. 335-349.
67. Statistics Canada. *op. cit.*, p. 41.
68. _____ . *op. cit.*, p. 42.
69. Davis, Kingsley. "The American Family in Relation to Demographic Change." International Population of Urban Research, Institute of International Studies, University of California, Berkeley, Rpt. No. 425, 1973.
70. For summarization of relevant statistical data between 1966 and 1973, see Wakil, S.P., ed. *Marriage, Family and Society: Canadian Perspectives.* Scarborough: Butterworth and Co., 1975.
71. Benjamin Schlesinger. "Remarriage," in G.N. Ramu. *op. cit.*, p. 158.
72. _____ . *op. cit.*, p. 159.
73. Ramu. *op. cit.*, pp. 4-5.

Part II
The Process and Dynamics of Marriage

In this section, marriage is examined as a dynamic, ongoing, social institution, with attention to some of the problems that have arisen in contemporary Canada in the functioning of this crucial institution. This section also attempts to see to what extent marriage is an adaptive institution, answering to the changing needs of the general society.

Charles Hobart explores one visible trend away from marriage in Canadian society today. His paper deals with an arrangement which he describes as "unmarried heterosexual cohabitation as an alternative to marriage in Canada." Conceding the absence of relevant statistical data, but indirectly using data on the number of married couples and the proportion of households with two or more persons not related to the head of the household, he arrives at the general conclusion that unmarried heterosexual cohabitation increased between 1961 and 1971. But the main objective of the paper is to analyse the survey data collected at Canadian universities and technical schools during 1967-68 and 1976-77 on student attitudes toward extramarital cohabitation arrangements. The later data register a significant increase in the approval of the arrangement. In particular, the data show that no significant moral approbation was attached to the practice. In terms of regional differentiation, Hobart found Quebec society relatively more ready to accept such relationships. At the same time the data on the Prairies and the Atlantic Provinces showed that their societies were no more conservative in morals than those of Ontario and British Columbia. In sum, Hobart finds the Canadian situation tending towards the American; in any case, he argues that unmarried heterosexual cohabitation would continue to be a minority practice.

In a statistically rigorous paper, Basavarajappa uses the Canadian census data for 1971 to analyse the trends and interregional differences in the mean age at marriage. Making the reasonable assumptions that age at which sexual interaction starts is an important determinant in the fertility pattern and further that the age at marriage is a good index of this age, he finds that the mean age at marriage has been declining since the nineteenth century, now at 24.4 years for males and 22 for females. He argues that the decline up to the early twentieth century resulted from industrialization while the subsequent decline could be attributed to the availability of contraceptives and changing values. His projections are that the mean ages of the single and widowed would increase while those of divorcees might come down. He also finds some interregional differences. Overall he identifies as important variables in this context: degree of urbanness, level of post-secondary education, proportion of persons in professional, managerial, and white-collar jobs, the proportion of Roman Catholics, and income level.

Monica Boyd tries to unravel the mystery of the causal connection between marriage and death in Canada. She finds the Canadian data in this regard a confirmation of the Durkheim thesis on suicide updated by Gove in 1973. She finds that married persons have lower death rates. She suggests that this is attributable to the fact that married persons enjoyed a comparatively greater degree of social integration than the unmarried. But she also hypothesizes that there may be a host of other variables at work, such as socio-economic status, health care, male-female differences in illness behaviour, illness diagnoses, and life chances.

John Peters focusses attention on the single female. He finds that singles make up a significant group in society and yet have failed to earn wide social approval. In particular, they have come to be perceived as a minority and are stereotyped. The paper examines the reactions, both attitudes and behaviour, of the single female to society's conception of her role and status. Using a questionnaire and administering it to a cross-section of single females above 24, drawn from representative categories, he assembles and interprets data which show that a considerable number of women prefer a single status. They are not generally feminists, and they don't find any prejudice against the single status in the matter of employment. However, what discrimination there is stems from sex discrimination. He pleads for early socialization to reflect and accommodate this phenomenon.

Perlman takes up the theme of the premarital sexual standards of

Canadians. Its relevance to the working of the institution of marriage in Canada is that sexual attitudes and behaviour are important components in any marital system. For instance, it is arguable that a more permissive ethos would tend to weaken the commitment to marital norms. Lamenting the inadequacy and inaccessibility of earlier work on the problem, Perlman makes a brief survey of the changing sexual attitudes in Canadian society in general, from the Victorian emphasis on self-restraint to the more relaxed atmosphere of recent years. Then he surveys the literature on sexual attitudes of the general public and students, using the 24-item Premarital Sexual Permissiveness Scale, developed by Ira Reiss in the late 1960's. He finds that mainstream Canadian students are "moderately, but not extremely permissive in their sexual standards," but he calls attention to the fact that the situation has been changing all the time. The paper devotes considerable analysis to Reiss' sociological theory about this behaviour. He refers to the "autonomy theory" of permissiveness, first suggested by Reiss and Miller in 1974, in which courtship autonomy is central to permissive behaviour. Then he considers the importance of dyadic influences in premarital sexual behaviour. Then he examines the role of emotional intimacy in sexual behaviour, the individual or psychological approaches to premarital sexual standards, and physical attractiveness. On the whole, Perlman believes that no single perspective or theory is adequate in this area, that several such theoretical perspectives should pool their findings.

Dianne Looker and Peter Pineo attempt to uncover the relationship between marital relationship and the extent and type of participation in the labour force by married women in Canada. Their study is based on data gathered in 1975 for 400 male and female teenagers, responding to questions about occupational expectations. Interviews were conducted with the teenagers and questionnaires were administered to their parents, with whom the teenagers were living. The data allowed cross-generational analysis. The paper suggests that the teenagers believed that a working career came into conflict, not with a married life, but with the duties and responsibilities imposed by maternity. The data indicated that no radical changes could be expected in the occupational pattern of married women. The study also found that women were more flexible than men with regard to occupational satisfaction. It was also found that sexual stereotyping of occupations dominated the occupational expectations of both male and female teenagers.

Ishwaran and Chan discuss the issues of marital stability and marital commitment among the Holland Marsh community of Dutch Canadians. Their paper is more ecologically oriented and examines the interaction between the marital system brought by the immigrants into their new country and the environmental pressures of the new land. They find that, on the whole, the immigrants were able to preserve the original Dutch values of marital stability and marital commitment in the new environment, but they also point to changes that are taking place in the attitudes and behaviour of younger generations. However, they conclude that the strong community framework, embodying the original Dutch norms, reinforced by religious ideology, may postpone changes for some time to come.

1/Marriage or Cohabitation
Charles W. Hobart

This paper deals with married heterosexual cohabitation, sharing a bedroom most nights of the week with a person of the opposite sex for at least two consecutive weeks.[12] It is obvious from periodic reporting in the popular press, beginning a decade and more ago, that this pattern must have been on the increase (see *References: Newsweeek*, 1966; *Esquire*, 1967; Grant, 1968; McWhirter, 1968; Schrag, 1968; *Time*, 1968; Bloch, 1969; Karlen, 1969; Rollin, 1969; Sheehy, 1969; Coffin, 1971). However, it is difficult to obtain precise data, at least about Canadians.

Until recently, marriage has been increasingly popular in Canada. The proportion of the adult population, aged 15 years and over, which is married* has increased steadily throughout this century, from 52% in 1901, to 54% in 1911, and 58% in 1921. The Depression years caused this increase to falter, to 56% in 1931. Thereafter the upward trend resumed, moving to 57% in 1941 just at the end of the Depression, to 64% in 1951, reflecting the many post-World War II marriages, and to a peak at 67% in 1961. Since then the rate has slipped, to 65% in 1966, and to 64% in 1972.** The numbers for the proportion of the adult population never married show a similar trend, declining from 42% in 1901 to 40% in 1911, to 36% in 1921, rising to 38% in 1931, then falling to 36% in 1941, 29% in 1951, and bottoming out at 26% in 1961. In 1966 the proportion rose slightly, to 28%, and in 1971 very slightly more, to 28.2%. These data suggest a trend in Canada parallel to that in the USA where the number of adults aged 25 to 34 who have never married increased by 50% between 1960 and 1975, and where half of those aged 18 to 39 are married.[11]

A very rough approach to estimating the exact number of cohabitors can be made through census data. Under "Households,"

---

*Including persons separated.
**1976 Census data were not yet available when this paper was written in the spring of 1977; it was first published in 1978.

47

Table 1.1

Households Comprised of Two or More Persons Unrelated to the Head for Canada and the Provinces, 1961 and 1971 with Percentages

	1961			1971		
	Total Households	2 + Persons Not Related to Head	90% of Total	Total Households	2 + Persons Not Related to Head	90% of Total
Canada	4 554 736	100 520	2.2	6 041 305	165 605	2.8
Total Maritimes	419 938	7 336	1.8	504 890	9 885	2.0
Newfoundland	87 940	617	0.7	110 475	1 125	1.0
P.E.I.	23 942	452	1.9	27 895	535	1.9
Nova Scotia	175 341	3 875	2.2	208 420	5 070	2.4
New Brunswick	132 715	2 392	1.8	158 100	3 155	2.0
Quebec	1 191 439	24 521	2.1	1 605 750	44 620	2.8
Ontario	1 640 881	38 990	2.4	2 228 160	63 385	2.9
Manitoba	239 754	4 920	2.1	288 720	7 505	2.6
Saskatchewan	245 424	4 712	1.9	267 845	5 720	2.1
Alberta	349 816	8 149	2.3	464 940	13 435	2.8
British Columbia	459 534	11 588	2.5	668 305	20 580	3.1
Yukon/N.W.T.	7 920	304	3.8	12 690	485	3.8

Statistics Canada includes a tabulation of two or more persons who are not related to the head of the household. This category includes same-sex roommates, two or more men, or two or more women, sharing the same house or apartment, as well as situations where a single homeowner rented out a room to another of the same or opposite sex. It also includes cohabiting couples. We shall examine these data to see what they may imply.

Table 1.1 presents data on total households and those comprised of two or more persons not related to the head of the household, for 1961 and 1971, for all of Canada, and for the individual provinces. The data show that there was indeed a substantial increase in the proportion of such households for the country as a whole, from 2.2% in 1961 to 2.8% in 1971, an impressive 28% increase during the decade. The provincial data show that the proportions of such households were highest in British Columbia, Ontario, Alberta, and Quebec, which appears to accord well with where one might expect to find the highest incidences of heterosexual cohabitation—as well as of same-sex apartment sharing. These provincial data also show large increases in Quebec, Ontario, Manitoba, Alberta, and British Columbia in 1971, compared with 1961. However, we must emphasize that these figures are of unknown, but certainly rough value in indexing relative changes in cohabitation trends. Their chief usage may lie in illustrating how difficult it is to try to quantify cohabitation experience, using publicly available data.

The Author's Research

Research conducted by the author in 1967-68 and in 1976-77 sheds some additional light on the incidence of heterosexual cohabitation among Canadian post-secondary students and their attitudes toward this type of arrangement. Both studies dealt with various issues relating to changing orientations to courtship and marriage, and included questions dealing with attitudes and with experience. The earlier study collected data from 700 university students in Ontario and Alberta, and from technical school students in Alberta.[8] The 1976-77 study collected data from 2062 university and technical students enrolled in five universities and five technical schools in the Atlantic Provinces, Quebec, Ontario, the Prairie Provinces, and British Columbia. All three schools included in the earlier research were studied a second time. Random samples drawn from students enrolled in each of these schools consisted of equal numbers of men and women, for the earlier and the later study. Over 75% of the students contacted participated in the questionnaire study at all of the three schools included in the 1967-68 survey, and in eight of the ten schools surveyed in 1976-77.

A word should be said about the limitations of attitude and opinion research. We have no proof that the respondents to our questionnaires were telling us the truth, in respect to their attitudes toward cohabitation, their knowledge of other cohabitors, or the consequences of their own experience. How then can we be sure that many were not just "pulling our leg"? There are two relevant possible answers to this question; unfortunately neither of them particularly compelling. The first is that the questions we are dealing with here were part of a much longer questionnaire, dealing with attitudes and experience relating to premarital intercourse, conceptions of what the responsibilities and privileges of husbands and wives should be, and attitudes in regard to childrearing. There were 277 questions in all, and the questionnaire took a minimum of 50 minutes to answer. We are confident that uninterested people who were asked to participate in the study refused in the first place or turned in partially completed questionnaires, which were then discarded. In brief, we believe that it was just too much effort to complete a questionnaire of this length just to give frivolous answers. Furthermore, such answers would have been apparent in coding questions requiring written replies, and almost none were discovered.

The second answer to this question is that we had many indications from respondents of their serious interest in the issues that we were raising. These are times of revolutionary changes in sexual relations: frank and open glorification of sexual experience for its own sake, rapid increases in female premarital intercourse, experimentation with cohabitation, and other "alternative relationships" are products of the past ten to fifteen years. We obtained many indications that most of our respondents welcomed the opportunity that the questionnaire provided to think about such issues, and to tell us how they felt about these behaviours, what their experiences had been, and their reactions to these experiences. It seems very clear that these are matters far too serious for most young people today to take lightly. A few respondents either could not be bothered to fill out the questionnaire, or did so in such a way as to discredit their answers.

In the following pages we will first present information on the respondents' attitudes toward cohabitation, contrasting the responses of those surveyed in 1967-68 with those of the 1976-77 respondents to identically worded questions. Thereafter we will present data on knowledge of cohabitors, personal experience with cohabitation, and reactions to this experience, again contrasting the responses from the two surveys to identically worded questions. Finally, we will discuss the significance of the data presented.

Attitudes toward Heterosexual Cohabitation

Acceptance of Cohabitation. Both in 1967-68 and 1976-77 questionnaires included this item: "There is evidence that in many parts of North America it is not too uncommon for boy-girl couples to live together in semipermanent relationships without being married. How do you feel about relationships of this kind?"[11]

In answer to the first question only 6% of the 1967-68 sample members said that such relationships were definitely good, 19% said that they were good under certain circumstances, 31% voiced permissive or indifferent attitudes, one percent qualified their rejection, and 43% said that such relationships were definitely bad. Women were significantly more negative in their attitudes than men with 51% and 36% respectively rejecting these relationships.* The data further show that the earlier university samples were significantly more accepting of trial-marriage relationships than were members of the trade school sample, with 40% of the university and 54% of the trade school samples rating them as definitely bad. This difference is equally large for the male and the female components of these two samples.

By contrast, an inclusive 61% of the 1976-77 sample members said that these relationships were definitely good (19%) or good under certain circumstances (42%), 27% were permissive or indifferent, and only 12% expressed qualified or unqualified rejection. There were no differences between men and women in the attitudes expressed, nor between university and trade school students. Quebec students were least rejecting of such relationships (5%) and Prairie Provinces and British Columbia students were most critical (16%).

Half of those in the earlier sample who approved of these

---

*Differences between subsample statistically different at the 5% confidence level are described as differing significantly.

relationships (22 persons) gave reasons for their approval. Of these, 13 gave reasons expressing criticism or rejection of the marriage institution, many arguing that trial-marriage relationships were more moral or sacred than marriage.

The 279 subjects who expressed permissive, conditional, or indifferent attitudes, were evenly divided by sex, and there were few differences between males and females in the reasons given. More men (46%) than women (36%) said that it was up to the individual to decide, while 29% of both sexes felt that these were quite acceptable relationships, except that parents would be hurt in many cases. Women more often than men (18% versus 11%) said that, given the attitudes in our society, such relationships are acceptable if they result in marriage. Eight percent said that they were acceptable if the people involved were mature and responsible, and the same percentage approved if birth control procedures were used to prevent conception of children.

Only 150 subjects in the earlier sample gave reasons for rejecting trial-marriage relationships, and in this group women outnumbered men two to one. The most frequent remark by about half of both sexes was "why not get married?", made often with the observation that the only apparent reason was irresponsibility. Sixteen percent said that such relationships were morally wrong, and 8% mentioned the danger of "being caught" and subjected to society's reaction.

Eighty-four percent of the respondents in the later sample (a much higher proportion than in the earlier study) gave reasons for their attitudes, with 868 (50%) giving reasons for favouring cohabitation, 245 giving reasons for opposing it, and 624 stating that it should be a matter of individual choice. The most frequently cited favourable reasons were that: it permitted couples to reach greater understanding of each other (17%); it was a good trial period prior to marriage (14%); it was a healthy relationship (7%); a marriage certificate was unnecessary for such sharing (6%); and that it gave people a freedom of choice that conventional marriage does not (5%).

The unfavourable reasons mentioned were that: cohabitation shows a decline in moral standards (7.5%); it is bad because it leads to emotional dependence in the absence of commitment (4%); it shows lack of a sense of responsibility (3%).

Equal proportions of men and women (42%) mentioned reasons for favouring cohabitation, and there were no differences between men and women in proportions giving reasons for opposing it. Thirty percent of each said that it should be up to the individual. Men more often mentioned the trial period for marriage and asserted that such relationships were "healthy" as favourable reasons, while women, half again more often than men, said that trial marriage permitted couple members to reach greater understanding of each other. There were no differences in proportions stating that cohabitation reflects declining moral and religious standards.

There were no significant differences between trade school and university students in the later sample in attitudes toward cohabitation. In terms of region, Quebec students often gave favourable reasons (59%), and Atlantic Provinces students did so least often (43%). Atlantic Provinces students most often gave permissive ("leave it up to the individual") responses, while the British Columbia students did so least often (44% versus 30%).

A question designed to "strike close to home" asked "What would be your reaction if you had a nineteen-year-old sister living away from home and you discovered that she and a university student were living together, though not married?" Respondents were asked to place an X on a 10-point rating scale labelled "very much shocked" at one extreme and "not at all shocked" at the other extreme. Forty-eight percent of respondents in the earlier sample checked the first three strongest-shock positions while 20% checked the three least-shock positions.

The data show that women reported significantly more "shock" than men. The differences between schools were more sizable with university students reporting less shock than the technical school students. This is due only to differences between female technical school and university students; the differences between the male students were negligible. These data are in accord with other findings of this study[8] in signifying that male and female university students share the same norms relating to sexual behaviour more commonly than do men and women in technical schools.

In response to this same question, the members of the later sample voiced much more acceptance of such a relationship involving a sister. Thus only 15% checked the three strongest-shock positions while almost two-thirds (63%) checked the three least-shock positions. There were no significant differences by sex. However, very many more

Quebec students said that they would be not at all shocked (66%) as compared with Prairie Provinces and Ontario (27%) and Atlantic Provinces and B.C. students (33%).

Perceived Disadvantages and Advantages. To the question "What would you say are the disadvantages of such relationships?" only 3% of the 1967-68 sample members said there were no disadvantages. The responses of men and women tended to be very similar. About 30% of both groups said that the main disadvantage was the attitude of others, including gossip, loss of respect or reputation, and the cost to the feelings of parents. About one-quarter of both said that the major disadvantage was the risk of pregnancy in these relationships. More women than men mentioned the instability of such relationships (18% versus 11%), with the possibility of sudden break-up as the most important disadvantage.* This pattern was reversed (8% versus 15%) among those who said that such unions were incompatible with the organization of society, and among those who cited legal problems and consequences for persons in high office.** There were no differences between men and women in proportions when referring to emotional-problem consequences: guilt, shame, fear, etc.

To the question about the disadvantages of cohabitation relationships, 11% of the 1977 respondents said that there were no disadvantages. The most frequently cited disadvantages were the emotional hurt after breaking up (19%), the lack of security in such relationships (19%), family and social pressures (18%), followed by the risk of pregnancy (12.5%), the weakness of the cohabitation bond (10%), and the loss of sexual freedom (6%).

Men more often than women said that there were no disadvantages (15% versus 8%).*** There were no other significant differences in response by sex or by type of school.

However, there are substantial differences between the students by region. Far more Quebec students said that there were no

---

*The differences between the responses of men and women are relatively slight, but they are statistically significant because the number of respondents is large.
**Idem.
***Idem.

disadvantages (22%) than Atlantic Provinces students (5%), and than Prairie Provinces, Atlantic Provinces, or B.C. students together (about 9%). Family pressures were mentioned most often by Ontario students (26%) and least by Prairie Provinces and B.C. students (about 14%); lack of security in the relationship was mentioned most by Quebec and least by Atlantic Provinces students (24% versus 15%); weakness of the cohabitation bond was mentioned most by B.C. and least by Quebec students (15% versus 5%); the risk of pregnancy was mentioned most by Quebec and least by B.C. students (17% versus 9%); and the emotional hurt after breaking up most by B.C., Atlantic provinces, and Ontario students, and least by Quebec students (about 24% versus 8%).

Twenty-two percent of the early sample members said that trial-marriage relationships had no advantages, including a higher proportion of women (26%) than of men (17%). Otherwise there were few differences between the two sex groups. The most often mentioned advantage, cited by 22% of both groups, was that such relationships served as a marriage trial by permitting couple members to test their compatibility under conditions when they could see each other at their worst. Almost one-fifth mentioned as the major advantage the freedom of such a relationship from the tyranny of a "*paper* marriage certificate." Compulsion for mates to live together when married and unable to get a divorce was also mentioned in this context. The fullness of sharing, of "real communication," and of knowing the other person that is possible in such trial relationships was mentioned by one in eight of men and women. Men more often than women spoke of the sexual satisfaction in cohabitation relationships (13% versus 5%).

Only 6% of those in the later sample said that there were no advantages to cohabitation, as compared with 22% in the 1968 sample. Sharing of experience in cohabitation leading to better understanding was the advantage cited by 33%, followed by appreciation of the trial period for marriage and/or compatibility that such relationships offer (21%), the flexibility and freedom of choice in such relationships (13%), the absence of legal complications if the relationship ends (11%), and the companionship enjoyed (10%). There were no sex differences in responses to this question, nor were there significant differences between trade school and university students in the advantages mentioned. While there were no differences between the regional samples in proportions asserting that cohabitation had no advantages, there were substantial differences in the kinds of advantages specified. The benefits of a trial period were most often cited by Ontario and Atlantic Provinces students (about 28%) but by only 8% of Quebeckers; and the resulting better understanding was mentioned most by Quebec and least by Atlantic Provinces students (40% versus 25%).

Perceived Justifications. To the question "Would you say that such a relationship is justified?" 56% of the early sample respondents said "yes," 52% qualifying their answers in various ways. The data show that affirmative answers were given only slightly more often by men than women, the proportions being 58% and 53% respectively. Almost all of the remaining answers were negative without qualification, with 41% of subjects answering in this way.

Again our data point to significant differences in acceptance of trial-marriage relationships between the earlier school samples, with 42% of the technical school as compared with 60% of the university students saying that they felt that cohabitation relationships could be justified. There were no differences between the male and female respondents.

The kinds of justifications mentioned by the earlier respondents have already been hinted at earlier. About half of the male and female samples said that it was entirely up to the people involved. Significantly more women (30%) than men (15%) felt that such relationships were justified if the partners were for some reason prevented from marrying each other. Eleven percent of both men and women said that such relationships were justified if the people involved were exploring the possibilities of marriage, and 9% said that they were justified if the partners were in love.

In the later sample, 87% of the respondents said that cohabitation relationships were justified, three-fifths qualifying their answers in various ways, as compared with 56% in the earlier sample. The data show that affirmative answers were made insignificantly more often by men than women. There were no significant differences in responses to this question by type of school, or by region, although justification of cohabitation was most frequently affirmed by Quebeckers (91%) and was least supported by Prairie Provinces students (83%).

The most common qualification suggested was that if the partners were in love, or needed each other (17%). Eleven percent inserted the qualification "if they were planning to marry," 7% said "if they were willing to accept the full consequences of their relationship," and 6% said "if they were prevented from marrying (as by a separation agreement) or were unsure about marriage." More men than women, 39% as compared with 30%, said that no justification was necessary; but, surprisingly, there was no sex difference in the proportions inserting the qualification "if the couple was planning to marry."

Somewhat more Quebeckers than Prairie Provinces and Atlantic Provinces respondents asserted that no justification was necessary (43% versus about 27%). There were differences in qualifications proposed by region as well. Quebeckers least often qualified "if the couple planned to marry" (8% versus 17% for the Atlantic Provinces), "if the couple accepts full responsibility" (2% versus about 11% for the Prairie Provinces and Atlantic Provinces) and most often qualified "if the partners love each other" (25% versus 16% for Ontario).

Information about Cohabitation Relationships

Subjects were asked "Do you know of any couples living together in this way? If so, how many? Are any of them friends of yours? How many? Were, or are, any of your brothers or sisters involved in such relationships?"

A total of 43% of the first sample, equally divided by sex, knew of cohabitation relationships at the time they filled out the questionnaires. Fifteen percent knew of two or more couples, and nine respondents said they knew of nine or more. Most of these, 28% of the total sample, reported that some of their friends were involved in such relationships. Nineteen subjects said that they had brothers or sisters who had participated in such relationships.

There were few differences between male and female members of the early sample in proportions knowing couples living together in this way. Women in the sample reported having siblings in these relationships more than twice as frequently as did men, but the frequencies were very small. There are more sizable, but yet insignificant differences between the school samples, however. Only 35% of the technical school students knew of couples living in trial-marriage relationships, as compared with 47% of the university students.

Among members of the later sample, no less than 87% reported knowing cohabiting couples, equally distributed between men and women. About three-fifths said that they knew of three or more couples, and one-third said they knew of five or more couples. Almost all those knowing people so involved said that some of their friends were in such relationships and 19% said that they had brothers and/or sisters so involved.

There were no significant differences between male and female members of the later sample in proportions knowing of cohabiting couples, or having friends or siblings so involved. The regional data show that there were no differences between regional subsamples in proportions knowing of cohabiting *couples* or having cohabiting *siblings*. However 94% of Quebec respondents said that they had cohabiting *friends*, as compared with 85% of the Ontarians, and about 90% of those in the other three regions.

Experience with Cohabitation Relationships

Sample members were asked: "Have you ever been involved in such a (cohabitation) relationship?" Thirty-eight subjects, in the 1968 sample, 21 men and 17 women, comprising 6% of the respondents reported that they had been. University students reported such experience more than twice as frequently as did the technical school students, but the difference is not statistically significant because of the small number of cases.

In the 1977 sample a total of 307 subjects, 15% of those responding including 157 men and 150 women, said that they had experience in cohabitation relationship. It is particularly significant that a further 70% said that they had not had such experience "because the situation has not arisen." Only 15% said that such a relationship would be wrong.* There were no differences in proportions of university and technical school students reporting cohabitation relationships. Although the Quebec students were the most favourable in their attitudes toward cohabitation, it was the B.C. students who were the most experienced sample (21%), followed by Quebec and Prairie Provinces (15.5%) and Ontario and Atlantic Provinces students

---

*These last two reponse alternatives were not included in the 1967-68 questionnaire.

(about 13%). However, the Quebec students most frequently and B.C. and Prairie Provinces students least frequently reported lack of experience because the situation had not arisen (76% versus 63%). Moral opposition to cohabitation was most strongly expressed by Prairie Provinces students (21%), followed by Ontario and B.C. (about 17%), Atlantic Provinces (12%), and least of all Quebec (8%), students.

Durations, Advantages, and Disadvantages. Respondents who said they had themselves been involved in trial-marriage relationships were asked: "How long did the relationship last? What would you say were the advantages of it? What would you say were the disadvantages of it?"

In the earlier sample, the 38 experienced respondents reported that the relationship had culminated in marriage in ten cases, that it was still continuing in 14 cases, and that it had ended in the remaining 14 cases. Of the 28 cases which had not ended in marriage, six had lasted less than a month, 14 had lasted from one to six months, four had lasted from seven months to a year, and four had lasted for more than a year.

Thirty-one subjects commented on the advantages of their relationships. A plurality of both sexes, 14 in all, said that it permitted each to get to know and appreciate the other better. Five out of eight women, and three out of eighteen men said that they learned in the relationship to become more co-operative, to experience life more deeply, etc. Three men, but no women, said that there were no advantages.

Thirty subjects commented on disadvantages of their relationships. Nine said that there were no disadvantages, and the same number mentioned the fear of being "caught." Four said that the relationship became unsatisfactory because it was too constraining.

Among the 1976-77 sample members, 10% reported that their cohabitation relationships had resulted in marriage. Among the remainder, the median duration of the first relationship was nine months, with 9% lasting no more than a month, 34% lasting from two to six months, 18% from seven to 12 months and 39% lasting more than a year.

There were no differences in duration of the first relationship by type of school. In terms of region they lasted longest in B.C. and the

Prairie Provinces where 63% had lasted at least seven months, and were shortest in Ontario and the Atlantic Provinces where 50% had lasted seven months.

In response to a question about the advantages of the first relationship, over one-third (37%) said that they grew closer to their partners; 20% said that it was a learning experience; 12% said that it was enjoyable or satisfying; 10% said that they enjoyed the different lifestyle. Only 6% mentioned sexual freedom, 4% reported economic advantages, and 4%, equally distributed, said that it had led to marriage. Only 10 people said there were no advantages.

There were significant regional differences but not university/ technical school differences in perceived advantages. Growing closer to the partner was mentioned most by Ontarians, and least by Prairie Provinces and Atlantic Provinces respondents (49% versus 32%). Value of the relationship as a learning or growing experience was emphasized most by B.C. and least by Ontario students (25% versus 13%). The pleasurable, satisfying aspects were cited most by Prairie Provinces and B.C. and least by Atlantic Provinces students (15% versus 5%). Enjoyment of the different lifestyle was mentioned most by Atlantic Provinces and least by Ontario students (17% versus 4%). This latter seems clearly to reflect regional differences in subcultures, as they impinge upon students.

To the question dealing with the disadvantages of the first relationship, the largest proportion, 29%, said that there were "none." Twenty-one percent mentioned difficulties in coping with bad times, 15% referred to parental rejection, 11% cited incompatibility, 9% mentioned social pressures ("people talk"), and the remainder referred to other disadvantages.

There were significant differences in disadvantages specified between the regional subsamples, but not between school types. Thus Quebeckers most often and Prairie Provinces students least often said that there were no disadvantages (35% versus 22%); Quebec and Prairie Provinces students most often, and Ontarians least often reported parental rejection (19% versus 9%); Atlantic Provinces most often and B.C. students least often cited social pressures (20% versus 4%). B.C. and Quebec most often and Atlantic Provinces students least often mentioned coping with bad times (23% versus 13%), and Ontarians most often and Quebeckers least often mentioned incompatibility with partner (21% versus 2%).

Emotional Involvement with Partners. Respondents with cohabitation experience were asked: "Were you in love with your relationship partner? Would you have liked to marry your relationship partner?" Of the 38 cohabitors in the 1968 sample, 48% (18 respondents), including 65% of the women and only 33% of the men, said that they definitely were in love. By contrast half of the men and none of the women said that they definitely were not in love with their partners.

Twelve out of thirty-three of the early respondents said that they definitely did not want to marry their partners, and this included half of the men but only one-quarter of the women. Ten subjects (7 of the women, and 3 of the men) had married, and eight said that they definitely would like to get married. This response was slightly more characteristic of women than men. Ten of the eleven men who said they did not want to marry their partners and all three of the women who made this response gave reasons for not wanting to marry their partners. Six men said that they were not in love with their partners; two said their partners were "easy makes" whom they would not want to marry; and two said their attitudes were not compatible. One woman made this latter response as well; one said her partner was too immature; and one was against marriage in principle.

When asked if they were in love with their first relationship partner, 81% said that they were, and 8% said that they were not, while 11% were not certain. Women more often than men said that they were in love—90% versus 72%, but note that the differential is far less than in the 1968 sample (65% versus 33%). There were no significant differences in this respect between the technical school and the university students, but there were differences between the regional samples. Quebec students most often said that they were in love (95%), followed by those from the Prairie Provinces (81%), Ontario and B.C. (77%), and the Atlantic Provinces (71%).

To the question "Would you have liked to marry your first relationship partner? Why or why not?", 43% of those in the later sample said "Yes," and the rest said "No." By contrast with the earlier samples, only 3% more of the women than of the men said "Yes." Reasons given for wanting to marry the partner included love (60%) leading to marriage in the case of half of them, and the fact that they got along well (17%). Only four people said that they wanted to marry because there were children involved.

Reasons given for not wanting to marry included: the partner did not meet standards for a mate (23%), did not wish to marry at the time (19%), did not know if marriage would work (14%), and did not feel that marriage was necessary (21%)—evenly divided by sex.

There were no differences by type of school in proportions wanting to marry their first cohabitation partner, nor in reasons given for not wanting to marry.

Again there were striking significant differences between regional subsamples. The Quebec students were least interested in marrying (30%), followed by those in the Atlantic Provinces and B.C. (39%), in the Prairie Provinces (51%), and in Ontario (59%). There were few differences in reasons for wanting to marry: B.C. and Atlantic Provinces students mentioned valuing the companionship less frequently than did those from the other regions (8% versus 23%). However, there were many differences in reasons given for not wanting to marry. Twice as many students in Quebec than in any other region said that marriage was unnecessary (37% versus about 18%). No fewer than 42% of the Prairie Provinces respondents said that the partner did not meet their standards, as compared with only 13% of those in Ontario and Quebec. Not wishing to marry at the time was reported most often by B.C. and least often by Prairie Provinces and Quebec respondents (27% versus 14%), and uncertainty about how marriage to the partner would work out was reported most often by Ontario and Quebec and least often by Prairie Provinces students (20% versus 8%).

Stresses in the Relationships, Terminations. Respondents were asked: "If the relationship is now ended, how and why did it end? If you are still in the relationship, can you see any difficulties developing that are likely to end it? If so, what are they?"

Of the 38 cohabitation relationships reported by the early sample members, as noted, ten subjects did marry their partners and in 14 cases the relationship was continuing at the time the respondent answered the questionnaire. The 14 subjects whose relationships had ended gave the following reasons: the partner had moved away (four); couple members became bored—"it was a drag" (five); incompatibility, (three); pregnancy (one); and intervention of parents (one).

Fourteen subjects—eight men and six women—whose relationships were continuing responded to the question "Can you see any difficulties developing that are likely to end the relationship? If so, what are they?" Seven subjects, five men and two women, said that they could anticipate no such difficulties. Others mentioned the possibility of one member having to move away, the negative reaction of society to their relationship, and the possibility of a change in attitude of the partners.

In the 1977 sample, 238 respondents provided information on how their last relationships had ended. Two-thirds (66%) said that the relationship was still continuing. Of the 81 with terminated relationships, 41% said that they had lost interest in the other person or vice versa; 24% said that they and their partners had differing goals; 23% reported that their partners moved away; and 5% reported economic problems. The remainder gave a variety of other reasons. There were no differences between the responses of men and women or of university and technical school students.

About 74% of the students in the Prairie Provinces, Atlantic Provinces, and B.C. said that their last relationship was yet continuing, as did about 57% of those in Ontario and Quebec. In terms of reasons for separating, one partner moving away was mentioned most frequently in Ontario and least often in the Atlantic Provinces (19% versus 0%), and loss of interest by one partner was mentioned most frequently by B.C. and Quebec and least often by Prairie Provinces students (about 19% versus 9%).

To the question "If you are still in the relationship, can you see any difficulties developing that are likely to end the relationship? If so, what are they?", about two-thirds of the 157 respondents said that they could not anticipate any such difficulties. Fifty-four percent of the remaining 56 respondents mentioned such problems as pursuing different interests and life goals, jealousy, partner's moving away, difficulties from differences in intelligence, parental pressure, and marriage as the termination. Men and women responded similarly, and there were no significant regional differences.

Discussion
These data reflect a number of fascinating contrasts between the 1967-68 and the 1976-77 samples. The earlier data show that there was limited approval of such relationships (26%) but a great deal of tolerance (31%), as well as of rejection of them (43%). The recent data show that only 13% of the sample members reject these relationships

for themselves or for others. The acceptance is particularly apparent in responses to the question concerning involvement of a sister in heterosexual cohabitation. Whereas earlier 48% had said that they would be much shocked, in the recent sample only 15% gave the same responses.

Awareness of such relationships in general had doubled, during the nine-year interval between the studies, but awareness of such relationships among friends had increased more than threefold, and awareness of such involvements among siblings had increased more than sevenfold. Personal involvement in such relationships had increased about threefold.

At least equally impressive is the erosion of sex differences in attitudes relating to cohabitation from 1968 to 1977. Generally the earlier study showed that women were more marriage-oriented and more concerned about the security or persistence of the relationship than were men. Thus, while women in the first sample were generally less favourable toward cohabitation than were men, they more often said cohabitation was acceptable if it resulted in marriage. Among those who had themselves experienced heterosexual cohabitation, twice as many women as men reported that they either had married or would like to marry their partners. By contrast, in the later sample, women were as favourable toward cohabitation as were men. They did mention disadvantages of such relationships slightly more often than men. However the distinctive concern among women in the early sample that cohabitation should lead to marriage was entirely lacking among women in the later sample.

Our search for differences in attitudes and experience relating to cohabitation between university and technical school students has revealed none of significance. It would thus appear that the cohabitation alternative has penetrated university and technical school subcultures about equally.

The same cannot be said for the regional subsamples. On the basis of our data, it would appear that if a revolt against marriage is brewing anywhere in Canada, it is brewing in Quebec. The consistency of the picture that has emerged from the data is indeed impressive. As compared with the other regional samples, the Quebec respondents most frequently asserted that: cohabitation relationships were good and gave reasons in support, there were no disadvantages to cohabitation; no justification was needed for such relationships or that mutual love was the only justification needed (and least often gave planning to marry as a justification); they would be not at all shocked if a sister was cohabiting; they had as yet had no cohabitation experience only because the situation had not arisen (and least often said that it was morally wrong); they had cohabiting friends; those with cohabiting experience were in love with their partners; they had no interest in marrying their cohabitation partners; and that marriage was unnecessary. The only exception to this pattern is that a slightly higher proportion of B.C. respondents than Quebec respondents reported actual cohabitation experience.

It is also noteworthy that there were few, if any, consistent differences between patterns of responses for the remaining four regions. One might have anticipated that students from the "Bible Belt" Prairie Provinces or the "backwater" Atlantic Provinces might have been more moralistic or conservative than those from "metropolitan" Ontario or "swinging" British Columbia. However, no such differences are to be detected in our data, with any degree of regularity.

What are the implications of these data for the future of marriage in Canada? Perhaps the first point to be made is that we have found relatively little moral opposition to cohabitation. Thus, only 15% reported that they felt it would be wrong for themselves; 13% said that they could not justify such relationships; and particularly noteworthy is the fact that only 7% said that cohabitation relationships were unconditionally bad, when asked how they felt about such relationships. Note also that women were not significantly more rejecting of cohabitation relationships than were men. This is particularly important because women have traditionally been ascribed special responsibility as "guardians of morality." Nor does our sample reflect the existence of pockets of moralistic resistance in some parts of the country. Thus, increasingly it would appear that the obstacles to the spread of cohabitation are practical, relating to the intrinsic disadvantages or limitations of this relationship rather than to principle or morality. This is, of course, particularly true of Quebec where there is more evidence of rejection of marriage as being unnecessary and acceptance of cohabitation as intrinsically good, than in any other part of the country.

We can further explore the implications of these data for the future by extrapolating from our data to the post-secondary school population of Canada. Thus we can draw some inferences about the current number of cohabitors and check these inferences against what is known about cohabitation in the United States and in European countries.

The most-recent enrolment statistics available at this writing for Canadian universities and other post-secondary schools are for the 1973-74 school year.[21/22] The estimated enrolments for the 1976-77 school year are about 325 000 for universities and about 200 000 for full-time enrolments in other post-secondary schools. If we extrapolate the 16.0% rate of cohabitation experience for university students and the 15.7% rate for technical school students to these total enrolments, about 83 400 post-secondary school students across Canada may have had cohabitation experience as of the end of the 1976-77 school year.

We may further extrapolate to the entire Canadian "early adult" population, aged 18 through 25 years, by assuming that a cohabitation experience rate of 15% is a reasonable estimate for this age category. On the basis of the approximately 350 100 young people in this age range,[20] no fewer than half a million young Canadians would have had cohabitation experience. This number seems realistic in view of Cole's report[4] that 1970 US census data show that approximately 11% of the total population aged 18 and over were cohabiting with an opposite sex person, when the census was taken. Further, he suggests that this is probably an underestimate since university student populations would not be systematically represented in that number.

It seems probable that Canadian experimentation and involvement with cohabitation will parallel the American experience—this has generally been true of technology, of food, dress, and sport fads, and of sexual morality generally. There is no reason to believe that the rate of cohabitation in the United States had peaked as of 1970. The conditions facilitating cohabitation—easy availability of the birth control pill, relatively easily available abortions, increasingly permissive attitudes toward premarital sex—were yet relatively new at that time. There was not yet a generation that had grown to maturity under these favourable conditions. However, in Sweden a 1974 national survey showed that no more than 12% of all couples living together were cohabiting out of wedlock.[24] Given the longer-standing, stronger permissiveness which is characteristic of Scandinavian countries, it is perhaps surprising that this proportion of cohabitors is not higher. Again it seems more important to remember that the first generation to have grown up under conditions optimally facilitating cohabitation is just reaching maturity.

Trost[24] cites evidence from Sweden and Denmark which suggests that as the marriage rate decreases, the rate of non-marital cohabitation increases. It seems probable that the marriage rate will continue to decline in Canada for at least five to ten years. Government projections of increasing unemployment in Canada during the next two years, leaked to the press in May 1977, continuing trends toward women's liberation, declining birth rates, and the growing popularity of childlessness, all tend to erode marriage rates.

And yet the high proportion of Swedish cohabiting couples who were married, 88%, points to the continued existence of strong forces sustaining the popularity of marriage. The two strongest of these must be the desire for, and/or birth of children, and the desire for security or permanence in the relationship. The latter is a strong consideration as our questionnaire data show. High and rising divorce rates demonstrate that marriage itself is certainly far from permanent for many. But, by contrast with cohabitation, it does involve making a formal, often ritualized commitment to permanence, and the routines which must be fulfilled for divorce preclude precipitous dissolution. On the other hand there is evidence that cohabitation is increasing among people who have been divorced or legally separated, including middle-aged people.[16]

The data reviewed and the arguments advanced appear to lead to the following conclusions which should prove valid for at least the short run. Heterosexual cohabitation will continue to increase significantly in Canada as it becomes increasingly socially acceptable, and as more people encounter others who have entered into this kind of relationship. The tendency to postpone, if not to avoid childbearing, economic insecurity—particularly of the young, which is now approaching an all-time high[2]—and high divorce rates, will all accentuate this trend. However, it will certainly remain a minority practice, at least among the general population, because most people will eventually want to be parents and to raise their children within wedlock. Many people, parents or not, will want security in relationships which cohabitation agreements by definition cannot provide. There is probably little chance that cohabitation will pose a widespread challenge to marriage, at least until the society is able to socialize generations which are more personally secure than are very many young people today.[10]

References

1. Block, Donald. "Unwed Couples: Do They Live Happily Ever After?" *Redbook* (April 1969), pp. 90ff.

2. Canadian Council on Social Development. *Youth and Unemployment: A Sourcebook.* Ottawa, Ontario: Publications Section, Canadian Council on Social Development, 1977.

3. Coffin, Patricia. "Young Unmarrieds: Theresa Mommett and Charles Walsh, College Grads Living Together." *Look* (January 26, 1971), pp. 634ff.

4. Cole, Charles Lee. "Cohabitation in Social Context," in Libby, Roger W., and Whitehurst, Robert N., eds. *Marriage and Alternatives, Exploring Intimate Relationships.* Glenview, Ill.: Scott, Foresman and Company, 1977, pp. 62-79.

5. Dominion Bureau of Statistics. 1961 Census of Canada. *Households and Families, Households by Type,* Vol. 2, Part 1, Bulletin 2.1-2, 1963.

6. *Esquire.* "Room-Mates." (September 1967), pp. 94-98.

7. Grant, A. "No Rings Attached: A Look at Premarital Marriage on Campus." *Mademoiselle* 66 (April 1968), pp. 208ff.

8. Hobart, Charles W. "Trial Family Living: A Study of Student Attitudes and Experience," in Wakil, S. Parvez, ed. *Marriage, Family and Society.* Toronto: Butterworth and Co., 1975, pp. 401-415.

9. Karlen, Arno. "Those Unmarried Marrieds on Campus." *New York Times Magazine* (January 26, 1969), pp. 29ff.

10. Levinger, George. Letter to Roger W. Libby, cited in Libby, Roger W. "Creative Singlehood as a Sexual Life-Style," in Libby, Roger W., and Whitehurst, Robert N., eds. *Marriage Alternatives.* Glenview, Ill.: Scott, Foresman and Co., 1975.

11. Libby, Roger W. "Creative Singlehood as a Sexual Life-Style," in Libby, Roger W., and Whitehurst, Robert N., eds. *Marriage and Alternatives,* Glenview, Ill.: Scott, Foresman and Co., 1975.

12. Maclin, Eleanor D. "Heterosexual Cohabitation Among Unmarried College Students." *The Family Coordinator* 21, No. 4, (1972), pp. 463-472.

13. McWhirter, William A. "The Arrangement at College." *Life* (May 31, 1968), pp. 56ff.

14. *Newsweek.* "Unstructured Relationships: Students Living Together," 68 (July 4, 1966), p. 78.

15. Rollin, Betty. "New Hang-up for Parents: Coed Living." *Look* (September 23, 1969), pp. 22ff.

16. Safire, W. "On Cohabitation." *The New York Times* (September 24, 1973), p. 31.

17. Schrag, Peter. "Posse at Generation Gap: Implications of the Linda LeClair Affair." *Saturday Review* 51 (May 18, 1968), p. 81.
18. Sheehy, Gail. "Living Together: The Stories of Four Young Couples Who Risk the Strains of Non-marriage and Why." *Glamour* (February 1, 1969), pp. 136ff.
19. Statistics Canada. *1971 Census of Canada, Household Composition*, Vol. 2, Part 1, Bulletin 2.1-4. Ottawa: Statistics Canada, 1973.
20. _____. *1971 Census of Canada, Population by Age Group*, Vol. 1, Part 2, Bulletin 1.2-3. Ottawa: Statistics Canada, 1973.
21. _____. *Students in Public Trade Schools and Similar Institutions 1973-75*. Ottawa: Information Canada, 1976.
22. _____. *Universities and Colleges of Canada, 1975*. Ottawa: Information Canada, 1976.
23. *Time*. "Linda, The Light Housekeeper." April 26, 1968, p. 51.
24. Trost, J. "Married and Unmarried Cohabitation: The Case of Sweden With Some Comparisons." *Journal of Marriage and the Family* 37 (1975), pp. 677-682.

2/Trends and Differences in Mean Age at Marriage in Canada*

K.G. Basavarajappa

Age at entry into sexual union is an important variable influencing fertility. As necessary data are usually not available in this variable, the age at marriage provided a closely related variable. Hence studies of differences in fertility have made use of this variable extensively. It has been shown generally that the age at marriage is inversely related to fertility. Censuses in Canada and the United States of America provide sufficient evidence on this aspect.[5/10]

It is of interest to see how the mean age at marriage has varied over time in Canada and whether there have been any differences in mean ages at marriage among ethnic groups, religious groups, residence groups, etc. Trends in mean age at marriage are examined by using data from both censuses and Vital Statistics records. The differences in mean age at marriage are examined on the basis of data from the 1971 Census.

Trends in Singulate Mean Age at Marriage Canada, 1851-1971

As vital statistics (births, deaths, marriages, etc.) on a more uniform basis became available for Canada only since 1921, a study of long-term trends in mean age at marriage involving the latter half of the nineteenth century must rely mainly on censuses.

Using the proportions of single by age obtained from the census enumerated age-sex marital status distribution, it is possible to estimate an index which is roughly equivalent to the mean age at first marriage. The estimate thus obtained is termed "singulate mean age at marriage." It represents the mean age at first marriage of a

---

*This paper is based on a more detailed work of the author entitled *Marital Status and Nuptiality in Canada* published by Statistics Canada. The views expressed are those of the author and not of Statistics Canada.

hypothetical cohort of persons passing through life, not subject to mortality, and marrying at various ages before their fiftieth birthday. The marriage rates are those implied in proportions single as shown in the given census.

Table 2.1 presents the singulate mean age at marriage of males and females as calculated from proportions single by age obtained from Canadian censuses of 1851 to 1971.

Table 2.1
Singulate Mean Age at Marriage, Canada, 1851-1971

Census	Male	Female	Difference
	Mean Ages		
1851	26.8	23.8	3.0
1861	27.6	25.2	2.4
1871	28.4	25.9	2.5
1881	28.5	25.8	2.7
1891	29.2	26.1	3.1
1911	28.5	24.4	4.1
1921	27.3	23.8	3.5
1931	27.7	24.6	3.1
1941	27.7	24.8	2.9
1951	26.0	23.0	3.0
1956	25.0	21.8	3.2
1961	24.7	21.9	3.3
1966	24.7	21.9	2.8
1971	24.4	22.0	2.4

Period	Changes in Mean Age[1]	
1851-1891	–2.4	–2.3
1891-1971	–4.8	–4.1
1851-1971	–2.4	–1.8

[1]A plus indicates an increase and a minus a decrease.

Source: Computed from Proportions single by age obtained from the respective censuses. For method of computation, see Appendix V in K.G. Basavarajappa, *Marital Status and Nuptiality in Canada*, Statistics Canada, Profile Studies, Demographic Characteristics, Bulletin 5.1-4, Catalogue 99-704, Ottawa, 1978.

It may be seen that for both males and females, the mean ages increased until 1891, and have shown declining trends since then with minor fluctuations. From 1851 to 1891 the increases in mean ages were roughly the same for both males and females. In Canadian, as in other Western societies, one of the traditional obstacles to marriage was the requirement of ability to support a family. This means that when the basis of family support was mainly agricultural, the couple had to have agricultural land of its own. As land was available in plenty in Canada, the couple could work the land and support the family. Hence the age at marriage was relatively low during the middle of the nineteenth century. As industrialization increased, the basis of family support was altered. To support a family a man had to have a steady job. Women's work participation was either low or non-existent and the man had to be the main breadwinner. This is probably the reason for an increase in the mean age at marriage until the beginning of the twentieth century. For the decline in mean age at marriage since the early years of the twentieth century, the wider availability of contraceptives (which enables couples to control the numbers and spacing of their offspring), the willingness of young married women to work outside the home, and various social and welfare measures (such as home ownership assistance, medical and health insurance, family allowances, etc.) may all have contributed their share.

The difference between the mean age at marriage of males and that of females increased until 1911, and has shown a declining trend since then with minor fluctuations. During 1891-1971, and during 1851-1971 as a whole, the decreases in mean ages were higher for males than for females.

Trends in Mean Age at Marriage of Brides and Grooms by Previous Marital Status

Trends in "singulate mean age at marriage" (which could be considered as roughly equivalent to the trends in mean age at first marriage) examined in the preceding section showed that the mean ages gradually increased from the middle of the nineteenth century to the early years of the twentieth century. Since then, they have declined for both sexes. It is of interest to see how the mean ages at marriage of single, widowed, and divorced brides and grooms have varied over time. Unfortunately, the published data needed to calculate these go back in time only to 1940.

An examination of these statistics showed that the levels for the three categories varied a great deal: the single, as expected, having the lowest mean age at marriage, and the widowed, the highest. The widowed level was nearly twice or slightly more than twice the level of the single. The divorced level was in between the levels observed for single and widowed. Although the relative values of the three categories changed slightly during 1940-1974, the relationship observed above (i.e., the widowed having the highest, the divorced, the second highest, and the single, the lowest) would continue in the future for two main reasons: (i) the already low levels of mortality are likely to continue to be low or decline further in future years, and (ii) the age at remarriage after divorce cannot be lower than the age at first marriage. However, the difference between the mean age at marriage of the single and that of the divorced may decrease in future years. In what follows, the trends in each of these categories are examined separately.

Single
It was found that the mean ages at marriage of single brides and grooms declined during 1941-1974. The declines amounted to two years for brides (from 24.4 years in 1940 to 22.4 years in 1974) and three years for grooms (from 27.7 years in 1940 to 24.7 years in 1974). Several factors may have influenced these declines. First, with the increased spread of knowledge and practice of contraception, marriage did not automatically lead to children. Couples were able to control the numbers and spacing of their offspring much more effectively than before, thus encouraging early marriages. Second, women were willing to work outside the home. The labour-force participation rates for females ages 14 years and over increased from about 22.9% in 1941 to 37.0% in 1971.[4] Consequently, the necessity of male earning power to support the family had been reduced, and men and women married earlier. Third, for those who wanted to have children immediately after marriage, many social programmes came to their aid. Family allowance, unemployment compensation, welfare payments, medical and health insurance benefits, etc., all probably encouraged early marriage. The proportions of brides and grooms aged 19 years or under (i.e., teenage marriages) increased during 1921-1974, and the increases were much more marked among males than among females. The levels for bridegrooms increased from 1.9% in 1921 to 7.8% in 1974 and those for brides from 21.9% in 1921 to 27.0% in 1974.

What is likely to be the future course in mean age at marriage of single persons is hard to say. If more and more young people begin to live together in the future without being legally married, the mean age at marriage may increase slightly for this group. In fact, such a trend has already been noticed in the United States [see also Chapter 1 in this book]. At the moment at least, it appears as though the declines in Canada have bottomed out.

Widowed

As may be expected, the mean ages at remarriage of widows and widowers increased during the period. The increases amounted to 6.8 years for these brides (from 45.9 years in 1940 to 52.7 years in 1974) and 8.9 years for these bridegrooms (from 49.4 years in 1940 to 58.3 years in 1974). These increases were brought about mainly by declining mortality. The expectation of life increased by 10.06 years for females and 6.38 years for males.* Thus, the increase in mean age at remarriage of females was lower than the increase in life expectation for them (6.8 years versus 10.06 years), whereas, in the case of males, it was higher (8.9 years versus 6.38 years). Why this difference? An important reason seems to be that older widows do not marry to the same extent as do older widowers. In fact, it has been shown elsewhere that not only did the widowers show higher marriage rates than widows, but also the increase in marriage rates during 1941-1971 at ages 50 years and over were higher for widowers than for widows.

The lowest values of mean ages at marriage of widows were observed during 1945-1948. This was obviously brought about by higher proportions of widows marrying during those years as compared with other years. Who were these younger widows and why were they found in larger numbers during those years when compared with other years? A plausible explanation is that the deaths of enlisted men during the Second World War were responsible for increases in numbers of widows during those years.

---

*Here the implicit assumption is that the expectation of life at birth observed for the general population is applicable to all marital status categories. Although this is not strictly correct, the errors involved especially in terms of expectation of life are negligible. For levels of expectations of life at birth during 1941-1971, see *Canada Year Book*, 1972, page 281, and 1975, page 184.

What about the future course in the mean ages at marriage of widows and widowers? If the already low levels of mortality in Canada further decline, the mean ages at widowhood are likely to increase further, and consequently the mean ages at marriage of widows and widowers may be expected to inch upwards in coming years.

Divorced

Unlike the mean ages at marriage of single persons (which showed declining trends) and those of widowed persons (which showed increasing trends), the mean ages at marriage of divorced persons fluctuated from year to year. These fluctuations were small except for noticeable declines during 1942-1946 for brides and 1944-1947 for bridegrooms, and noticeable increases during 1968-1969 for both brides and grooms.

Why did the declines in mean ages at marriage of divorced persons occur during 1942-1947? It should be remembered that the crude divorce rate increased much faster immediately after the Second World War to reach a high level of 65.4 per 100 000 population in 1947, a level which was not again reached until 1969.[2] These more numerous divorces undoubtedly occurred because of marital disruptions associated with the war and occurred mainly to relatively younger persons when compared with earlier or immediately succeeding periods. Thus the age distributions of divorced brides and grooms consisted of greater proportions of younger persons during 1942-1947, thereby giving rise to declining mean ages at marriage during those years. With the situation becoming relatively more stable after 1947, the divorce rates declined and the mean ages at marriage of divorced persons showed increases until the early 1950's. Thereafter, the mean ages fluctuated slightly and remained roughly at the same levels until 1968. Suddenly there was a noticeable jump in the mean ages (i.e., about 2 years for brides and 2.4 years for bridegrooms) during 1968-1969. Indeed, the mean ages reached their highest levels during 1969. Why did this sudden jump occur? Again, one should look at the divorce rate during 1968-1969. The rate more than doubled during this one-year period. Many people who had been waiting for their divorce that had been filed under old regulations were probably suddenly helped by the new divorce regulations with expanded grounds for divorce, which came into effect on July 2, 1968.

In some cases, informally separated persons may have already been living in consensual unions and remarriage in such cases might be expected to follow immediately after the divorce decree. Consequently, they were able to obtain the divorce speedily and go ahead with their remarriages. It is implied here that the increased divorce rate during 1968-1969 is associated with increased marriage rates of divorced persons. This assumes that the waiting time before marriage of divorced persons is small. This seems to be a reasonable assumption because, in many cases, a complete breakdown of marriage may well be the result of a new relationship that has already been established, and the remarriage in such cases is likely to occur without much delay. It was found in an American study that nearly 34% of divorced men and women born between 1900 and 1949 remarried within two years after divorce.[11] Again, many older persons who may not have wanted to go through the divorce proceedings under the restrictive old regulations may have decided to seek divorce under the new regulations (which were based on expanded grounds for divorce) and legalize their existing or budding relationships by marrying their new partners. Indeed, the numbers of divorced brides and grooms increased by about 55% during 1968-1969 and the increases at older ages were even greater.[2]

It should be noted that the increases in divorce rates during 1942-1947 and 1968-1969 were associated with mean ages at marriage of divorced brides and bridegrooms during those two periods in opposite ways. During 1942-1947, the mean ages at marriage declined and, during 1968-1969, they increased.

As noted above, the reasons were that during 1942-1947 it was mostly the younger persons who were affected because of the Second World War; and during 1968-1969, it was persons of all ages, but especially those of older ages because of the changes in divorce regulations which came into effect on July 2, 1968.

What will be the future trend in age at marriage of divorced persons? Given that the divorce rates are likely to increase further, especially at younger ages, and the fact that the mean age at divorce is likely to decline further in coming years, the mean ages at marriage of divorced persons may be expected to decline further. The mean ages at marriage since the early 1970's already indicate this phenomenon.

Differences in Mean Age at First Marriage, 1971

Unlike the censuses of 1941 and 1961, when the information on age at first marriage of only ever-married women was collected, the Census of 1971 collected this information on all ever-married men and women. In the absence of detailed data on the characteristics of brides and grooms from vital statistics, these data provide very useful information on differences in mean ages at first marriage of various subgroups of population. It should be noted here that, in 1941, information on the age at first marriage was asked in completed years. In 1961 and 1971, this information was derived by combining the information on months and years of birth and marriage. The following analysis is, however, confined to the data from the 1971 Census.

Regions

Table 2.2 presents the mean ages at first marriage of ever-married persons for Canada and the regions.

It may be seen that Yukon and Northwest Territories showed the lowest mean ages for both males and females. The highest mean ages were shown by the Prairies and British Columbia for males and by Quebec for females. The difference between the highest and the lowest

Table 2.2
Mean Age at First Marriage of Ever-married Persons, Canada and Regions, 1971

	Males	Females
Canada	25.4	22.6
Atlantic	25.2	22.1
Quebec	25.5	23.0
Ontario	25.3	22.6
Prairies	25.7	22.2
British Columbia	25.7	22.7
Yukon and Northwest Territories	25.2	21.9

Source: 1971 Census of Canada, unpublished tabulations.

amounted to about 0.5 years in the case of males, and 1.1 years in the case of females. In general, the regional differences with regard to males were smaller than those with regard to females.

It has been shown that education is one of the most important variables associated with age at marriage of females. The higher the education, the higher the mean age at marriage of females.[5] The proportion of population with post-secondary education was one of the lowest in Yukon and Northwest Territories.[9] This, coupled with the high concentration of Inuit and Native Indian populations (nearly 40%), who generally show lower mean ages at marriage, probably explains the lowest mean ages at marriage in these territories. The Atlantic Region also showed one of the lowest proportions with post-secondary education and the mean ages at marriage in the Atlantic Region were very close to those observed in Yukon and Northwest Territories. The higher mean age at marriage of males in British Columbia could similarly be explained by one of the highest proportions with post-secondary education shown by this province. The highest mean age at marriage of females in Quebec, on the other hand, has to be explained by other factors because the proportion with post-secondary education was one of the lowest in this province. As Roman Catholics have been shown to marry later than non-Catholics,[5] the higher proportion of Roman Catholics in Quebec's population probably explains the higher mean age at marriage of females in that province.

The differences in mean ages at marriage do not always reflect the differences in distribution of ever-married males and females by age at marriage. For example, Yukon and Northwest Territories showed the same mean age at marriage for males as the Atlantic Region. However, an examination of the proportional distributions by age at first marriage showed that the proportions marrying at ages under 20 years and over 35 years were higher, and those marrying at age 20-35 years lower in Yukon and Northwest Territories as compared with those in the Atlantic Region.

British Columbia and the Prairies showed slightly higher mean ages at marriage for males when compared with that for Quebec. However, British Columbia and the Prairie Provinces also showed higher proportions (than Quebec) marrying at ages under 20 years, whereas normally one would have expected the opposite. These two regions further showed slightly lower proportions marrying at prime age 20-29 years and higher proportions at ages 30 years and over when compared with Quebec. Thus, the higher mean ages for males in British Columbia and the Prairie Provinces were mainly caused by higher proportions in these two regions marrying at ages 30 years and over when compared with those in Quebec.

The lower mean ages for females observed in the Prairie Provinces and British Columbia when compared with Quebec were clearly caused by higher proportions marrying at ages under 20 years and lower proportions at ages 20 years and over in these two regions.

The lower mean ages for females observed in Yukon, Northwest Territories, and the Atlantic Region, when compared with other regions, were again the results of considerably higher proportions marrying at ages under 20 years in these regions when compared with other regions.

Urban/Rural Residence

Table 2.3 presents the mean ages at first marriage for urban, rural, and census metropolitan areas (CMA's).

Table 2.3
Mean Age at First Marriage of Ever-married Persons, Canada and Urban/Rural Residence, 1971

	Males	Females
Canada	25.4	22.6
Rural	25.6	22.0
Rural non-farm	25.4	21.9
Rural farm	26.2	22.1
Urban	25.4	22.8
CMA's	25.5	22.9

Source: 1971 Census of Canada, unpublished tabulations.

It may be seen that the urban areas and the CMA's showed nearly the same mean ages. In the case of males, except for "rural farm" where a very high mean age at marriage was observed, those in "rural non-farm," urban areas, and CMA's were nearly the same. In the case of females, the mean ages at marriage in "rural farm" and "rural non-farm" were not very different from each other. However, higher values were observed in urban areas and CMA's than in rural areas.

Although the differences in mean ages at marriage of females between urban and rural areas could be explained in terms of higher proportions of population with post-secondary education observed in urban areas than in rural areas,[9] the highest mean age at marriage of males in "rural farm" could not be explained.

An examination of proportional distributions by age at first marriage showed that:

1) the proportion of males marrying at ages under 25 years was lowest, and that at ages 25 years and over the highest in "rural farm";
2) the proportion of females marrying at ages under 20 years the lowest, and that at ages over 20 years in the highest in the CMA's;
3) for both males and females, the proportions marrying under 20 years were the highest, and those marrying at ages over 20 years, generally lower in "rural non-farm" than in other areas;
4) the proportions of males marrying at ages under 25 years were lower and that at ages 25 years and over higher in "rural farm" than in "rural non-farm." The proportions of females marrying at ages under 20 years and over 35 years were lower, and that at age 20-34 years higher in "rural farm" than in "rural non-farm."

The maximum difference between the mean age at marriage of males and that of females (i.e., 4.1 years) was observed in "rural farm."

Table 2.4
Mean Age at First Marriage of Ever-married Persons,
Selected Religious Groups, by Birthplace, Canada, 1971

Population group	Male		Female	
All Religions				
Canadian born	25.1		22.4	
Foreign born		26.7		23.2
No Religion				
Canadian born	24.5		21.6	
Foreign born		26.0		22.6

Anglican
    Canadian born 24.9   22.3
    Foreign born 26.7   23.8

United Church
    Canadian born 25.0   22.4
    Foreign born 27.1   23.6

Roman Catholic
    Canadian born 25.1   22.6
    Foreign born 26.4   22.8

Jewish
    Canadian born 25.8   22.7
    Foreign born 27.9   23.6

Greek Orthodox
    Canadian born 25.7   21.7
    Foreign born 27.5   22.7

Baptist
    Canadian born 24.7   22.1
    Foreign born 26.5   23.4

Lutheran
    Canadian born 25.1   21.8
    Foreign born 27.5   23.6

Presbyterian
    Canadian born 25.7   23.0
    Foreign born 26.7   23.8

All Other
    Canadian born 24.8   21.8
    Foreign born 26.6   22.9

Source: 1971 Census of Canada, unpublished tabulations.

Religious Groups by Birthplace

Table 2.4 presents the mean ages at first marriage of ever-married persons for selected religious and birthplace categories. Among Canadian- and foreign-born males, the highest mean ages were shown by Jewish groups. The highest ages observed resulted mainly from the lowest proportions marrying at ages under 20 years, generally lower proportions marrying at ages 20-29 years, and the highest proportions marrying at ages over 30 years among Jews when compared with other groups. The explanation seems to hinge on the fact that the Jewish population is highly urbanized (99.2% living in urban areas in 1971), having one of the highest proportions engaged in professional, managerial, and other white-collar occupations* (27.1%), and having one of the highest average incomes ($7703) when compared with other groups.

Among Canadian- and foreign-born females, the highest mean ages were shown by the Presbyterian group. The foreign-born Anglican females also showed the same mean age as the foreign-born Presbyterian females. The highest ages observed resulted mainly from the generally lower proportions marrying at ages under 30 years and the higher proportions marrying at ages over 30 years among these groups as compared with other groups. Here again, the proportions living in urban areas, the proportions engaged in managerial, professional, and other white-collar occupations, and the mean income were all higher for Presbyterian and Anglican groups than those for many other religious groups.

Both for males and females, the "No Religion" group showed the lowest mean ages. It was observed that the proportions marrying at ages under 25 years were higher and those marrying at ages over 25 years lower than most other groups. This group seemed an exception because the proportions living in urban areas, the proportions engaged in white-collar occupations, and the mean income were all higher than those for many other groups.

Within each religious group, the foreign-born always showed higher mean age than Canadian-born, both among males and females. The differences between Canadian-born and foreign-born, however, were higher among males than among females. A detailed comparison of the distributions by age at first marriage showed that the proportions marrying at ages under 25 years were always lower, and those marrying at ages over 25 years always higher among the foreign-born as compared with the Canadian-born. There are two factors

---

*The occupations included are (i) managerial, administrative, and related occupations, (ii) occupations in natural sciences, engineering, and mathematics, (iii) occupations in social sciences and related fields, (iv) teaching and related occupations, and (v) clerical and related occupations.

which seem mainly responsible for this phenomenon. One is that the foreign-born showed a higher proportion with post-secondary education than Canadian-born (24.9% versus 18.0%[9]). The second factor is that a higher proportion of foreign-born is resident in urban areas than Canadian-born (87.8% versus 74.1%, Reference 3, Table 8).

The differences in mean ages at first marriage among birthplace groups were more marked than those among religious groups.

As is well known, the average for males was higher than that for females within each religious and birthplace category. The difference in the mean age between males and females was higher among foreign-born than among Canadian-born within each religious category. The maximum differences occurred among Jewish and Greek Orthodox groups.

Ethnic Groups by Birthplace

The mean ages at first marriage for various ethnic groups by birthplace are presented in Table 2.5.*

Among Canadian-born males, the Jewish group showed the highest mean while the Scandinavian and Polish groups did so among the foreign-born males. A detailed comparison showed that among the Canadian-born males, the Jewish males showed the lowest proportions marrying at ages under 20 years and the highest proportions marrying at age 25-29 years. On the other hand, among the foreign-born males, the Polish and the Scandinavian showed the lowest porportions marrying at ages under 30 years, and the highest proportions marrying at ages over 30 years. These patterns have undoubtedly given rise to the highest mean ages observed for these groups.

Among Canadian-born females, the Jewish group showed the highest mean, while the British Isles group did so among the foreign-born females. The proportional distributions by age at marriage showed that among Canadian-born females, the Jewish showed the lowest proportion marrying at ages under 20 years and the highest proportion marrying at age 20-24 years. On the other hand, among

---

*For a study of ethnic differences in age at marriage based on "singulate mean age at marriage," see Reddy and Krishnan, 1976, pp. 55-63.[7] Unfortunately, the method for computing singulate mean age at marriage seems to have been applied in an incorrect manner.

foreign-born females, the British Isles group showed the lowest proportion marrying at ages under 20 years and the highest porportions at ages over 30 years. At age 20-29 years, generally, the proportions marrying were higher. These patterns have given rise to the highest mean ages for these two groups.

As in the case of religious differences in mean ages at marriage, some of the factors observed, e.g., higher proportions urban, higher proportions in managerial, professional, and other white-collar occupations,[6] which imply higher educational attainments among Jewish, British, Polish, and Scandinavian, probably explain higher mean ages at marriage amongst them when compared with other groups.

Table 2.5

Mean Age at First Marriage of Ever-married Persons, Selected Ethnic Groups, by Birthplace, Canada, 1971

Population group	Male		Female	
All ethnic groups				
Canadian born	25.1		22.4	
Foreign born		26.7		23.2
Jewish				
Canadian born	25.8		22.7	
Foreign born		27.8		23.6
Italian				
Canadian born	24.9		22.2	
Foreign born		25.8		21.8
German				
Canadian born	24.7		21.8	
Foreign born		26.3		23.1
French				
Canadian born	25.1		22.6	
Foreign born		26.3		23.2
Indian and Inuit				
Canadian born	24.5		21.0	
Ukrainian				
Canadian born	25.3		21.7	
Foreign born		28.2		22.6

Scandinavian
    Canadian born 24.9   21.8
    Foreign born 28.8   23.5

Polish
    Canadian born 25.2   21.9
    Foreign born 28.8   23.5

Netherlands
    Canadian born 24.6   21.7
    Foreign born 25.5   22.9

British Isles
    Canadian born 25.0   22.5
    Foreign born 26.6   23.8

All other
    Canadian born 25.1   22.1
    Foreign born 26.8   22.9

Source: *1971 Census of Canada*, unpublished tabulations.

Among Canadian-born males and females, the Indian and Inuit group showed the lowest mean ages. The proportional distribution by age at first marriage showed that for both males and females, the proportions marrying at ages under 20 were highest and those at age 20-34 years the lowest of all ethnic groups. These patterns have given rise to the minimum ages at marriage observed for this group. The factors which seemed to have given rise to such low ages at marriage are the lowest proportion urban (30.7%), and the lowest proportion engaged in professional, managerial, and white-collar occupations (7.1%) of all ethnic groups,[6] which imply lower educational attainments.

Among foreign-born males, the Netherlands group showed the lowest age at marriage. Among foreign-born females, the Italian group showed the lowest. A detailed examination of proportional age distributions showed that the Netherlands males showed the lowest proportions marrying at ages 30 years and over, and the Italian females, the highest proportions marrying at ages under 20 years and the lowest proportions marrying at ages 25 years and over. These patterns have obviously given rise to the minimum ages observed among these two foreign-born groups. Although the Italian group showed one of the highest proportions of urban, the proportions engaged in managerial, professional, and other white-collar occupations were the second lowest.[6] This implies lower educational attainments, and this is probably what has given rise to lower mean ages at marriage among them. On the other hand, among the Netherlands group, both the proportion of urban and the proportion engaged in professional, managerial, and other white-collar occupations were lower than those for many other groups and the national averages, which may be expected to give rise to lower mean age at marriage among them.

As in the case of religious groups, within each ethnic group, the foreign-born always showed higher mean ages than Canadian-born. The differences were more marked in the case of males than females.

As is well known, the mean ages at marriage for males always exceeded those for females. The differences between males and females were higher among foreign-born than among Canadian-born except for the Netherlands group which showed the opposite.

Conclusions

Trends in Mean Age at Marriage

1) For both males and females, "the singulate mean ages at marriage" increased slightly during 1851-1891 and declined thereafter. Since 1940, the mean age at marriage of single persons declined while those of the widowed increased mainly as a result of rise in age at widowhood brought about by declining mortality. The levels in 1974 were 24.7, 22.4, 58.3, and 52.7 years for single males, single females, widowers, and widows, respectively. The mean ages at marriage of divorced persons fluctuated slightly and have been declining since 1969. The levels in 1974 were 38.4 and 35.0 years for divorced males and females, respectively. The indications are that these will continue to decline in coming years.

2) The increase in divorce rates during 1942-1947 appeared to have been associated with declines in mean age at remarriage of divorced persons during that period, and the phenomenal increase in divorce rates during 1968-1969 with increase in mean age at remarriage of divorced persons during that period. The explanation seems to be that during 1942-1947, it was mainly the younger persons who had been affected by the Second World War; and, during 1968-1969, it

was persons of all ages, especially those of older ages, who were affected by changes in divorce regulations which came into effect on July 2, 1968.

Differences in Mean Ages at First Marriage, 1971

1) Among regions, while the western provinces showed the highest mean ages at first marriage for males, Quebec did so for females. Yukon and Northwest Territories showed the lowest mean ages for both males and females.

2) Among residence groups, "rural farm" showed the highest mean age for males while CMA's did so for females. "Rural non-farm" showed the lowest for both males and females.

3) The differences in mean ages at first marriage among birthplace groups (Canadian-born and foreign-born) were more marked than those among religious or ethnic groups. With each religious or ethnic group, the foreign-born always showed higher mean age at first marriage than Canadian-born.

4) The differences observed in mean ages at first marriage were largely explained in terms of differences in proportion of urban, proportion with post-secondary education, proportion engaged in professional, managerial, and other white-collar occupations, proportion of Roman Catholics, and income. These factors appeared to be positively associated with mean age at first marriage.

References

1. Basavarajappa, K.G. *Marital Status and Nuptiality in Canada*. Ottawa: Statistics Canada, 1971 Census of Canada, Profile Studies, Demographic Characteristics, Bul. 5.1-4, Catalogue 99-704, 1978.

2. Canada, Statistics. *Vital Statistics 1974*, Vol. II, Marriages and Divorces, Ottawa: Statistics Canada, 1976.

3. George, M.V. *Place of Birth and Citizenship of Canada's Population*. Ottawa: Statistics Canada, 1971 Census of Canada, Profile Studies, Demographic Characteristics, Bul. 5.1-11, Catalogue 99-711, 1978.

4. Gnanasekaran, K.S. "The Labour Force." Ch. 5 in L.O. Stone and A.J. Siggner, eds. *The Populations of Canada: A Review of the Recent patterns and Trends*. C.I.C.R.E.D. Monograph, 1974.

5. Henripin, Jacques. *Trends and Factors of Fertility in Canada*. 1961 Census

Monograph, Catalogue 99-541, Information Canada. Ottawa: Statistics Canada, 1972.

6. Kralt, John. *Ethnic Origins of Canadians.* 1971 Census of Canada, Profile Studies, Demographic Characteristics, Bul. 5.1-9, Catalogue 99-709. Ottawa: Statistics Canada, 1977.

7. Reddy and Krishnan. "Ethnic Differentials in Age at First Marriage, Canada, 1961." *Journal of Comparative Family Studies* VIII, No. 1, Spring 1976.

8. Scott, Jack. *Canada's Religious Composition.* 1971 Census of Canada, Profile Studies, Demographic Characteristics, Bul. 5.1-10, Catalogue 99-710. Ottawa: Statistics Canada, 1976.

9. Tetlock and Mori. *Educational Attainment in Canada.* 1971 Census of Canada, Profile Studies, Demographic Characteristics, Bul. 5.1-8, Catalogue 99-708. Ottawa: Statistics Canada, 1977.

10. U.S. Bureau of the Census. *Census of Populations: 1970 Subject Reports.* Final Report PC(2)-3A, Women by Number of Children Ever Born. Washington, D.C.: U.S. Govt. Printing Office, 1973, Tables 23 and 25.

11. _____, *Current Population Reports*, Series P-20, No. 297, "Number, Timing, and Duration of Marriages and Divorces in the United States: June 1975." Table 0. Washington, D.C.: U.S. Govt. Printing Office, October 1976.

3/Marriage and Death*

Monica Boyd

> As the winter storm raged, a solitary, ill-clad figure was seen
> shuffling from garbage bin to bin. From time to time a flask
> would emerge from beneath the ragged overcoat and the contents
> were soon drained. Inside a cosy bungalow, the flickering fire cast
> a rosy hue upon the enraptured faces of three small children and
> their parents as they gazed upon their bountiful meal. "Oh,
> Papa," said the woman, "aren't we lucky to have each other."

Although much of the imagery is created in novels, the association of
solitude with death and marriage with life has long intrigued
sociologists. As early as 1897, the French sociologist Emile Durkheim
showed that the suicide rate of the married is lower than that of the
single, widowed, or divorced, even after adjustments are made for the
differing age distributions (and hence the different susceptibility to
suicide) of these groups. His findings still hold today (see References:
Cummings, et al., 1975; Gove, 1972a; Heer and Mackinnon, 1974;
Newman and Whittemore, 1973; Rico-Velasco and Mynko, 1973),
and similar findings have been observed with respect to other causes of
dying. In one of the more complete studies to date, Gove[12] has shown
that rates of death from additional causes such as homicide, accidents,
cirrhosis of the liver, diabetes, lung cancer, tuberculosis, and accidents
are lower for the married compared to the non-married United States
population.

These findings raise two questions which are of interest to
students of marriage and the family in Canada. First, "What is the
relationship between marriage and mortality in Canada?" Are the
results of studies conducted on European and United States
populations applicable to Canada? Secondly, "Why are the mortality
rates of the married population lower than those observed for non-

---

*The analysis was funded by a grant from the Department of Sociology and
Anthropology, Carleton University. Gillian MacKelvie served as the research
assistant for the project. This paper was completed July, 1977.

married persons?" If marriage confers some kind of advantage in warding off death, what explains this advantage?

Table 3.1
Mortality Rates[a] and Indexes of Preservation[b] by Sex, Age, and Marital Status, Canada 1971

| Sex and Age | Mortality Rates[a] | | | Indexes of Preservation[b] | |
	Single	Married	Divorced and Widowed	Single	Divorced and Widowed
Males					
Age Standardized total[c]	1538.8	1029.9	2 168.2	1.49	2.11
15-24	165.4	114.1	268.2	1.45	2.35
25-44	389.0	179.7	523.8	2.16	2.91
45-64	1867.9	1084.4	2 308.5	1.72	2.13
65+	7457.6	5628.4	11 257.3	1.32	2.00
Females					
Age Standardized Total[c]	814.0	537.5	1084.3	1.51	2.02
15-24	61.9	45.1	164.4	1.37	3.67
25-44	189.2	103.7	278.7	1.82	2.69
45-64	783.4	521.6	931.3	1.50	1.79
65+	4525.0	3038.2	6022.1	1.49	1.98

[a]Deaths per 100 000 population, specific to each age and sex group.

[b]The ratio of the death rate, specific to each age and sex group for single persons to the death rate for the comparable married group. Similarly, the ratio of the death rate for the divorced and widowed population to the death rate of the married.

[c]The total 1971 census population of age 15 and over is the standard population.

Source: Statistics Canada, *Vital Statistics*, Volume III. Deaths, 1974. Table 13. Statistics Canada, 1971 Census of Canada. *Population Marital Status by Age Groups.* Volume 1 — Part 4. Table 1.

Marital Status and Death

A quick look at Table 3.1 answers the first question by showing that in 1971 married persons in Canada of both sexes have a lower rate of early death compared to single persons or persons who once were married but who now are not (the divorced or widowed). The last two columns of Table 3.1 show how many times higher the mortality rates are for the single or the divorced and widowed population compared to the married population. These Indexes of Preservation, as they are called in Durkheim's study of suicide, are calculated by taking the ratio of the single mortality rate to the married mortality rate specific to each sex and age, or the ratio of the "other" category mortality rate to the mortality rate of married persons, again specific to each sex and age. A ratio of 1.00 thus indicates that the death rate for the group in the numerator is identical to that observed for the married population in the denominator. However, Table 3.1 shows that, after adjusting for differences in age, single men have a mortality rate about one and a half times that of married men and divorced and widowed men are about twice as likely to die early as married men. Similar conclusions are reached for women. Across all age and sex groups, the non-married have higher mortality rates than the married, and the differential is largest for widowed and divorced persons.

Explanations

What accounts for the Canadian differentials in mortality by marital status? Are the data in Table 3.1 spurious, perhaps the result of a yearly fluctuation, or the result either of some error in recording information on the marital status of the deceased or of under-enumerating the population at risk? No. These findings are not idiosyncratic to 1971; the same conclusions are reached for every year on which there are data, notably from 1951 to 1972.[25] Nor does it appear likely that the differences in marital status reflect some systematic errors in classification or under-enumeration of the population at risk.[16/27]

What then explains the findings that married persons in Canada have a lower rate of dying early compared to the single, divorced, and widowed populations? At least three possible reasons exist:

1) married persons have higher socio-economic status than the non-married;

2) marriage is selective of healthier persons; and/or
3) marriage has an integrative function.

The first explanation observes that marital groups may differ in their mortality simply because they differ in their orientation toward health-care, illness prevention, and illness treatment, all of which are associated with socio-economic status, which includes education and income. In particular, if married persons are economically better off than the non-married, this and the related health-care behaviour might account for the lower mortality rate of the married compared to the non-married. Unfortunately, it is difficult to assess the validity of this explanation. The authors of two United States studies[12/6] have refuted it by arguing that although never-married men are better off economically than never-married women, the latter have lower rather than higher mortality rates with respect to selected causes of death. However, their interpretation ignores the fact that women in general have lower rates of mortality than men, and hence a more favourable mortality regime. In any event, the possibility that differences in mortality by marital status may reflect socio-economic and related health-care differences has never been systematically examined, quite probably because of the difficulty of obtaining information on these characteristics of the deceased.

In addition to differences in socio-economic status among marital groups, the selectivity of marriage for healthy individuals may also be a reason for the lower mortality rates of the married compared to the non-married. This view holds that marriage is a competitive process in which the physically handicapped and the psychologically disturbed are unlikely to find "buyers" and hence mates. Alternatively, marriage can be said to be selective of the physically and emotionally healthy. Obviously, if married persons are healthier than the non-married, and if health in turn is associated with a lower risk of dying, then the selective nature of marriage alone will account for the mortality differentials by marital status. Seductive as this explanation is, however, it appears to have little validity. Gove[12] and Geerken and Gove[6] note that if the selective nature of marriage accounted for mortality differentials by marital status, then differences should also be found in all types of mortality, particularly those which are not affected by psychological factors. However, their studies of deaths by marital status in the United States in 1959-1961 reveal that differences among marital status groups in rates of death caused by leukemia and aleukemia are extremely small, thus tending to cast doubt upon the validity of this selectivity hypothesis. In addition, in studying the health of divorced and married persons in the United States, Renne[20] finds no evidence for the argument that the healthiest of the divorced persons remarry, leaving the ill and infirm as the residual divorced population.

The reason that has received the most attention in the sociological literature is one which posits that married persons have an advantage in avoiding death because they are more socially integrated. More precisely, married persons are viewed as having more social roles and involvement in meaningful personal relationships, and hence greater social integration relative to the non-married who lead a more isolated existence.[12/15] This argument derives from Durkheim's study of deaths from suicide, in which he argues that the suicide rate varies inversely with the degree of integration of social groups in which the individual forms a part (see Reference 4. Durkheim, page 209). Durkheim never gave a precise definition of social integration and the lack of conceptual clarity over this term persists to this day,[8] but it is clear that he envisioned society as a collectivity which was greater than the sum of the individual members and which exercised a control over individual behaviour as a result of religious, moral, and political beliefs. His approach is compatible with a definition of social integration provided by the German sociologist Max Weber, who suggests that social integration occurs when a person's behaviour conforms to the demands or expectation of others. Because the degree to which a person's behaviour is required to conform to the demands and expectations of others increases with the number of social relationships in which the persons are involved (see Reference 15. Henry and Short, pages 59-61), it is argued that married people who have at least one more meaningful relationship (with spouse and/or children) than do non-married, are likely to be more socially integrated.

Durkheim, of course, was seeking to explain the association between marital status and one cause of death, notably suicide. But the argument that married persons have lower rates of mortality than non-married because they are involved in more meaningful relationships has been extended to account for deaths in which emotional states play a part, albeit more indirectly than in the case of suicide in which a person takes his or her own life. Here it is posited that the more isolated and less socially meaningful existence of non-married persons underlies the findings that non-married persons compared to the married report themselves as less happy and they have higher rates of mental illnesses.[11/12] Emotional and psychological states, however, are associated with illness across all marital status groups.[20] And, if the non-married are more likely to be unhappy psychologically and physically ill than are the married, it is reasonable to argue that they are more likely to die early as well, particularly from emotionally or psychologically induced illnesses.[12]

This "social integration" explanation for mortality differentials by marital status is invoked in a United States study using data for 1959-1961 and in a recent study of suicide in Canada, using data from 1961 and 1971. The latter study examines suicide rates in British Columbia for working and non-working women by marital status and finds that non-married women have higher rates of suicide than married.[3] However, the risk of suicide is lowered across all marital status groups when women work, and there is greater protection from suicide afforded by work than by marriage. Why should involvement in the labour force make a difference in suicide rates? Cummings et al.[3] suggest that as an additional social role, work enlarges the contacts and social relationships of women, and hence counterbalances the isolation, loneliness, and lack of social integration of the housewife role (see Reference 3. Cummings et al., page 468). As such, working also appears to reduce emotional and physical illness, which underlie not only suicide but also other causes of death. In this regard, Feld[5] has found that employed women are in better health than the non-employed, not only with respect to major illnesses but also for minor neurotic symptoms (also see Reference 19. Pratt).

Social integration also is used to explain differentials in mortality by marital status and sex in the United States. Using 1959-1961 data, Gove[12] finds that variations in mortality rates by marital status are particularly large for those causes of death in which psychological states appeared to exert some influence. In particular, the non-married population had higher rates of death from stress-related causes, such as suicide, homicide, and accidents, and from causes related to tension or self-abuse such as lung cancer and alcoholism. Higher rates for the non-married are also observed for deaths from tuberculosis or diabetes where extended and careful treatment requiring the tacit co-operation and involvement of the patient are required. In contrast, there is little difference between marital status groups with respect to diseases such as leukemia or aleukemia where psychological states would have little effect on the etiology of the disease or on the success of its treatment (see Reference 12. Gove, page 61). Gove attributes these findings to the fact that non-married persons, compared to married persons, lack the sense of well-being derived from close family and personal ties and hence are more likely to experience emotional stress and psychological distress.

Marital Status, Psychological Stress, and Death in Canada

Given the results from Cummings et al.,[3] investigation of variations in deaths from suicide for British Columbia women and Gove's analysis of mortality in the United States,[10/12] what can be said about the causes of death of marital status groups in Canada? Do the married and non-married die from similar causes? Or, as suggested by the social integration argument, are non-married persons more likely than married to die from causes in which psychological factors play a part? These questions are answered by examining cause of death data for Canadian men and women age 25-64 by marital status for the period 1970-1972. The 1970-1972 period is chosen not only because it represents the most recent data on cause of death by marital status, but also because averages based on a three-year period smooth out the effect of yearly fluctuations in the data. Likewise, there are two reasons for focussing upon the age group 25-64. First and foremost, the age group 25-64 represents that stage of the life cycle in which marriage and family procreation are both normatively prescribed and likely to provide the adult roles of spouse and/or parent. Thus the impact of marriage as integrative mechanism should be most clearly evident for this age group. Secondly, although marriage also may affect the risk of dying for younger and older age groups, its impact is more difficult to assess. Data comparisons by marital status are not very reliable for ages below 25 because there are very few deaths in general and very few persons who are divorced or widowed in this group. Conversely, groups age 65 and older will have increased probabilities of dying because of degenerative diseases, and this increased risk of dying will partly obfuscate the impact of marital status.[12]

Although not presented here, cause of death data, using the Eighth Revision of the Cause of Death Classification categories for deceased Canadian men and women, ages 25-44 and 45-64, clearly confirm the association of marriage or non-marriage with cause of death in Canada. In general, when compared to the married deceased, a larger proportion of single, divorced, or widowed deceased persons dying in 1970-1972 died from infectious diseases, endocrinal, nutritional, or metabolic diseases, mental disorders, vague symptoms, diseases of the nervous system, respiratory system, and digestive system, and from accidents. In contrast, the deceased married men and women are more likely to have died from diseases of the circulatory system or from neoplasms.[22]

If the causes of death differ according to marital status, are non-married persons, compared to the married, more likely to die from causes associated with psychological stress and/or illness? To answer this question, a detailed analysis is needed because the major categories used in the Eighth Revision of Causes of Death are broad and subsume many more specific causes of death. Thus, they lack the detail needed to determine if differences in cause of death by marital status reflect the hypothesized greater social integration of the married compared to the non-married. Using the index of preservation, Table 3.2 compares the mortality of rates of the single, divorced, and widowed populations in Canada to that of the married for the specific causes of death examined in Gove's analysis of marital status and mortality in the United States.[12] According to Gove, these are the causes of death which can be linked to the psychological sense of well-being of individuals and hence to their social integration. Suicide is a self-inflicted cause of death and occurs in the absence of social integration.[4] Psychoses and neuroses also are causes of death which automatically imply psychological stress. Acts of risk-taking can be viewed as "death wishes" and hence may also reflect suicidal actions as well as psychological states. According to Gove, a lack of social integration and the absence of any sense of well-being may mean that such individuals are more likely to place themselves in dangerous situations vulnerable to the risk of being murdered, or killed in accidents, particularly traffic accidents. Thus, to the extent that non-married persons are less likely to have meaningful social ties, they would be more likely to engage in such behaviour and to have higher rates of mortality from not only psychoses, neuroses, and suicides, but also from accidents and murder.

What do the Canadian data suggest? The indexes of preservation (Table 3.2) indicate that for all age and gender groups, with the exception of single women age 45-64, non-married men and women are at least twice as likely to die from these five causes of death as are their married counterparts. Even in the case of single women age 45-64 the indexes of preservation are above unity (an index of 1.00 indicating that the married and non-married groups have identical mortality rates) and in many instances the mortality rate is more than twice as high. For example, compared to married men and women, divorced or widowed persons age 25-44 have a mortality rate from neuroses which is over seven times higher than that of married persons.

In addition to psychoses, neuroses, suicide, homicide, and accidents, psychological ill-health may, by physical abuse and neglect, lead to deaths from lung cancer, alcohol, diabetes, and tuberculosis. Cigarettes and other forms of tobacco-smoking are known to have a narcotic effect, and for this reason their usages are associated with stress and tension. In his United States study, Gove (see Reference 12, page 54) invokes the imagery of heavy users of alcohol as trying to drown their troubles and suggests that such behaviour may be more typical of the non-married persons than the married. If this is the case, then rates of dying from cirrhosis of the liver should be higher for the non-married than for the married. Gove also looks at mortality data for tuberculosis and diabetes, arguing that emotional states are related to the willingness to undertake the prolonged and methodical care required in the treatment of these diseases. Thus, if the non-married find their roles less satisfying than the married, this should be reflected in the higher rates of mortality from these diseases for the non-married compared to the married (see Reference 12. Gove, page 56).

Once again, the indexes of preservation, comparing the mortality rates of the non-married to the married, for cirrhosis of the liver, diabetes, and tuberculosis, show that in Canada, as in the United States, the non-married are more likely to die from these causes than are the married. The only exception is in the case of single females age 45-64 who are about as likely to die from cirrhosis of the liver as are married women (the index of preservation equals 1.02). However, of the single persons, only males age 45-64 are more likely than the married to die from lung cancer, whereas persons who are divorced or widowed have an index of preservation greater than unity, indicating that their mortality rate from lung cancer is higher than that observed

Table 3.2

Ratios of Death Rates[a] by Marital Status, Sex, and Age for specified causes of Death, Canada 1970-1972.

Cause of Death	Males 25-44 Single	Males 25-44 Other	Males 45-64 Single	Males 45-64 Other	Females 25-44 Single	Females 25-44 Other	Females 45-64 Single	Females 45-64 Other
All Causes	2.08	2.84	1.73	2.17	1.80	2.33	1.47	1.73
Psychoses	2.62	—	3.30	4.24	2.17	—	1.27	2.32
Neuroses	4.74	7.74	5.31	6.25	1.86	7.32	1.69	3.15
Suicide	2.88	4.69	2.20	2.95	1.95	3.06	1.16	1.98
Homicide	4.20	8.26	5.08	4.53	1.82	4.49	1.09	2.39
Accidents, Total	2.52	3.25	2.42	2.89	2.19	3.55	1.35	2.17
Accidents, Traffic	2.31	1.95	2.32	2.21	2.00	1.15	3.32	1.83
Cirrhosis of the Liver	2.40	7.25	2.53	4.54	2.06	5.16	1.02	2.18
Tuberculosis	3.73	8.77	5.79	4.82	2.75	2.08	2.90	1.32
Diabetes	2.62	2.56	2.10	2.54	1.88	2.96	1.09	1.84
Lung Cancer	.69	2.88	1.20	1.88	1.02	2.55	.93	1.74
Leukemia	1.14	.89	1.06	1.33	1.33	1.12	1.16	1.09

[a]The ratios or "Indexes of preservation" are computed with reference to average-cause specific death rates for the years 1970-1972, using the married population for each age-sex group as the population of reference. Thus the ratio of 2.88 for suicide of single males age 25-44 is calculated by dividing their death rate from that cause during 1970-1972 (49.99 per 100 000) by the death rate from suicide for married males age 25-44 (17.35 per 100 000). The resulting ratio of 2.88 indicates that the death rate from suicide for single males age 25-44 is 2.88 times that observed for married males, age 25-44.

Sources: Statistics Canada. *Vital Statistics, 1970. Vital Statistics 1971, 1972,* Volume III. Deaths.
Statistics Canada. *Population Estimates by Marital Status, Age and Sex for Canada and Provinces, 1972.*

for the married. These findings differ from those of Gove's in the United States,[12] who found that single persons as well as the divorced and widowed had a higher rate of lung-cancer deaths compared to the married.

With the exception of mortality from lung cancer, Canadian data, like that of the United States, shows that married men and women for the most part are less likely to die from psychoses, neuroses, suicide, homicides, accidents, cirrhosis of the liver, diabetes, and tuberculosis, all of which are diseases affected by psychological factors. Such findings thus appear to reflect the relative lack of social integration of the non-married compared to the married. However, it is also possible that such findings merely reflect the overall greater tendency of the non-married compared to the married to die (see Table 3.1), perhaps as the result of their socio-economic status or the selective nature of marriage. If this is the case, the indexes of preservation for causes of death not related to psychological factors also should be greater than 1.0 for the non-married. Leukemia is a disease where psychological factors are unrelated to the overall etiology of the disease and the effectiveness of its treatment (see Reference 12. Gove, page 58). As in Gove's United States study, the mortality rates from this disease for married and non-married can be compared. Data in Table 3.2 show the mortality rate from leukemia to be greater than unity for the non-married compared to the married. But the indexes are not as large as the overall differential between the married and non-married from all causes. This suggests that the higher indexes observed elsewhere may at least partly reflect the psychological states of non-married persons, which in turn are viewed as resulting from their social isolation and lack of social integrations.

If the social roles associated with the married or unmarried state affect psychological well-being, which in turn influences mortality, then the data in Table 3.2 would appear to suggest that divorced and widowed persons are the least emotionally healthy. Data in Table 3.2 show that divorced and widowed persons have indexes of preservation which, for the most part, are higher than those observed for single persons. For example, widowed and divorced males age 25-44 have a mortality rate from cirrhosis of the liver which is eight times that of married males, whereas single males have a mortality rate from that disease which is twice as high as that of married males. The social integration theory used to account for mortality differentials between the married and non-married would interpret these findings as reflecting the greater psychological instability of persons who once were married but now find an alteration in, if not a diminution of, their social roles and social relationships. Is this indeed the case? Possibly, for mental-illness data show that the widowed and divorced populations have higher rates of first admissions to institutions in Canada than do the single and married population.[24] However, age-composition differences may partly account for the higher indexes of preservation for the divorced and widowed. The published mortality data by marital status, on which Table 3.2 is based, give data in broad 20-year groups. It is possible that, within these broad 20-year age groups, most of the widowed and divorced persons who have died are simply older than either the married or the single population, and hence have a higher risk of dying irrespective of their marital status. This contention is supported by the age composition within each 20-year group for the population at risk of dying, for each marital status group enumerated in the 1971 census. In 1971 less than half of the single or married population age 25-44 was between 35 and 44 years old compared to nearly 60% of the divorced or widowed population. Similarly, of the population age 45-64, less than half of the single or married population was age 55 and older compared to 56% and 63% of the divorced and widowed male and female population, respectively.[23]

Gender, Marital Status, and Mortality

Overall, the most popular explanation invoked by sociologists to account for the lower mortality rates of the married compared to the non-married stresses the integrative function of marriage, despite the possibilities that such differentials might also be explained by the improved health care and/or socio-economic status of the married. Differences in social integration and hence in psychological well-being are also hypothesized to underlie a second finding of studies into mortality of marital status groups—notably that differentials in mortality by marital status are not as pronounced for women as they are for men. Bernard[1] and Gove[11/12] argue that compared to married men, married women experience greater unhappiness and higher rates of mental illness as a result of the constriction and frustration of their roles. As a result, marriage does not reduce the mortality levels of married women relative to other women as it does for married men, compared to other men.

What aspect of the married women's role causes a greater degree of frustration, unhappiness, and mental illness compared to men? One possibility is that confinement to the house, a state which characterizes about 50% of Canadian married women of working age, reduces the number of social contacts and increases the degree of social isolation. Such isolation in turn increases emotional and physical illness and may increase the probability of death. A second possibility is that frustration, mental illness, and ill-health arise from the low status and diffuseness of the housewife's role, as well as from the various conflicts between the roles of wife, mother, and housekeeper. In particular, role conflict arising from conflicting statuses is hypothesized to be associated with variations in suicide.[7/8]

If, as a result of their greater social isolation and/or role conflict, married women compared to married men are more unhappy and have higher rates of mental illness, and if illness and death are related, then marriage will not give women the same benefit in mortality reduction as it gives to men. Is this hypothesis true in general, and does it hold for Canada? Looking at causes of death where psychological factors play a part, Gove[12] finds that differentials in marital rates by marital status are smaller for women than for men in the United States, and on the basis of his findings, he argues that the hypothesis is supported. Similarly, Table 3.2 shows that the indexes of preservation are smaller for non-married women compared to non-married men in Canada, thus indicating that mortality differentials across marital status groups are smaller for females.

However, rigorous proof of the hypothesis that marriage does not give women the same advantage as men with respect to mortality reduction demands showing the following relationships: 1) that married women compared to married men experience greater social isolation and frustration; 2) that, as a result, married women compared to married men are more unhappy and have higher mental-illness rates; 3) that illness and death are associated; and 4) that married women have higher death rates than they would if they were less socially isolated, unhappy, and subjected to mental illness. To examine mortality differentials and then to explain variations *ex post facto* does not necessarily prove the hypothesis in question. As is the case in the earlier examination of mortality differentials in Canada by marital status, the data are compatible with other explanations.

What kind of support can be offered for the hypothesis that marriage does not lead to as great a mortality reduction for women as it does for men, and what kind of alternative explanations exist for male-female differentials by marital status? Much of the argument stressing the disadvantage of marriage focusses on the propositions that married women compared to married men experience greater social isolation and frustration and hence unhappiness and higher mental illness. Based on a review of the literature, Bernard,[1/2] Gove,[11] and Gove and Tudor[13] maintain that married women are indeed more unhappy than married men, and they show that married women have higher rates of mental illness than married men. However, these findings may be spurious, or may reflect factors other than isolation, loneliness, and frustration with the housewife role. Glen[9] notes that marital happiness is a motherhood question, the questions to which must be viewed with scepticism. After re-analysing data, Glen[9] suggests that even if marriage is stressful for women, the benefits cancel the costs. With respect to mental illness, there is no question that married women have higher mental-illness rates compared to married men. But, these higher rates may not only reflect a greater social isolation and frustration for married women, but also sex biases in diagnosing illness. Verbrugge[26] notes that physicians diagnose illnesses in women as psychosomatic more so than they do for men. In addition, gender differences in mental-illness rates may arise simply because of differences in how stress is handled, with women tending to express stress through psychological illness and men tending to express stress in external ways, through drinking, violence, and drug abuse (see Reference 26. Verbrugge, page 41). Data on first admissions to mental institutions in Canada suggest that men and women do indeed convert stress into different physical symptoms. The rate of first admissions from neuroses for married women is twice that for married men but the rate of admissions from alcoholism for married men is six times higher than that for married women during the 1970-1972 period.[24]

Factors other than isolation and role-strain also explain gender differences in marital happiness and mental health for the married population. The same is true for the smaller differences by marital status in mortality rates observed for men and women in the United States[12] and in Canada (Tables 3.1 and 3.2). In fact, the explanation given for mortality differentials is dependent upon which marital group is used as the basis of comparison. Gove[12] observes that the indexes of preservation are smaller for the non-married female population than they are for the non-married male population, and, as noted earlier, similar findings are observed for Canada (Tables 3.1 and 3.2). That such findings reflect the greater isolation, frustration, unhappiness, and psychological stress of married women compared to married men, assumes that the mortality rate of married women is higher than it would otherwise be despite the fact that, of all marital status groups, married women have the lowest mortality rates, even for those causes related to psychological factors. Thus the argument used by Gove appears to take the non-married population as the standard and to ask why the mortality rate of married women is not proportionately as low as it is for men. But, the converse strategy can be used. The mortality rates of married women can be used as the basis of comparison and the question posed as to why the mortality rates of the non-married female population are not, relative to these rates of the married population, as high as those observed for non-married men. Demographers have a ready explanation for this finding. In general, Canadian women live longer than men with an average life expectancy of 76 years in 1971 compared to that of 69 years for men—and across all age groups they have lower overall rates of mortality than men. Why is this the case? As a result of their physiology and social roles, women compared to men are more likely to monitor illness and to restrict their activities when ill; thus, for women, illness is acute rather than chronic and is less likely to become a cause of death.[26] Also, women may have a genetic advantage over men in terms of being resistant to infectious diseases and to the acquisition and progress of degenerative ones (Reference 17, and see Reference 26. Verbrugge, pages 42-43). If rates of death are lower, and if women have greater immunity to dying, then the impact of social factors may be less, thus narrowing the differentials in mortality rates by marital status. Conversely, men have higher risks of dying, less genetic protection, and thus their death rates by marital status may be more influenced by health care, which in turn is associated with marital status—the view generally being held that married persons eat more nutritious foods, are more likely to practise preventive medicine, and to seek medical assistance for illness when it occurs.

Conclusions

Are marriage and death associated in Canada, and if so, how? What explains the association? Data presented in this paper answer the first question, and sociological theory addresses the second. Average mortality rates over the three-year period 1970-1972 for men and women age 25-64 clearly show that the non-married population in Canada has higher mortality rates than the married, both in general and for causes of death in which psychological factors play a role. What explains the finding that married persons in Canada have lower rates of dying compared to the single or the divorced and widowed populations? The reason that has received the most attention in the sociological literature is one which posits that married persons, compared to the non-married, have an advantage in avoiding death because they are more socially integrated. The Canadian data are consistent with the hypothesis, which was developed by Durkheim with respect to suicide and recently extended by Gove.[12] But, since a number of other explanations may also account for the finding, the data do not prove the hypothesis that mortality differentials by marital status reflect differences in social integration between marital status groups. The fact that the Canadian differentials in mortality by marital status are both consistent with the social integration hypothesis and with other alternative explanations is particularly true when considering the indexes of preservation of women compared to men. As a result, three answers are required for the two questions posed earlier. First, mortality differentials by marital status do exist in Canada, such that married persons have lower death rates than non-married. Secondly, this pattern may reflect the greater social integration of the married compared to the non-married. But, thirdly, the pattern may also reflect the operation of various other factors, ranging from differences among marital status groups with respect to socio-economic status and health care to the male-female differences in illness behaviour, illness diagnosis, and life chances.

References

1. Bernard, Jesse. *The Future of Marriage.* New York: Bantam Books, 1972.
2. —————. "Comment on Glenn's Paper." *Journal of Marriage and the Family* 37 (August, 1975), pp. 600-601.
3. Cummings, Elaine, Lazer, Charles and Chisholm, Lynne. "Suicide as an Index of Role Strain Among Employed Married Women in British Columbia." *Canadian Review of Sociology and Anthropology* 12 (1975), pp. 462-470.
4. Durkheim, Emile. *Suicide.* Glencoe: Free Press, 1951.
5. Feld, S. "Feelings of Adjustment," in Nye, I., and Hoffmand, Lois, eds. *The Employed Mother in America.* Chicago: Rand-McNally, 1963, pp. 331-352.
6. Geerken, Michael, and Gove, R. Walter. "Race, Sex and Marital Status: Their Effect on Mortality." *Social Problems* 21 (April 1974), pp. 567-580.
7. Gibbs, Jack P. "Marital Status and Suicide in the United States: A Special Test of the Status Integration Theory." *American Journal of Sociology* 74 (March 1969), pp. 521-533.
8. Gibbs, Jack P., and Martin, Walter T. "Status Integration and Suicide," in Anthony Giddens, ed. *The Sociology of Suicide.* London: Frank Cass, 1971, pp. 67-86.
9. Glenn, Norval D. "Contribution of Marriage to the Psychological Well-Being of Males and Females." *Journal of Marriage and the Family* 37 (August 1975), pp. 594-601.
10. Gove, Walter R. "Sex, Marital Status, and Suicide." *Journal of Health and Social Behaviour* 13 (June 1972), pp. 204-213.
11. —————. "The Relationship Between Sex Roles, Marital Status and Mental Illness." *Social Forces* 51 (September 1972), pp. 34-44.
12. —————. "Sex, Marital Status and Mortality." *American Journal of Sociology* 79 (July 1973), pp. 45-67.
13. Gove, Walter, and Tudor, Jeanne. "Adult Sex Roles and Mental Illness." *American Journal of Sociology* 78 (January 1973).
14. Heer, David, and Mackinnon, Douglas. "Suicide and Marital Status: A Rejoinder to Rico-Velasco and Mynko." *Journal of Marriage and the Family* 36 (February 1974), pp. 6-10.
15. Henry, Andrew F., and Short, James. "Suicide and External Restraint," in Anthony Giddens, ed. *The Sociology of Suicide.* London: Frank Cass and Company, Ltd., 1971, pp. 58-66.
16. Lee, J.A.H., Chin, Pearl G., and Wutrich, Karen J. "Relationships in Canada Between Mortality of the Gastro-Intestinal Tract and Marital Status." *Canadian Medical Association Journal* 113 (November 8, 1975), pp. 839-843.
17. Madigan, Francis C. "Are Sex Mortality Differentials Biologically Caused?" *Milbank Memorial Fund Quarterly* 35 (April 1957), pp. 202-223.
18. Newman, John F., Whittemore, Kenneth R., and Newman, Helen G. "Women in the Labour Force and Suicide." *Social Problems* 21 (Fall 1973), pp. 220-230.
19. Pratt, Lois. "Conjugal Organization and Health." *Journal of Marriage and the Family* 34 (February 1972), pp. 85-95.

20. Renne, Karen S. "Health and Marital Experiences in an Urban Population." *Journal of Marriage and the Family* 33 (May 1971), pp. 338-350.
21. Rico-Velasco, Jesus, and Mynko, Lizbeth. "Suicide and Marital Status: A Changing Relationship?" *Journal of Marriage and the Family* 35 (May 1973), pp. 239-244.
22. Statistics Canada. *Vital Statistics*, 1970; *Vital Statistics*, Volume III. Deaths, 1971, 1972.
23. _____. 1971 Census of Canada. *Population: Marital Status by Age Groups.* Table 1.
24. _____. *Mental Health Statistics.* Volume I, 1972. Table 2.
25. _____. *Vital Statistics.* Volume III. Deaths, 1973. Table 18.
26. Verburgge, Lois M. *Sex Differences in Illness and Death in the USA.* Baltimore: Johns Hopkins University: Center for Metropolitan Planning and Research, 1975.
27. Weiss, Noel S. "Marital Status and Risk Factors for Coronary Heart Disease." *British Journal of Preventive and Social Medicine* 27 (February 1973), pp. 41-43.

4/The Single Female*

John F. Peters

Despite the significant social and economic contribution of single females in our society, this population is stereotyped, stigmatized, and treated as a minority. The research examines the lifestyle and stereotyping as perceived by the never-married female. The random sample, chosen from a medium-sized urban community was not found to be antifamily, strongly career-oriented, nor feminist. The majority had an opportunity to marry, had friends of both sexes, and respected the mother role. Such findings, besides stimulating further research, should modify socialization patterns concerning the single female in our society.

A neglected field of research in family and futuristic studies is that of the single person. A quick survey of the more recent numerous texts or readings on the family found that only six (Delora and Delora,[14] Kirkendall and Whitehurst,[25] Lasswell,[29] Cox,[11] Scanzoni and Scanzoni,[39] and Skolnick and Skolnick[40]) gave at least slight recognition to the subject of singles. It is anticipated that the current interest in futuristic studies will stimulate further research into this subject.

Research in the United States indicates that the increased involvement of single women in higher education and in employment has encouraged singlehood. The percentage of single women between ages 20 and 24 has jumped by one-third between 1960 and 1970.[21] Some of this population will marry, but this delay in marriage will also mean that some will not marry. The probability of a single person marrying after 25 is inversely related with age. In Canada each year 72% of the brides and 57% of the grooms are under 25. After several decades of a declining average age at marriage for both bride (22.4) and groom (24.7), the age at marriage has now stabilized, and may show a gradual increase in the years ahead. In 1971 there were approximately

*The author acknowledges with gratitude that this research was funded by a Canada Council Grant, 1975–76.

42 000 females and 48 000 males single and never married who were over 30 years of age.

The non-married females do make a sizable contribution to our society. Their services have been traditionally found in the fields of public education, health care, food services, office personnel, and factory labour in the garment and electronics industry. They contribute considerably to both the production and consumption of goods.

The presence of the non-married females is seen in other areas of our social system than that of economics. The socialization of children is affected to some degree by the non-married in the public and secondary schools. Women in religious orders establish lasting values in young children. In the health profession, non-marrieds care for the ill, facilitating physical and mental recuperation.

But the non-married minority population finds itself dominated by a majority which is married. The religious, economic, and political institutions appear to control legislation and social behaviour, often to the disadvantage or exclusion of the non-married single female. In fact, married life, whether happy or unhappy, is viewed as normative, while the single life is perceived as deviant. This has led to misrepresentation, misunderstanding, discrimination, and stereotyping. This study seeks some empirical evidence of these perceptions and social expectations, as well as a better understanding of the lifestyle of the non-married.

This research has been stimulated because of three factors: (a) the lack of research in the area, (b) the probing of a number of single female teachers, over 30 years of age, who tolerated the biasses of the married in several classes of Sociology of the Family, and (c) acquaintances who are not married and obviously uncomfortable in activity sponsored and controlled by marrieds.

The theoretical value of the research is found in terms of stereotyping and socialization processes inherent within our society, as well as anomie caused by loneliness. The practical significance penetrates the area of understanding the unmarried female within our society, as well as exposing existing societal inequalities.

Existing Research and Literature

Research done in the area of the non-married has focussed upon the single female. This may result from the fact that there are more non-married females than non-married males and that single females are more concentrated in some professions such as teaching and secretarial work than are single males. It may also be the case that our society views the non-married male as socially much more "manageable" or normal than the non-married female. Baker suggests that the perception of society is that women need men to assist them and that a woman's fulfilment comes only through marriage (see Reference 2, pages 115-130). If the feminine mystique[20] is true, then it is likely that the single woman is socially pitied or considered unfulfilled.

Baker (*loc. cit.*) used the California Test of Pesonality with 38 non-married and a matched sample of 38 married women. He found no difference in personality adjustment in his sample of married and non-marrieds. Rallings (see Reference 34, pages 485-494) used a sample of 100 never-married males and an equally numbered matched sample of married males, all of whom were 40 years of age or more. Rallings' area of investigation was the home background, hypothesizing a difference between the married and single men. He found no difference in their home background with regard to affection, co-operation, discipline, intellectual stimulation, scientific and rationale orientation, and economic status. On the other hand Cox has found a higher rate of mental illness among non-married than among those who are married (see Reference 11, page 132). He states the "living together causes interaction and a corrective function of keeping one closer to reality" (*op. cit.*, page 133). Statistics on suicide show a higher rate for single males than single females and a higher rate for singles than for marrieds. The divorced and widowed exceed the rate of the singles.[10]

It is Moran's observation that encounters for singles in singles' clubs and bars have not always been as exciting and constructive for the single female as one would assume. Computer dating programmes have often programmed the same date for a group of friends (see Reference 32. Moran, page 339). The singles' societies have received considerable mass media attention but, "many females are not at all happy with the new singles' society, stating that it caters to men but virtually gives women a degrading role" (*loc. cit.*). Moran further comments that males often circulate at these parties from one female to another, so as to maximize their own personal interests (see also Reference 45). Judy McKeown, a television personality and a single, observes that: "You can go out every night with a different guy, but after a while you're bound to get tired of it, because all the running around you're doing is in a circle. Really, you don't get anything. You don't learn anything about people. You'll find six months of it is a very long time. After that, you're asking yourself, 'What's going on? What's it all about?'" (*Time* essay in Reference 29). The singles' bar has been referred to as the "body shop" or "meat market" and as a "humiliating atmosphere."[22]

From US demographic data Glick gives evidence that singlehood will increase in the future.[21] Two factors are that men no longer have to marry to get sex and that women do not have to marry to get financial support. Stein argues that the emphasis upon human growth and an increasing demystification of marriage in our society will appreciably increase the number of singles. Canadian statistics show an increase in the number who divorce. Though many of this number remarry, many remain single.

Spreitzer and Riley have researched the factors associated with singlehood.[41] There is a higher rate of singles among Roman Catholics than among non-Roman Catholics. Single females with high education were most likely to remain single. Srole et al. suggest that these women tend to be rejected because "... many males in their active courting roles tend to choose a wife who enhances their culturally conditioned self-image or masculine dominance" (see Reference 42, page 180). The David study showed that female "scientists and engineers are six times as likely not to have married than are their male counterparts" (see Reference 13, page 82). With the influence of greater equality between the sexes, and as more women achieve educational and economic levels comparable to men, the number of singles will increase. The relationship of these variables, particularly among the middle and upper classes, are consistent with Centers'[8] and Rubin's[37] research. Women tended to marry hypergamously, that is, males in a class equal to or higher than themselves. This would place the female achiever at a relative disadvantage among the marriage eligibles.

Spreitzer and Riley also show that family or orientation characteristics are significant to singlehood. A male "only child" is significantly more likely to remain single (see Reference 41, page 537). The only child is socialized to higher achievement, and with females this seems to militate against marriage (see Srole et al. research, Reference 42). Females reared by only one parent are more likely to remain single. An early age of departure from the home to work is related to singleness (see Reference 41, page 537). A female's poor relationship with her mother, while having a good relationship with her father and siblings, is related to singlehood. Males from a democratic family are less likely to remain single than females from a democratic family, according to the Spreitzer and Lawrence study.

There are proportional differences, by ethnicity, in the percentage who remain single. Among females in Canada the proportion is highest for the Asian, native Indian, Inuit, and French.[17] The proportions of single females has increased between 1961 and 1971, while the proportions of single males has declined.

The Cruikshank work among the matrifocal Athapaskan Indian family shows that less than half of the Indian men and women over 21 are married.[12] Among unmarried women, 55% are unmarried mothers living with their children. The intrusion of the white man into the Athapaskan culture altered the traditional family form of these people.

Adams shifts the discussion to the social milieu in which the single female finds herself.[1] She faces problems of social role, acceptability, and self-esteem. The single woman who fends for herself is fair game for any exploitation that the male-dominated working world chooses to exact (see Reference 1, page 779). The "devalued social definition of single women and the distorted self-images of inferiority that it creates can exert a subtly damaging effect on the quality of social relationships with peers, the opposite sex, and married couples. The insidious conviction of being only second best makes it hard for single women to put a proper value on themselves: they tend to approach relationships in an over-diffident, if not apologetic, frame of mind...." She may have "some residual uncertainty about her own identity" (see Reference 1, pages 779-780). She is clearly defined in a minority group that demonstrates a conspicuous pattern of functioning in terms of the dominant value system and the organizational goals of American society (*op. cit.*, page 778).

Stereotyping of single females is prevalent. The most common ideas are those of lack of sexual attractiveness, unresolved early psychosexual conflicts, and narcissistic unwillingness to be closely committed to another individual.[1] More's empirical work with 176 summer school students in 1951 sought to differentiate the subject's perception between a known-married and a non-married woman.[31] The student perceived the non-married woman as hard to get along with, wanting to be boss, independent, self-centred, and void of sex appeal. Behaviourally she was considered extremely religious, professionally ambitious, fussy about order and time, moody, and not fond of children. With respect to men, her expectations were viewed as unrealistic—she distrusted men and was afraid of sex.

More recently Wakil[48] did a similar Canadian study with 300 college students. The study generally verified Moore's earlier work. The non-married were perceived as introverted, unsocial, and as lacking confidence and beauty. At the same time Wakil's subjects perceived the non-married as more intelligent and sophisticated, more extensive in travelling experience, more interested in the arts, and better read than married women.

This research further investigates the stereotypes of the single female, not from the perspective of the college student (audience) but rather the perception of the actor, that is, the single female. These perceived stereotypes are compared to the actual behaviour of single women. The study does not pursue any causal analysis of variables. This study is more exploratory in nature.

For the purposes of this research, the single woman is defined as the never-married, and therefore excludes the married, widowed, or divorced. Since marriage is a high potential for those women in their early twenties, no one under 25 was included in the research.

Because it was anticipated that respondents might differ considerably by age, where relevant, comparison has been made between those under 35 years of age and those over 40 years of age.

Sampling Procedures

A total of 990 names and addresses was selected from a current provincial voters list in an urban community of an estimated population of 160 000 in Southwestern Ontario. Names from the voters list were randomly selected from addresses in which (a) one woman, (b) a multiple of women, or (c) a multiple of women plus one male were listed. This research was focussed upon those with the status of single, and therefore excluded those who were married, divorced, widowed, or under 25 years of age. This was done by sending an introductory letter to the 990 addresses and requesting those who were not defined as single by our definition to return the letter in the self-addressed stamped envelope. A total of 186 indicated that they did not qualify and 39 had been sent to incorrect addresses.

The remaining sample of 765 were sent questionnaires in the winter of 1976. Those who did not respond received a second questionnaire with a cover letter three weeks later. In these mailings of the questionnaire some had the wrong address (N = 22) while some were not interested (N = 24) or were too old or handicapped (N = 12). A large number (N = 264) indicated that they did not qualify. One can assume that there were other ineligibles among the remaining nonrespondents. A total of 65 eligible subjects returned a completed questionnaire.

Findings

The occupations of the respondents ranged from secretary (17%), nurse (9.5%), factory worker, retired (8%), to unemployed, etc. The ages of the respondents are found in Table 4.1.

Table 4.1
Age of Respondents

Age	Absolute Frequency	Relative Frequency	Cumulative Frequency
25-29	21	32.8	36.5
30-34	11	17.5	50.8
35-39	2	3.2	54.0
40-49	5	7.9	61.9
50-59	8	12.7	74.6
60 and over	16	25.4	100.0
missing	1	—	100.0
Total	64	100.0	

Fifty-two percent of the respondents were under 39 years of age and 48% were 40 years of age or more. The level of formal education is found in Table 4.2. Younger respondents (under 35) had a marked higher education than older respondents.

Table 4.2
Education of Respondents

Education	Absolute Frequency	Relative Frequency
8 years or less	5	7.8
9-12 years	11	17.8
High school completed	12	18.8
2 yr. college or university	23	30.8
University degree	13	20.4
Total	64	

Association with another resident, if any, is found in Table 4.3. Older respondents were more likely to be living alone than were younger respondents (Level of significance = .08). In only a few cases, the subjects resided with relatives who required their aid. The mean years of residence with associations as indicated in the above table was 12 years. In 27% of the cases the subject owned the residence and in 73% of the cases the dwelling was rented. Older subjects were much more likely to own their dwelling. The type of rented dwelling is indicated in Tables 4.4 and 4.5. Among those renting, the older respondents were more likely to be renting a house. The mean years of living in the current residence was just over two years. The younger

Table 4.3
Association of Fellow Resident

Residence	Absolute Frequency	Relative Frequency
Alone	35	54.7
With one or both parents	13	20.3
With brother(s) and or sister(s)	2	3.1
With someone of the same sex, not related	7	10.9
With someone of the opposite sex, not related	1	1.6
With dependent child	3	4.7
Other	4	6.2

subjects showed much more residence mobility. The mean time of residence in any one location in the previous four years was three years (S.D. = 13 mo.).

Table 4.4
Type of Residence of Renters and Frequency

Residence	Absolute Frequency	Relative Frequency
House	12	18.8
House with apartments	6	9.4
Apartment building	27	42.2

Table 4.5
Type of Apartment of Renters and Frequency

Apartment Number	Absolute Frequency	Relative Frequency
One	4	6.2
2-4	4	6.2
5-11	1	1.6
12-24	5	7.8
over 24	20	31.3

Seventy-five percent of the subjects had sisters and 73% had brothers. (Note that 25% of the subjects were over 60 years of age.) In 34% of the cases the subject was the oldest in the family. The mother was considered the one chiefly responsible in "raising" the respondent during early childhood in 39% of the cases.

The religious affiliations were Protestant (64%), Roman Catholic (30%), and Orthodox (3%).* Protestants were more highly represented among the older subjects. Thirty percent considered themselves "very religious," 45% as "somewhat religious," and 17% as "minimally religious." In the preceding year, 47% had attended church at least once a week, 22% once or twice a month, and 14% about 6 times. The older respondents considered themselves more

---

*The population of the area was 46% protestant and 36% Roman Catholic.

religious and attended church more frequently than did the younger subjects.

Yearly income is indicated in Table 4.6 with a mean of about $8000 (1975). Younger subjects had a higher income than did older subjects.

Table 4.6
Income by Frequency

Income	Absolute Frequency	Relative Frequency
0 - $3999	10	15.7
$4000 to $6999	10	15.6
$7000 to $11 999	26	40.6
$12 000 to $18 000	13	20.3
Over $18 000	3	4.7

Twenty-nine percent of the respondents' mothers and 20% of their fathers preferred or expected that their single daughter would still marry. As the age of the respondent increased, the parent showed less concern that she marry. Sibling concern for the subject's marriage was identified by 20% of the respondents. Married friends also showed concern that the respondent marry (39%).

Table 4.7 indicates the respondent's perceptions of acquaintances with regard to the respondent's single status. A fairly high percentage considered themselves as being viewed by acquaintances as having much more money (47%), as having much more spare time (51%), and as more dedicated to work (47%) because of their single status.

Nineteen percent felt they were more closely observed by neighbours because they were single. A sizable number (45%) felt that marrieds considered the respondents "lucky" to be single. A few (28%) felt that the married considered them as unfortunate in singlehood. Some (22%), particularly the younger respondents, felt that married women considered them a threat to their marriage. Twenty-three percent felt that their brother(s) or sister(s) wanted them to take greater responsibility for the caring of parents, because of their being single.

The sample showed concern because of societal inequality between the status of being married and being single. Sixty-two percent felt that our society was primarily geared to families. Forty-seven percent felt that a greater attempt should be made to educate young people to view singlehood as an option.

Table 4.7
Respondent's Perception of Acquaintances' Views of Respondent's Single Status, in Percentages

Trait	Strongly Disagreed	Disagreed	No Impression	Agreed	Strongly Agreed
I have much money because I am single	4.7	12.5	35.9	37.5	9.4
I have much time because I am single	3.1	25.0	20.3	39.1	12.5
More dedicated to work because I am single	3.1	12.5	29.7	42.2	4.7
Active social life because I am single	7.8	20.3	29.7	28.1	7.8
Active sex life because I am single	29.7	10.9	40.6	6.2	3.1
Out to "Trap a man" because I am single	34.4	26.6	26.6	3.1	3.1
Self-centred because I am single	23.4	25.0	31.3	15.6	—
Selfish because I am single	26.6	31.3	35.9	—	1.6
Treat me with suspicion because I am single	25.0	28.1	14.1	14.1	1.6

The advantages of being single were seen as being able to travel (36%), participation in hobbies (13%), independence (13%), pursuit of a career (11%), and education (9%). Disadvantages were seen as having to make decisions alone (particularly by the older respondents), having no companion to share feelings (53%), and having to pay more taxes (6%). Thirty-six percent felt that their life had been unfulfilled because they were single. A sizable number (31%) regretted that in being single they were not likely to have children. This was particularly true of younger subjects. A higher percentage (66%) felt that single people should be legally permitted to raise children.

A high percentage kept in touch with between one and five single female friends at least once every two months (72%). Many had mostly married friends and others had their friends equally distributed between singles and marrieds (39%). Thirty-nine percent kept in touch with one or two male friends at least once every two months, though older subjects had fewer male friends and less contact with male friends. Only 14% did not keep contact with males. A high percentage (70%) had been invited for a meal to a married couple's home in the preceding three months (excluding Christmas and New Year's Day). An equally high number (70%) had been invited to a social gathering at a married couple's home. Most (91%) felt at ease in visiting a home with children. Many were not looking for more invitations to homes with children.

The subjects were asked whether the life of a mother with two young children and not working outside the home was viewed as boring or stifling. The response was strongly "No" (69%).

Most felt that there was greater social stigma for single females than for single males (64%). Few felt that they had been restricted in employment advancement because of being single (9.4%), although some felt restriction had been present because of their sex (20%). Jobs that required considerable travelling were viewed as particularly open to single women (11%). A high percentage (31%) considered that no job was closed to them because of being single.

Eighty-one percent felt lonely at times, and 54% of this group felt that it was because they were single. Few (17%) felt the non-married were more lonely than the married. Loneliness was overcome by calling or writing a friend (34%), being involved in sports (22%), or being involved in the community (8%). A few (16%) had pets.

A high proportion of the group (69%) had had an opportunity to marry and, with one exception, did not regret declining marriage. Reasons for refusing included being too young or immature (18%), lack of love (8%), lack of interest (8%), and incompatibility (6%). Fifty-six percent stated that they would opt to remain single if they had to relive the past 20 years again. A fairly high percentage, particularly among the younger respondents (67%) still anticipated marrying. The respondents' reason for the consideration of marriage was companionship (36%). A few were very satisfied with their present status of singlehood.

Sex was not viewed as a major problem. Only one subject reported having had a "bad" sex experience. Two subjects stated that they did not want to commit themselves exclusively to one sex partner.

A classmate's wedding, a broken engagement, or a heterosexual-friendship termination were social events which forcibly reminded the subjects of their own single status (44%). A few were concerned about the increasing probability of not marrying. Respondents were sometimes stimulated to marital hopes when a friend became engaged or a male gave an approving glance.

Several questions concerning cohabitation were asked. Nineteen percent, all younger subjects, had lived with a person of the opposite sex in a sexual relationship for at least a week in the preceding five years. The younger respondents were more likely to approve of sex outside marriage as well as cohabitation. Living together was not a common occurrence among their friends (11%), but was generally viewed as a threat to the institution of marriage by the older respondents. Some approved of living together as a form of "trial marriage" (17%). Others felt that the two lifestyles were not readily comparable (11%). Some (16%) were strongly opposed, and others (8%) expressed caution. Most felt that the more liberal sex norms would increase the percentage of adult singles in our society (66%).

The respondents were asked what they viewed as the largest problem in being single. Responses ranged from stigma (19%), to social restrictions (14%), to being viewed as failures (12%), being lonely (11%), and imposed systemic financial sanctions (8%). These were expressed as "society believes that there is something odd about singles," "a couple-oriented society," "pressures to explain to friends why you aren't married," or "people setting up dates."

Discussion

Previous studies on singlehood have used a highly selected sample, such as from a college campus[31/48] or of a few upper middle-class urbanites who included the previously married.[45] The present research was drawn from a random sample of never-married singles over 25 years of age in a medium-sized urban community.

Congruent with the Spreitzer and Riley work, there was a high number of single females who were raised by the mother and/or had no siblings. Single females did not tend to have an unusually high level of education as suggested by Srole et al. They were generally quite religious, a factor possibly peculiar to this city population.

The findings of this research about single females were not consistent with stereotyping generally found in society by other researchers.[1/31/48] The respondents were not social isolates. They had friends of both sexes. There was no evidence of "sex hang-ups" or lack of sex appeal. A majority had had at least one opportunity to marry, but declined this option for quite mature reasons: youth, lack of interest, incompatibility. Marriage was still viewed as an option for many of the sample who were under 35 years of age.

The respondents realized that the bliss of marriage is often a myth; however, they were not opposed to marriage or childrearing. Most respected the role of motherhood. Many regretted that they likely would not have the opportunity to raise a child. (Three subjects were raising their own child.) Some of the respondents under 35 years of age had had the experience of cohabitation. The younger respondents were tolerant of sex outside marriage.

The subjects were not highly career-oriented, not did they appear to be devout supporters of the women's liberation movement.

Social Implications

This research suggests there are some gross misrepresentations regarding singles in our society. Stereotypes of the single female are not supported. The research also suggests that the more liberal lifestyles of single females, as frequently portrayed by the popular news media, may be a selected population in highly urbanized and upper-middle-class areas, comprised of those possibly in the 24-30 age cohort.

Sex norms have changed. Young singles are more tolerant of cohabitation than are older singles. The single woman respects childrearing and in many cases regrets its denial because of singlehood. She would also appreciate companionship but not at any cost. Many singles are highly selective and willing to wait for the correct choice, thus possibly avoiding an ill-suited match in marriage.

This research also reveals some peculiar problems for older single women. They have less income and education while showing more loneliness and religious dedication than younger singles. In many cases the higher frequency of church attendance may be a significant social link.

The single woman functions in a social system that is highly family-oriented. The single woman finds herself a minority, and therefore quite frequently subject to stigmatization. The respondents resent the social stigma of their status and wish to be treated with dignity and respect. Rather than attempting to resocialize the singles, our society would do well to place greater effort and concern upon resocializing the public to treat all humans as individuals, whether married or single. Myths of marriage need to be dispelled and stereotyping of the singles should be terminated.

Reflections by the Researcher

This research has a number of limitations. The sample is small. Though random selection procedures were rigorously followed, it is possible that the respondents were older, more religious, and more permanent in residence than is normally found among single females in Canada.

The social scientist is continually faced with a series of decisions that must be made in doing research, particularly in an area that has previously been minimally studied. In this case it was a choice between a random selection or a depth interview with a few subjects. The latter technique of data-gathering might be criticized for the narrow selection of a small sample, likely those familiar to the investigator. Similarly, investigator-bias might be evident in the interpretation and coding of the data.

This researcher chose the survey technique of data-gathering, using randomness in the selection of the sample. Permission to use the voters' list was obtained from the authorities. Letters and question-naires were printed and mailed. Ineligible subjects were excluded from the research. A second mailing of questionnaires was made. Responses were coded and the data analysed.

The researcher was disappointed with the small return rate. This fact limited the degree of causal analysis that could be validly made from the study. Thus, percentages were used.

However, the data do yield a number of interesting points which now can be further researched. Possibly a subsequent research would focus upon a more specific population such as those single females in their thirties, or those in their sixties. Or there might be more advantage in studying singles by profession; such as teachers or nurses. Whatever the unit of analysis, variables such as social-class differences, renters versus owners, large-apartment versus smaller rental-unit respondents, rural versus urban respondents, and parent versus childless subjects could be further studied.

A subsequent study would also clarify some questions or statements which were not clearly defined. What is meant by "Did you have an opportunity to marry?" "Do you feel that your life as a single is unfulfilled?" "Would you consider yourself religious?" These questions cover a wide range of subjectivity.

This study showed a seeming ambivalence: a preference for being single, yet a desire for some of the advantages, such as childbearing and companionship, which are generally attributed to those in the married state. How is such divergence accommodated by the respondent?

References

1. Adams, Margaret. "The Single Woman in Today's Society: A Reappraisal." *The American Journal of Orthopsychiatry* 41, No. 5 (1971), pp. 776-786.
2. Baker, Luther G. (Jr.). "The Personal and Social Adjustment of the Never Married." *Journal of Marriage and the Family* (August 1968).
3. _____. "Sex, Society and the Single Woman," in Lester A. Kirkendall and Robert N. Whithurst, eds. *The New Sexual Revolution.* New York: Brown, 1971, pp. 115-130.
4. Bell, Robert R. "Those Who Never Marry," in *Marriage and Family Interaction.* Homewood, Ill.: Dorsey, 1975, pp. 156-171.
5. Bernard, Jesse. "Note on Changing Life Styles, 1970-1974." *Journal of Marriage and the Family* 37, No. 3 (August 1975), pp. 582-593.
6. Brooks, Marjory, and Hillman, Christine H. "Parent-Daughter Relationships as Factors in Non-marriage Studied in Identical Twins." *Journal of Marriage and the Family* (1964), pp. 383-385.
7. Carter, Hugh, and Glick, Paul C. *Marriage and Divorce.* Cambridge: Harvard University Press, 1970, pp. 298-357.
8. Centers, Richard. "Marital Selection and Occupational Strata." *The American Journal of Sociology* 54 (May 1949), pp. 530-535.
9. Coffin, Patricia. "The Young Unmarrieds," in Joann S. Delora and Jack R. Delora, eds. *Intimate Life Styles: Marriage and its Alternatives.* Pacific Palisades: Goodyear, 1972, pp. 316-317.
10. Coleman, James. *Abnormal Psychology and Modern Life,* 4th ed. Glenview, Ill.: Scott, Foresman, 1972.
11. Cox, Frank D. *Youth, Marriage and the Seductive Society.* Dubuque: Brown, 1974.
12. Cruikshank, Julie. "Matrifocal Families in the Canadian North," in K. Ishwaran, ed. *The Canadian Family.* Toronto: Holt, Rinehart & Winston, 1971, pp. 39-53.
13. David, Deborah. *Career Patterns and Values: A Study of Men and Women in Science and Engineering.* New York: Columbia University, Bureau of Applied Social Research, 1973.
14. Delora, Joann S., and Delora, Jack R. *Intimate Life Styles: Marriage and its Alternatives.* Pacific Palisades: Goodyear, 1972.
15. Densmore, Dana. "On Celibacy." *No More Fun and Games: A Journal of Female Liberation* I (October 1968).
16. Department of National Revenue. *Taxation Statistics, 1971.* Ottawa: Queen's Printer.
17. De Ruyter, Barbara. "Ethnic Differentials in Age and First Marriage." Edmonton: Population Research Laboratory, Department of Sociology, University of Alberta, 1971.
18. Dominion Bureau of Statistics. Vol. 1, Bulletin 1. 2-5 and 1. 2-6, October and April 1973. Ottawa: Queen's Printer.
19. Doty, Carol N., and Hoeflin, R. "A Descriptive Study of 35 Unmarried

Graduate Women."*Journal of Marriage and the Family* (February 1964), pp. 91-94.

20. Frieden, Betty. *The Feminine Mystique.* New York: Dell, 1963.
21. Glick, Paul C. "A Demographer Looks at American Families." *Journal of Marriage and the Family* 37, No. 1 (February 1975), p. 24.
22. Goldfield, Evelyn, Maunaker, Sue, and Weisstein, Naomi. "A Woman Is a Sometime Thing," in P. Long, ed. *The New Left.* Boston: Porter Sargent, 1969.
23. Hutton, Laura. *The Single Woman.* London: Barrie and Rockliff, 1960.
24. Kostash, Myrna. "The Single Girl Rip-off." *Chatelaine* (February 1974).
25. Kirkendall, Lester A., and Whitehurst, Robert N. *The New Sexual Revolution.* New York: Brown, 1971.
26. Kubat, David, and Thornton, David. *A Statistical Profile of Canadian Society.* Toronto: McGraw-Hill Ryerson, 1974.
27. Kuhn, Manfred. "How Mates Are Sorted," in Howard Becker and Ruben Hill, eds. *Family Marriage and Parenthood.* Boston: Heath, 1955.
28. Kuhn, Margaret E. "Female and Single—What Then?" *Church and Society* (March-April 1970).
29. Lasswell, Marcia E., and Lasswell, Thomas E. *Love Marriage Family—A Developmental Approach.* Boston: Little, Brown, 1974.
30. Lichtenberger, J.P. *Divorce—A Social Interpretation.* New York: Whittlesey House, McGraw-Hill, 1931.
31. Moore, H.K. "The Wife and Spinster." *Family Life* 11, No. 5 (May 1951), pp. 1-4.
32. Moran, Rosalyn. "The Singles in the Seventies," in Joann S. Delora and Jack R. Delora, eds. *Intimate Life Styles: Marriage and its Alternatives.* Pacific Palisades: Goodyear, 1972, pp. 338-344.
33. Proulx Cynthia. "Sex as Athletics in the Singles Complex." *Saturday Review/Society* (May 1973).
34. Rallings, Elisha M. "Family Situations of Married and Never-Married Males." *Journal of Marriage and the Family* (November 1966), pp. 485-494.
35. Rappoport, Allan E., Payne, David, and Steinman, Anne. "Perceptual Differences Between Married and Single College Women for the Concepts of Self, Ideal Woman, and Man's Ideal Woman." *Journal of Marriage and the Family* (August 1970), pp. 441-442.
36. Rosenteur, Phyllis. *The Single Woman.* New York: Popular Library, 1961.
37. Rubin, Zick, "Do American Women Marry Up?" *American Sociological Review* 33 (October 1968), pp. 750-760.
38. Scanzoni, Letha, and Hardesty, Nancy. "The Single Women," in *All We're Meant to Be.* Waco, Texas; Word, 1974, pp. 145-168.
39. Scanzoni, Letha, and Scanzoni, John. *Men, Women and Change.* New York: McGraw-Hill, 1976, pp. 150-156.
40. Skolnick, Arlene, and Skolnick, Jerome. *Intimacy, Family and Society.* Boston: Little Brown, 1974.
41. Spreitzer, Elmer, and Riley, Lawrence. "Factors Associated with Singlehood."

Journal of Marriage and the Family. (August 1974), pp. 537-542.

42. Srole, Leo, Langer, Thomas, Michael, Stanley, Opler, Marvin, and Rennie, Thomas. *Mental Health in the Metropolis: The Midtown Manhattan Study.* New York: McGraw-Hill, 1962.

43. Starr, Joyce R., and Carns, Donald E. "Singles in the City," in Helena Z. Lapata, ed. *Marriage and Families.* New York: Van Nostrand Co., 1973, pp. 154-161.

44. Statistics Canada. *1974 Perspective Canada.* Cat. No. 11-507. Ottawa: Information Canada, 1974.

45. Stein, Peter J. "Singlehood: An Alternative to Marriage." *The Family Coordinator* 24, No. 4 (October 1975), pp. 489-503.

46. Sullenger, Thomas E. *Neglected Areas in Family Living.* North Quincy, Mass.: Christopher Publishing House, 1960.

47. *Time* (Magazine) Essay. "The Pleasures and Pain of the Single Life," in Marcia and Thomas Lasswell, eds. *Love Marriage Family—A Developmental Approach.* Glenview, Ill.: Scott, Foresman, 1973, pp. 210-214.

48. Wakil, Parvez. "To Be or Not To Be Married. . . ." Unpublished paper, University of Saskatchewan, 1967.

49. *Weekend Magazine.* "It Takes Two to Tango, It Takes 5000 to Bash." Vol. 24, No. 31 (August 3, 1974), pp. 2-4.

5/The Premarital Sexual Standards of Canadians[*]

Daniel Perlman

The purpose of this paper is to provide a social scientist's view of the sexual standards of Canadians. The paper is divided into two major sections. The first section presents descriptive information about Canadians' sexual standards. This section will deal with a variety of questions such as: How do students and members of the general public feel about premarital sex? Have these feelings changed in recent years? What proportion of students actually engage in sexual intercourse? Are students' sexual attitudes consistent with their behaviour?

Naturally, there are individual and group differences in sexual mores. The second part of the paper focusses on factors useful in predicting and explaining these differences. For didactic purposes such factors are divided into three broad categories: a) sociological (or cultural) influences, b) dyadic influences, and c) individual influences.

Probably the first sociological study of the sexual standards of Canadians was conducted by Mann[15] in the 1960's. It is unfortunate that earlier research isn't available. Historical accounts[3] suggest that a dramatic "sexual revolution" has undoubtedly occurred since the late nineteenth century. To shed light on earlier norms, Bliss[3] analysed a series of pamphlets entitled *Self and Sex*. With endorsements from such groups as the Methodist Church and the Christian Temperance Union, this series claimed to be Canada's best-selling sex manual in the period 1900-1915.

[*]It is a pleasure to indicate the contributions others have made, directly or indirectly, to this paper. I have especially appreciated the collaboration of William Barker, Stephen Eyres, Wendy Josephson, and Kenneth Martens in my own sexual standards research. Our work has been supported by grants from the Canada Council and the University of Manitoba Research Board. While I was preparing this paper, Dr. Charles Hobart generously provided, prior to their publication, results from his 1977 survey. Finally, the Canadian Institute of Public Opinion made available the data from their February 1975 poll for further analysis and reporting.

A few of the views expressed in the series will suffice to indicate the tenor of their advice and of that period. Co-author Sylvanus Stall offered "very strong arguments" for sexual abstinence in marriage except for the purpose of procreation. Furthermore, he strongly warned adolescents about the dangers of masturbating, suggesting that

> if persisted in, masturbation will not only undermine, but completely overthrow the health. If the body is naturally strong, the mind may give way first, and in extreme cases imbecility and insanity may and often do come as the inevitable result.

He devoted not one but rather three chapters to the "evils" and "dreaded consequences" of sex outside of marriage. One of his primary concerns was venereal disease. In a similar vein, co-author Mary Wood-Allen gave the example of a young woman disfigured by syphilis because she once innocently let a young man kiss her goodnight. "I do not need to multiply such cases," wrote Dr. Wood-Allen. "You can be warned by one as well as by a hundred."

Needless to say, many of the statements in this series have subsequently been proven erroneous. Nonetheless, the Victorian views expressed by Stall were undoubtedly widely accepted before World War I. This paper will focus on sexual standards in the late 1970's. Obviously the tenor of the times has changed. But, how much? To provide a perspective on contemporary sexual standards, I will rely heavily on evidence collected in surveys and questionnaires.

Naturally, in asking people about their sexual standards, social scientists face a number of ethical and methodological problems. For instance, researchers must ask themselves such questions as: Are the people who answer sex questions different from the people who refuse to do so? Are the answers that people give influenced by the interviewer's characteristics and behaviour? Do people answer honestly?

Let us consider some evidence bearing on these questions. First, volunteer bias does not appear to be a greater problem in sexual standards surveys than it is in any other type of research: potential respondents have been as willing to participate in sex surveys as they have in investigations of other topics.[18/1] Research does, however, suggest that volunteers usually have more permissive standards than non-volunteers.[6/13] Second, with regard to interviewer effects, interviewer characteristics other than age appear to have little or no impact on the sexual standards reported by respondents.[12] And, obviously, in questionnaire studies, the potential problem of interviewer effects is almost completely circumvented by not having an interviewer. Third, converging bits of evidence testify to the validity of respondents' answers. For instance, when separate interviews are held with sexual partners, they give very similar reports of their joint sexual activities. Similarly, at the end of one sexual standards questionnaire, Reiss[25] asked respondents to assess the truthfulness of their fellow students' answers. About 80% felt that the questionnaire would be answered honestly by other students and that it had got at the essence of their own beliefs.

In weighing the evidence, I have come to believe that sexual standards surveys are about as valid as most other types of surveys—not perfect, but reasonably good. I am convinced that opinion polls are a more accurate indication of the public's "true" sentiment than are estimates given by individual observers. Taken collectively, the results of various studies have an admirable reliability and consistency.

Premarital Sexual Standards

The General Public's View
One of the most important sources of information about public attitudes is the Canadian Institute of Public Opinion (CIPO), or the so-called Gallup Poll. Several times a year, this institute interviews a sample of Canadian adults. Typically, each recent CIPO sample has contained over 1000 respondents representative of the non-institutionalized civilian population, 18 years and older, living in Canada.

Fortunately, during the 1970's, several Gallup polls have included questions to tap the public's attitude toward sexual matters. Furthermore, some of these questions have been presented to a second sample of Canadians interviewed at a different time. One question directly concerned with premarital sex was phrased as follows:

> There's a lot of discussion about the way morals and sex are changing in this country. What is your opinion on this—do you think it is wrong for a man and woman to have sex relations before marriage or not?

Of 1043 people interviewed in February 1975, 47.1% answered that premarital sex was acceptable, 16.6% were undecided, and 36.4% responded that premarital sex was unacceptable.

Table 5.1
Distribution of Responses to the Gallup Poll Question on
Premarital Sex by Year and Respondent's Gender

| | Male | | Female | |
Answer	1970	1975	1970	1975
No, Not Wrong	35%	51%	27%	39%
Undecided	14%	15%	10%	19%
Yes, Wrong	51%	34%	63%	42%

Note: The response "Yes, Wrong" indicates disapproval of premarital sexual relations.

Table 5.1 gives a more detailed breakdown of answers, showing the attitudes of men and women separately and how responses have changed over a five-year period. The time trends will be discussed in a subsequent subsection of this chapter. In the February 1975 survey, having an accepting attitude toward premarital sex was associated with: being under 30; being university educated; having an annual family income over $15 000; being a male; favouring NDP candidates; and living in a community of over 100 000. Conversely, having a restrictive orientation toward premarital sex was associated with: being older; being less-well educated; having an annual family income under $6000; living in a Prairie Province; living in a smaller community; being a female; and favouring PC candidates. Finally, among people in their forties, those with children living at home had more restrictive attitudes than those without children at home.

Many of these findings on the attitudes of various subgroups have been replicated in other surveys. For instance, other surveys[30] have consistently shown older Canadians to have more restrictive attitudes toward premarital sex than younger Canadians. Similarly, holding age constant, Reiss[25] found that being a parent, especially of teenagers, was associated with having a restrictive attitude toward premarital sex.

Students' Standards

Students' Attitudes. During the past dozen years, several social scientists (see References: Mann, 1967, 1968, 1970; Luckey and Nass, 1969; Hobart, 1970, 1972, 1974, 1979; Perlman and associates, 1973, 1978; Shymko, 1977) have investigated Canadian students' attitudes toward premarital sex. Most of these researchers have used questions from Ira L. Reiss' 24-item Premarital Sexual Permissiveness scale.[25] A typical item reads:

> I believe that full sexual relations are acceptable for the male before marriage when he is in love.

The items elicit the respondents' reactions to males (or females) engaging in three types of behaviour (kissing, petting, and full sexual relations) at four levels of interpersonal intimacy (when the couple is engaged, in love, feels strong affection, or does not feel particularly affectionate).

Naturally, as is illustrated by Hobart[9] and Perlman,[24] differences in the use of these questions exist between and even within various studies. Hobart conducted his 1968 survey at universities and trade schools in three provinces (Quebec, Ontario, and Alberta). At the English-speaking universities, he contacted a 16%-20% proportion of the third- and fourth-year students in several faculties (Arts, Science, Engineering, Nursing, Medicine, Law, and Education) by mail or telephone. Approximately 90% of the students contacted completed questionnaires. At the French-speaking university, generally comparable procedures were followed except that a research assistant personally picked up the questionnaires. Unfortunately, however, the research assistant only picked up questionnaires from 44% of the people originally contacted. In 1977, Hobart replicated his earlier study but also collected data in the Atlantic Provinces and British Columbia. Perlman et al.'s cross-cultural study[24] involved students from five "cultures" (four countries). As part of this larger study, 259 Introductory Psychology students at the University of Manitoba completed questionnaires in the spring of 1975. For these students, completing the questionnaire was one of several options for fulfilling a course research-participation requirement.

In Hobart's 1977 survey, approximately three-quarters of Anglophones and five-sixths of Francophones approved full sexual relations for a female in love. Similarly, in Perlman et al.'s University of Manitoba sample,[24] a clear majority of students accepted premarital sex involving partners with an emotionally intimate relationship. More detailed results for the Manitoba sample are shown in Table 5.2. Examination of this table supports the following three conclusions. First, males tended to have more accepting attitudes towards premarital sexual activities than females. This gender difference was especially pronounced for petting and intercourse "without strong affection." Second, petting was more widely accepted than full sexual relations. For instance, for a female in love, 91.8% of Manitoba students approved of petting, while only 77.4% of Manitoba students approved of sexual intercourse. Finally, each type of sexual activity was more widely accepted if the partners are emotionally close to one another.

Table 5.2
The Percentage of University of Manitoba Students
Agreeing with Each of Reiss' Sexual Permissiveness Items

Type of Activity and Relationship	Male Students		Female Students	
	Male Scale	Female Scale	Male Scale	Female Scale
Petting—Without Strong Affection	67.9	68.5	39.0	35.2
Petting—With Strong Affection	94.6	91.0	80.1	77.2
Petting—In Love	94.6	92.8	88.4	91.0
Petting—Engaged	97.3	94.5	95.2	91.7
Coitus—Without Strong Affection	46.4	43.5	20.7	19.3
Coitus—With Strong Affection	79.1	73.2	59.3	55.2
Coitus—In Love	83.9	81.3	76.6	74.5
Coitus—Engaged	84.7	82.1	75.2	77.2

Note: The "male scale" refers to the respondents' attitudes toward the behaviour of males; the "female scale" refers to the respondents' attitudes toward the behaviour of females.

Students' Premarital Sexual Behaviour. Data indicating the extent of premarital sexual intercourse among student samples are shown in Table 5.3. These percentages indicate that, in the mid-1970's, a majority of students across Canada reported being sexually experienced.

Furthermore, among Anglophones, the proportion of sexually experienced males was slightly higher than the proportion of sexually experienced females.

Table 5.3

The Percentage of Respondents Reporting Having
Experienced Premarital Intercourse

Sample	Sex of Respondent	
	Male	Female
University of Manitoba Studies		
Introductory Psychology Students—1975	62	45
Students in Personality Courses[a]—Circa 1970	~55	~37
Hobart's 1977 Study		
Anglophone Students	73	63
Francophone Students	59	65
Hobart's 1968 Study		
Anglophone Students	56	44
Francophone Students	63	30

[a]Source of Data: Perlman, 1973.

In their 1975 survey, Perlman et al.[24] collected data on the number of coital partners reported by each sexually experienced respondent. Of the sexually experienced males, 42% had only one coital partner; 45% had had two to five partners; and 13% had had six or more partners. Of the sexually experienced females, 57% had had one coital partner; 28% had had two to five partners; and 15% had had six or more partners.

Students' Contraceptive Practices. No particularly current data on the premarital contraceptive practices of Canadian students were available for inclusion in this paper. Of sexually experienced respondents in Hobart's earlier study,[8] only 31% of the English sample and 38% of the French sample regularly used contraceptives. Of Anglophones and Francophones, respectively, 13% and 30% never used contraceptives. While these percentages probably have changed somewhat since the late 1960's, one basic fact undoubtedly remains: Many sexually active students fail to use contraceptives. Why is this? Among the numerous contributing factors, I will mention three. First, many sexual encounters, especially initial sexual encounters, aren't planned. Thus, in these cases, failure to employ contraceptives results from lack of foresight and unwillingness to make sex a premeditated act. Second, the process of obtaining contraceptives may be aversive for some individuals. Finally, because of a personal sense of infallibility and a misunderstanding of the rules of probability, many contraceptive non-users underestimate their chances of instigating pregnancy.[4] As one adolescent girl commented retrospectively: "Pills? That's what I should have taken ... the thought I might get pregnant never entered my mind."

On Students' First Coital Experiences. Students' first sexual experiences have been investigated in several studies. In the mid-1960's, Mann[16] asked Ontario students what factors served to restrain their sexual activities. The three reasons students mentioned most frequently were: fear of pregnancy, respect of their partner, and respect for their parents' restrictive standards. Fear of pregnancy is an important restraint for both males and females. Other reasons for sexual abstinence, as shown in a recent American study of dating couples,[22] are gender linked. In that study, 64% of abstaining males (versus only 11% of females) gave as a restraint that "my partner does not wish to have sexual intercourse at the present time." Women were more likely than men (31% versus 11%) to give as a sexual restraint that "It is against my moral or religious convictions."

In interviewing 35 women at the University of Windsor, Whitehurst[31] found that their first sexual experiences tended to be a positive, satisfying event. He noted the following theme in their remarks:

> There was a general feeling that (losing virginity) had made the subject more a woman, an adult, a more fully participating member of society.

The Congruence between Students' Attitudes and Their Behaviours. Having separately reviewed both the sexual attitudes and practices of Canadian students, a natural question arises: Do students behave in a fashion consistent with their attitudes? The 1975 University of

Manitoba data indicate that premarital sex was more widely accepted than practised (see Tables 5.2 and 5.3). However, most individuals practise what they advocate. This has been found both by Reiss (see Reference 25, page 117) and by Hobart[10] and can be demonstrated with data from the 1975 University of Manitoba survey. Using the Reiss item about the acceptability of premarital sex for a couple in love, respondents were classified into four groups: 1) virgins who approved of premarital sex; 2) non-virgins who approved of premarital sex; 3) virgins who disapproved of sex; and 4) non-virgins who disapproved of sex. Approximately 70% of respondents were consistent in their attitudes and behaviours. Virtually all the inconsistent University of Manitoba respondents (73 of 78) were virgins who approved of intercourse before marriage. However, of the virgins who approved of coitus for a couple in love, over half had never themselves been in love. This lack of an appropriate partner may help explain the apparent contradiction in their attitude and behaviour.

Over 80% of students attending the Winnipeg religious colleges held attitudes consistent with their behaviour. But among the inconsistent members of that population, sexually experienced students who disapproved of premarital sex outnumbered approving virgins by a margin of more than four to one. Hobart (see Reference 10, page 37) found that "regretful non-virgins" tended to be "very devout, very romantic, (and) little experienced in drinking." Such students typically had intercourse with their "first love," sometimes after drinking, and often as a response to reported pressure from their partners.

Cross-Cultural Comparisons. Two sets of evidence are available for placing the sexual standards of Canadian students in a global perspective. The first set is from a five-nation study conducted in 1966 involving 2230 students (including 180 Canadians). The investigators, Luckey and Nass,[14] gathered data at 21 American schools, and one large university, with a geographically diverse student body, in each of the remaining four countries. The second set of evidence is Perlman et al.'s attitudinal data,[24] collected in five "cultures" (four countries) between 1972 and 1975. Three of Perlman et al.'s five samples were students at large, government-funded universities in Manitoba, Malaysia, and Bangladesh. The other two samples were obtained at small, private institutions believed to attract students with extreme sexual standards. The students attending the New York State College had a reputation for being particularly accepting of premarital sex. The students attending religious colleges in Winnipeg had a reputation for having very restrictive sexual standards.

Table 5.4
Percentage of Students Reporting Having
Experienced Premarital Intercourse

Sample	Sex of Respondents	
	Male	Female
Canadian	56.8	35.3
American	58.2	43.2
English	74.8	62.8
German	54.5	59.4
Norwegian	66.7	53.6

Source: Luckey and Nass.[14]

Table 5.5
Percentage of Students Approving of Premarital
Intercourse for an Engaged Female

Sample	Sex of Respondent	
	Male	Female
University of Manitoba	82.1	77.2
Canadian Religious Colleges	4.8	8.2
New York State College	95.5	97.7
Malaysia	43.3	14.7
Bangladesh	53.0	10.6

Results from these two cross-cultural studies are shown in Tables 5.4 and 5.5. In the earlier study by Luckey and Nass,[14] Canadian students, just as Americans, were generally less likely than Western European students to report having engaged in sexual intercourse. In Perlman et al.'s later study, a very marked difference emerged between the two Canadian populations. As expected, University of Manitoba students were more accepting of premarital sex than students at the religious colleges. The University of Manitoba students were also more likely to approve of premarital intercourse than were Malaysian or Bangladesh students. However, students at the University of Manitoba were less accepting of premarital coitus than were students at the New York State College. In general, these results suggest that the mainstream of Canadian students (i.e., those attending provincial universities) are moderately, but not extremely, permissive in their sexual standards.

Recent Changes in Canadian Sexual Standards

Before leaving this descriptive section on the sexual standards of Canadians, a few comments on how these standards have changed in the past decade are worth making. The mass media often suggest that we have just lived through a period of increasing sexual freedom. Evidence collected since the mid-1960's supports this view.

The trend toward increased acceptance of premarital sex appears true for both the general public and for student groups. For instance, between 1970 and 1975, there was a 16% increase in Gallup Poll respondents answering that premarital sex was acceptable. In 1968, 51% of Hobart's Anglophone and 46% of his Francophone students accepted premarital intercourse for a female in love. These figures, albeit based on a larger sample of schools, had increased by 1977 to 80% and 84%, respectively.

A second, more subtle, recent trend can also be detected in many sets of data (see, for instance, Tables 5.1 and 5.3). In the late 1960's, males generally had more accepting attitudes toward premarital sex than females. However, since that time the attitudes of females have changed more rapidly than the attitudes of males, so that today the gap between the attitudes of men and women is smaller. Thus, the existence of a "double standard" is declining.

Theoretical Perspectives for Understanding Premarital Sexual Standards

Reiss' Sociological Theory

It is fitting to begin by first examining Ira L. Reiss' explanations of our premarital sexual standards.[25/26] What Kinsey was to the area of sexual research generally and Masters and Johnson[19] were to the investigation of physiological aspects of sexual intercourse per se, Reiss has been to the area of people's premarital sexual standards. Reiss has been a pioneer, a sociologist whose extensive work provides a standard of excellence against which other contributions can be judged.

Reiss' Model. Reiss and Miller[26] have ordered the influences on our premarital sexual standards along a time line. First, there are the traditional norms in a society which are present before and throughout the individual's life. Second, there are long-term parental influences and one's responsibility to one's family. Third, there are the norms and structural factors which influence the courtship process. Finally, there are the individual's participation in courtship activities plus the perceived importance various groups (parents and peers) have for the individual.

Reiss and Miller[26] labelled their view an "autonomy theory" of permissiveness to denote the central importance of courtship autonomy in their model. They comment:

> There is presumptive evidence for assuming a general tension between a courtship subculture which furthers a high emphasis on the rewards of sexuality and a family subculture which stresses the risks of sexuality.... If youth culture stresses the rewards of sexuality, then to the extent young people are free from the constraints of the family and other adult type institutions, they will be able to develop their own emphasis on sexuality. The physical and psychic pleasures connected to human sexuality are rewards basically to the participants and not to their parents.... Thus, the autonomy of young people is the key variable in determining how sexually permissive one will be.

In terms of the temporal ordering of influences, courtship autonomy is in the third set of influences. As such, the amount of courtship autonomy individuals have is influenced by earlier factors such as societal norms, and in turn influences subsequent factors such as their participation in courtship activities. Reiss and Miller[26] did not predict a strong, direct relationship between courtship autonomy and premarital permissiveness. Rather, they claimed that courtship autonomy is a crucial link in a chain of influences.

Canadian Evidence Relevant to Reiss' Model. A number of results from the 1975 study of University of Manitoba psychology students are consistent with Reiss' view. First, greater participation in courtship activities as measured either by age of first date or number of steady dating partners went hand in hand with having more accepting attitudes toward premarital sex. Second, consistent with Reiss and Miller's postulates on the perceived importance of parental (and peer) sexual standards, students who spent less free time with their parents reported being more accepting of premarital sex. Third, younger siblings, who according to Reiss and Miller have less family responsibility, were more accepting of premarital sex.

Besides the data from the University of Manitoba sample, some comparative findings from the two different Canadian samples were consistent with Reiss and Miller's view. For instance, consistent with their historically more conservative norms, students attending the Winnipeg religious colleges were much less likely than University of Manitoba students to report being sexually experienced. Furthermore, among sexually experienced students, a higher percentage at the religious colleges than at the University of Manitoba reported having ever felt guilty about their sexual behaviour. This is consistent with an implication of Reiss and Miller's model that the negative consequences of having premarital sex increase with the restrictiveness of the sexual norms in the cultural group.

Not every facet of the available Canadian data supported the Reiss and Miller model. For instance, according to their theory, the socio-economic status-permissiveness correlation should be contingent on the degree of support for premarital permissiveness in the cultural group. In particular, in groups with permissive norms such as the University of Manitoba students, higher socio-economic status should be associated with greater permissiveness. In restrictive groups such as the students attending religious colleges, higher socio-economic status should be associated with less permissiveness. In fact, however, students from higher status backgrounds in both samples were more accepting of premarital sex.

Reiss himself has considered other studies whose evidence seemingly contradicted his initial predictions of 1967. In some cases, Reiss has maintained that other investigators have provided an inadequate test of his propositions. In other cases, Reiss has used the evolving body of evidence to revise his original position. Thus, despite some healthy controversy over a few of his specific predictions, I believe that Reiss has provided an extremely fruitful and generally successful way of explaining people's premarital sexual standards.

The Dyadic Approach

Dating partners constitute a dyad. These partners influence one another, and every dyad, as a dyad, has properties of its own. Every dyad develops various patterns of behaviour and has a history. Being in the presence of another person changes an individual's behaviour. A considerable body of evidence (see Reference 32, page 628) demonstrates that after interacting with one another, people make more extreme decisions than they would individually recommend. In essence, a dyad is different from the sum of its parts.

Some social scientists maintain that dyadic influences should be given a central role in explaining our premarital sexual behaviour. After all, sex is essentially a form of social interaction involving shared decision-making. Thus, advocates of this view argue that our sexual behaviour is shaped by our partners and our relationships with them. Naturally, this dyadic viewpoint is supported by studies which show that particular combinations of partners behave uniquely. For instance, consider a virginal male named John who forms an emotionally intimate, new relationship with Mary. If dyadic considerations made no difference, John would be equally likely to engage in sexual intercourse with his new partner regardless of her previous sexual experience. However, as available evidence clearly demonstrates, John will almost certainly engage in intercourse if his partner is sexually experienced. If she is inexperienced, this is much less likely to occur. These and other similar results testify to the importance of dyadic factors.

Equity Theory provides one dyadic analysis of premarital sexual relations. According to this perspective, people strive for fairness in their relationships. They want their inputs and benefits to be roughly equivalent to their partners'. Walster, Walster, and Traupmann[29] found that equitable relationships were characterized by greater sexuality than non-equitable relationships. For instance, where students felt that their relationships were fairly well balanced in terms of the benefits to the two partners, they reported more intimate sexual behaviours, knowing their partner only a short time before having intercourse, and having intercourse more frequently.

Two other illustrations of a dyadic approach merit attention. Another current example of research generated by the dyadic viewpoint is McCormick's work (in press) on the power strategies people use in sexual encounters. A final example is Peplau, Rubin, and Hill's study[22] on how three different types of couples interact sexually. Both of these studies are worth reviewing briefly.

Power Strategies in Sexual Encounters. McCormick (in press) asked 229 UCLA students to describe the tactics they would use to avoid or to achieve having sex with a partner. McCormick classified the students' answers into ten different categories. For instance, one category was called seduction. McCormick defined seduction as a step-

Table 5.6

Examples from Students Essays of Strategies for Having or Avoiding Sex

Major Strategies Used for Having Sex	Example
Seduction	First of all, I would put on some soft music and offer her some wine, then I would start kissing her gently and caressing her body. . .
Body Language	I would test the limits by holding hands, sitting closer . . .

Major Strategies Used for Avoiding Sex	Example
Coercion	If he still insisted on making love, I'd remind him that it's my apartment and he can just leave.
Logic	I would give reasons why I didn't want to make love . . . like fear of pregnancy.
Moralizing	I would state directly that that type of relationship is reserved for marriage.
Relationship conceptualizing	I would tell her the relationship had only just begun. I don't feel we are ready for sex at this stage.

Source: McCormick (in press)

by-step, sexually arousing plan for getting a date to have intercourse. Table 5.6 lists and gives examples of six important strategies.

Seduction was the strategy for having intercourse most frequently cited by both men and women. Men did, however, report this strategy more often than women. Women were also apt to report body language as a technique they would use for encouraging intercourse.

The most frequently mentioned way of avoiding sex was "relationship conceptualizing" (i.e., saying that the relationship wasn't advanced enough for having sex). Several strategies were cited more often as ways of avoiding sex than as ways of having sex. These strategies were direct, as opposed to indirect, forms of social influence. They included coercion, logic, and moralizing (see Table 5.6).

Sexual Behaviour and Emotional Intimacy. Peplau et al.'s study was based on 231 college-aged dating couples in New England. At the time the study began, all these couples defined themselves as "going together." On the basis of rational considerations, Peplau and her colleagues expected to be able to divide couples into the three groups (traditionals, moderates, and liberals) on the basis of their sexual behaviour. For traditionals, love alone would be an insufficient justification for intercourse; instead, abstinence should be considered a sign of respect and the more permanent commitment of engagement or marriage should be a necessary prerequisite for intercourse. The *moderates* should hold standards akin to what Reiss[25] calls "permissiveness with affection." For such couples, intercourse should be acceptable when strong affective bonds (but not necessarily long-term commitment) exist. The *liberals* should approve of sex on a more casual or recreational basis, and consider intercourse an expected part of dating relationships. For them, intercourse can, but doesn't need to be an expression of emotional sharing and intimacy.

As an illustration of one of these orientations, consider the case of a moderate couple, Tom and Sandy.[22]

Three weeks after their first date, Tom told Sandy that he loved her. She was in love, too, and their relationship grew quickly. In a few months, they were spending weekends together at one of their dorms. They slept in the same bed, but did not have intercourse. While Sandy was a virgin, Tom had had coitus with three different women. Although Tom was very attracted to Sandy, he was slow to initiate intercourse. "I didn't want to push it on her," he said. "I felt that we shouldn't have sex until our relationship reached a certain point. [Sex] is something I just can't imagine on a first date." For Tom, sex "added another dimension to our relationship; it's a landmark of sorts."

To study these ideal types, Peplau et al.[22] divided their sample into three groups: couples (N=90) who engaged in intercourse within one month of their first date, couples (N=92) who waited longer than one month before having intercourse, and abstaining couples (N=49). A number of differences between early- and later-sex couples emerged. Members of early-sex couples were more apt to have had prior coital experience in previous relationships. They had more accepting attitudes toward sex without affection and gave greater importance to sex as a dating goal. For early-sex couples, sex usually preceded "going together" by about a month's time. Early-sex couples preferred and engaged in sex more frequently.

Later-sex couples reported waiting an average of six months after they started "going together" before they had intercourse. Later-sex couples reported knowing their partners better and feeling closer to their partners. Not only were they more apt to say that they were "in love," but also they gave higher estimates of the probability that they would marry. Peplau et al. followed the progress of these relationships for two years. At the end of that time, there was no relationship between the couple's dating status (going together, married, or not going together) and their sexual type (early-sex, later-sex, or abstinence). The follow-up data on the later-sex couples is especially interesting. Despite their greater avowed emotional intimacy and expectations for marriage when the study began, these couples were no more apt to remain together.

Perhaps in the case of these moderates, sex and love are linked via two processes. First, given their beliefs, later-sex couples may delay coitus until their relationship is emotionally close. Thus, the development of emotional intimacy serves as a trigger or releasing mechanism for sexual behaviour. Also, having intercourse may require a process of emotional justification and/or create conditions for mislabelling one's feelings so that people exaggerate the intensity of their love.

Psychological Approaches

Individual or psychological approaches for explaining people's premarital sexual standards focus on personality traits as well as on other dimensions. Other types of individual differences include people's physical appearance, their moral values, and the like. Recently, Hans Eysenck,[7] the British psychologist, has been one of the leading exponents of this viewpoint.

One of Eysenck's most cogent arguments for using personality traits to predict premarital sexual standards is rather simple. Eysenck pointed out that many sex researchers such as Kinsey have tried to provide descriptive statistics for entire groups. For instance, Kinsey reported the average number of times per week that American males have sexual intercourse. However, Eysenck maintains that such statistical averages are virtually meaningless. The variability hidden by these means is so great that averages tell little, if anything. One person may have intercourse only two or three times a year, while another person may have intercourse two or three times a day. Eysenck concluded that sex researchers should examine these individual differences in behaviour. He also concluded that one of the best ways to account for the variability in people's sexual behaviour is through personality traits.

Eysenck's personality scheme involves three primary dimensions: neuroticism, extroversion, and psychoticism. Eysenck stresses the genetic determinants of personality and believes that there are important gender differences in sexuality. For instance, he believes the underlying basis of extroversion is a physiological factor, low cortical arousal. Because of this, Eysenck argues that extroverts typically seek above-average amounts of external stimulation. They are sociable, carefree, impulsive, and active.

One of the early investigations using Eysenck's concepts to study premarital sexual behaviour was done in Germany. Among the students sampled, extroversion was associated with greater premarital sexual activity (i.e., being non-virginal, having premarital sex more frequently, etc.). His book, *Sex and Personality*, provides a detailed report of Eysenck's own British findings. Further discussion of Eysenck's work will be curtailed so that attention can be focussed on evidence gathered in Canada. Although no Canadian researchers have used Eysenck's three dimensions, they have used a number of other, equally important personality traits.

Personality Correlates of Permissiveness. In a study done at the University of Manitoba[1] a sexual standards questionnaire plus Jackson's multidimensional personality scale were administered to 209 Introductory Psychology students. For 100 of these students, authoritarianism scores were also available. Around the same time that these data were gathered, a group of psychologists[33] at the University of Delaware administered Jackson's scale and a sexual standards questionnaire to a sample of American students. By and large, the results of the two studies were very similar.

Personality scores were correlated with both attitudinal and behavioural measures of permissiveness (see Reference 23. Perlman, Table 6). Some personality attributes correlated significantly with one type of permissiveness but not with the other. Overall, however, a gestalt emerged. Permissive males were characterized by eight personality attributes. They were high in autonomy, change, dominance, exhibitionism, play, and sentience; they were low in avoidance of harm and need for order. Thus, the permissive male can be described as trying to break away from restraints; liking new, different experiences; being willing to express his opinions forcefully to influence others; liking an audience and attention; spending time in leisure activities and doing things for fun; and being a sensually aware person who may maintain an essentially hedonistic view of life. Being low in harm avoidance, the permissive male likes exciting activities even if danger is involved. Finally, he is less concerned with being neat, organized, prompt, disciplined, and tidy.

Among females, those with sexually permissive attitudes were high in autonomy and impulsiveness but low in harm avoidance, orderliness, and cognitive structure. Thus, sexually permissive females tend to do things on the spur of the moment. Like their male counterparts, they try to break away from constraints; they enjoy activities even if they involve risk of bodily harm; and they are less concerned with neatness. Finally, girls with accepting attitudes toward premarital sex are more willing to make decisions without perfect information and they are more comfortable with ambiguous, uncertain information.

Regarding the personality correlates of women's sexual behaviour, the pattern of results was less clear. The results from the American and Canadian studies differed. For example, among the Canadian females, being low in dominance was associated with having a larger number of coital partners. The exact opposite was true for American females.

In addition to the reults they obtained with Jackson's personality scales, Zuckerman et al.[33] reported that more permissive students tended to be high in sensation-seeking (a trait somewhat akin to Eysenck's extroversion). Barker and Perlman[1] found that more permissive students tended to score low in authoritarianism. Highly authoritarian individuals are characterized by a syndrome of characteristics including rigid adherence to conventional values, submission to authority, a punitive attitude toward deviants, and several other components. These supplementary findings from the two studies held for both males and females, and for both attitudes and behaviour.

Morality as a Correlate of Permissiveness. Religiosity, moral development, and sex guilt can all loosely be considered as related to morality. Furthermore, each of these three factors has been successfully used in predicting people's premarital sexual standards.

For instance, among the 1975 University of Manitoba psychology students, frequency of church attendance was the single best predictor of attitudes toward premarital sex. Not surprisingly, highly religious people tend to have restrictive sexual standards. Across several samples studied at the University of Manitoba, this relationship has been one of the most consistent, most salient findings.

Mosher[2] has defined sex guilt as a general tendency to punish oneself whenever proper standards of sexual conduct are transgressed either in thought or in deed. For instance, if a high-sex-guilt boy believed pornographic pictures were taboo, he might experience anxiety when looking at a *Playboy* magazine centrefold. Mosher contends that high-sex-guilt people are less dependent on, and less sensitive to, external cues indicating social punishment for sexual behaviour. Instead, their own sex guilt serves as an internal control device (or conscience).

Ridley[27] administered Mosher's Sex Guilt Inventory to 238 Introductory Psychology students at the University of Manitoba. As expected, he found that high-sex-guilt students rated themselves as more conservative in their sexual attitudes, reported fewer sexual partners, and reported less voluntary exposure to pornographic materials. Mosher and his associates[21/5] have obtained similar results in the United States.

Besides administering Mosher's sex guilt scale, D'Augelli and Cross[5] also assessed each student's level of moral development. The results indicated that students in Kohlberg's conventional stage of moral development were less sexually experienced than students in either Kohlberg's premoral (hedonistic) or post-conventional (principled) stage of development. Conventional-level individuals, according to Kohlberg, strive to do what will please others and be within the limits of externally given social rules.

Physical Attractiveness. In addition to personality traits, per se, psychologists have also investigated how other personal attributes influence sexual standards. For instance, in my 1975 study of Manitoba students, I had each person rate his or her own physical attractiveness. For females, but not for males, being physically attractive was associated with: greater participation in courtship activities, more permissive attitudes toward premarital sex, and a higher number of coital partners. Kaats and Davis[13] conducted a similar study at the University of Colorado. However, instead of using self-reported physical attractiveness they had judges rate each girl's appearance. In their study attractive girls were more apt to be sexually experienced even though their attitudes toward premarital sex were no more liberal than those held by less attractive students.

Since highly attractive women date more and have been in love with more men, their greater number of sexual partners probably reflects two factors. First, attractive girls have more opportunities to engage in intercourse within emotionally intimate relationships. Second, males may bring greater pressure to bear on attractive girls to have sex.

Evaluation of the Personality Approach. During the past decade the personality approach has come under criticism from a number of directions. Vis-à-vis the study of premarital sex, three criticisms are noteworthy. First, the classic conception of personality traits assumes that people act consistently in different situations. But, this assumption isn't completely valid. Second, in a statistical sense, the predictive power of personality traits is usually weak rather than strong. Third, so many different personality traits exist that it is difficult to know which ones are the most important.

Advocates of the personality approach have offered a number of rebuttals to such criticisms. Regarding the first point, many personality theorists would agree that situational pressures are very important. However, they wouldn't consider this grounds for rejecting the usefulness of personality traits. Instead, they would argue that we need a better understanding of how the impact of personality influences is altered by situational and cultural forces. Regarding the second criticism, personality theorists have merely addressed the same question to their critics. Has the predictive strength of other approaches been that much greater? Despite some controversy, the answer is probably "No." Regarding the third criticism, personality theorists can point to various statistical methods for extracting a few basic dimensions from a more complex network of traits.

Personally, I believe our premarital sexual standards are determined by a number of influences. No one influence, or even type of influence, can completely explain the phenomena of interest. The most complete understanding will come from considering the contributions of different theoretical viewpoints and/or developing theories which simultaneously consider the influence of social, dyadic, and personality influences. Given the practices of most contemporary social scientists, I predict that progress is most apt to occur along several separate tracks by people with different perspectives, each simultaneously extending his or her own position.

References

1. Barker, W.J., and Perlman, D. "Volunteer Bias and Personality Traits in Sexual Standards Research." *Archives of Sexual Behavior* 4 (1975), pp. 161-171.
2. Barker, W.J., and Perlman, D. "Personality Traits and Students' Sexual Standards." Paper presented at the meeting of the Canadian Psychological Association, Victoria, B.C., 1973.
3. Bliss, M. "Pure Books on Avoided Subjects: Pre-Freudian Sexual Ideas in Canada." *Canadian Historical Association, Historical Papers* (1970), pp. 89-108.
4. Cvetkovich, G., Grote, B., Bjorseth, A., and Sarkissian, J. "On the Psychology of Adolescents' Use of Contraceptives." *Journal of Sex Research* (1975), pp. 256-270.
5. D'Augelli, J.F., and Cross, H.J. "Relationship of Sex Guilt and Moral Reasoning to Premarital Sex in College Women and in Couples." *Journal of Consulting and Clinical Psychology* 43 (1975), pp. 40-47.

6. Diamant, L. "Attitude, Personality, and Behavior in Volunteers and Non-volunteers for Sexual Research." *Proceedings of the 78th Annual Convention of the American Psychological Association* 5 (1970), pp. 423-424.

7. Eysenck, H.J. *Sex and Personality*. Austin, Texas: University of Austin Press, 1976.

8. Hobart, C.W. "Changing Orientations to Courtship: A Study of Young Canadians," in W.E. Mann, ed. *Social and Cultural Change in Canada*, Vol. 2. Toronto: Copp Clark, 1970.

9. Hobart, C.W. "Sexual Permissiveness in Young English and French Canadians." *Journal of Marriage and the Family* 34 (1972), pp. 292-303.

10. Hobart, C.W. "The Social Context of Morality Standards among Anglophone Canadian Students." *Journal of Comparative Family Studies* 5 (1974), pp. 26-40.

11. Hobart, C.W. "Courtship Processes: Premarital Sexual Behavior," in G.N. Ramu, ed. *Courtship, Marriage and Family in Canada*. Toronto: Macmillan Canada, 1979.

12. Johnson, W.T., and Delamater, J.D. "Response Effects in Sex Surveys." *Public Opinion Quarterly* 40 (1976), pp. 165-181.

13. Kaats, G.R., and Davis, K.E. "The Dynamics of Sexual Behavior of College Students." *Journal of Marriage and the Family* 32 (1970), pp. 390-399.

14. Luckey, E.B., and Nass, G.D. "A Comparison of Sexual Attitudes and Behavior in an International Sample." *Journal of Marriage and the Family* 31 (1969), pp. 364-379.

15. Mann, W.E. "Canadian Trends in Premarital Behavior." *Bulletin of the Council for Social Services of the Anglican Church of Canada* 198 (1967).

16. Mann, W.E. "Sex Behaviour on Campus," in W.E. Mann, ed. *Canada: A Sociological Profile*. Toronto: Copp Clark, 1968.

17. Mann, W.E. "Sex at York," in W.E. Mann, ed. *The Underside of Toronto*. Toronto: McClelland and Stewart, 1970.

18. Martin, R., and Marcuse, F. "Characteristics of Volunteers in Psychological Experimentation." *Journal of Consulting Psychology* 22 (1958), pp. 475-479.

19. Masters, W.H., and Johnson, V.E. *Human Sexual Response*. Boston: Little, Brown, 1966.

20. McCormick, N.B. "Come-ons and Put-offs: Unmarried Students' Strategies for Having and Avoiding Sexual Intercourse." *Psychology of Women Quarterly*, in press.

21. Mosher, D., and Cross, H.J. "Sex Guilt and Premarital Sexual Experiences of College Students." *Journal of Consulting and Clinical Psychology* 36 (1971), pp. 27-32.

22. Peplau, L.A., Rubin, Z., and Hill, C.T. "Sexual Intimacy in Dating Relationships." *Journal of Social Issues* 33, No. 2 (1977), pp. 86-109.

23. Perlman, D. "The Sexual Standards of Canadian University Students," in D. Koulack and D. Perlman, eds. *Readings in Social Psychology: Focus on Canada*. Toronto: Wiley of Canada, 1973.

24. Perlman, D., Josephson, W., Hwang, W.T., Begum, H., and Thomas, T.L. "A Cross-cultural Analysis of Students' Premarital Sexual Standards." *Archives of Sexual Behavior*, 1978.

25. Reiss, I.L. *The Social Context of Premarital Sexual Permissiveness.* New York: Holt, Rinehart & Winston, 1967.

26. Reiss, I.L., and Miller, B.C. *A Theoretical Analysis of Heterosexual Permissiveness.* Minneapolis: The Family Study Center, University of Minnesota, 1974.

27. Ridley, C.K. "Inhibitory Aspects of Sex Guilt, Social Censure, and Need for Approval." Unpublished Ph.D. dissertation, University of Manitoba, 1976.

28. Shymko, D.M. "Current Sex Research in Canada," in B. Schlesinger, ed. *Sexual Behaviour in Canada: Patterns and Problems.* Toronto: University of Toronto Press, 1977.

29. Walster, E., Walster, G.N., and Traupmann, J. "Equity and Premarital Sex." *Journal of Personality and Social Psychology* 36 (1978), pp. 82-92.

30. Weekend Poll. *Weekend Magazine* (December 3, 1977), p. 3.

31. Whitehurst, R.N. "Losing Virginity: Some Contemporary Trends." Unpublished manuscript, available from R.N. Whitehurst, Department of Sociology, University of Windsor, Windsor, Ontario.

32. Wrightsman, L.S. *Social Psychology*, 2nd ed. Monterey, California: Brooks/ Cole, 1977.

33. Zuckerman, M., Tushup, R., and Finner, S. "Sexual Attitudes and Experience: Attitude and Personality Correlates and Change Produced by a Course in Sexuality." *Journal of Consulting and Clinical Psychology* 44 (1976), pp. 7-19.

6/Looking Forward: Current Attitudes of Canadian Teenagers to Work, Careers, and Marriage*

E. Dianne Looker and
Peter C. Pineo

Although marriage involves the interaction between two individuals, the form and style of this interaction is strongly influenced by the kinds of obligations and constraints that the husband and wife incur in their roles outside the family. That is to say, the marriage relationship can be viewed as highly "adaptive" in the sense used by Clark Vincent, as he writes:

> The family, to a greater degree and more frequently than is true of the other major social institutions ... (adapts) its structure and activities to fit the changing needs of the society and other social institutions. (1966:29)

It follows from this view of marriage that when the wife undertakes the considerable role obligations that are involved in employment outside the home, one should anticipate a broad and pervasive effect upon the marital relationship.

The investigation of such effects has been the focus of much sociological research. Recent issues of the *Journal of Marriage and the Family* have been rarely without at least one article dealing with the effects of working wives or working mothers. Much of this research addresses the questions of the effect of the wife's employment on marital satisfaction. The early expectation, like that held by Blood and Wolfe in their 1960 US study,[2] was that working wives would report lower levels of marital satisfaction than their homebound counterparts. Employment outside the home was seen as a potential source of strain in the marriage. The data did not support this hypothesis; in fact

*Funds for this research came from the Department of Manpower and Immigration and from the Canada Council.

no difference was found in the levels of marital satisfaction of working and non-working wives* (see Reference 2. Blood and Wolfe, page 101). By the end of the decade considerably more sophisticated hypotheses were advanced, taking into consideration whether or not the wives worked by choice, and whether or not the work was full-time or part-time (see Reference 12. Orden and Bradburn, page 392). Under highly specialized circumstances, higher levels of marital satisfaction are reported by working wives as shown by a recent Canadian study (see Reference 5. Burke and Weir, page 285).

The more recent studies also show a concern with the level of satisfaction of the husband, and the complexity of this phenomenon is reflected in much of the research. The Canadian study cited above found that husbands of working wives were less content in their marital relationship (Burke and Weir, *loc. cit.*) but this result has been sharply challenged by another Canadian study (see Reference 3. Booth, page 649).

A separate, but related issue in studies of marital relationships is the question of the relative power of the male and female partners. Blood and Wolfe's study[2] contains relevant data on this topic as well. Viewing power as a reflection of control over personal resources, they see employment as an important source of marital power. This finding confirms the results of David Heer's earlier study (see Reference 7, page 341). Gillespie has challenged the conventional interpretation of these results, viewing the wife's employment as a source of power, but one which serves only to erode some of the male dominance of the marriage (see Reference 6, page 135).

Communication patterns and the content of communication may also be affected by the wife's employment. Baum focusses on the effects of role segregation on the marital relationship and hypothesizes an increase in communication potential when both husband and wife are employed outside the home.[1]

A considerable body of research has dealt with the interrelationship of family size, desired family size, and the employment of wives.[19/17] When both spouses work, married couples show less interest in having children, and a complex statistical analysis by Waite and

---

*"Non-working" means only that the wife does not have employment outside the home.

Stolzenberg[19] suggests that in many cases the decision of the wife to work precedes the decision to have few or no children. Other research shows that where there are children, the relationship between the parents and children is different if the mother works. Early concerns that the difference might result in serious maladjustment of the child proved unfounded (see Reference 11. Nye, page 244); more recent works, such as Propper's study of Toronto high school students,[14] find subtle differences in the communication and conflict patterns between parents and children in families where the mother works.

Most of the studies in this area focus on the simple dichotomy of working versus non-working wives (with occasional inclusion of part-time work as an additional consideration). Less attention has been paid to the specific type of occupation of the wife and how this affects the marriage relationship. The exceptions to this most frequently deal with high-status occupations, such as the work on "dual-career" families (see Reference 16 and Reference 10. Martin, Berry, and Brooke, pages 734-742).

While much of this research remains inconclusive, in reviewing it, one is struck by the range of topics covered. It is clear that the wife's employment is seen as a critical factor in the dynamics of the marital relationship, even though the details of the complex effects have not yet been fully unravelled by social scientists. The differences in the marital lifestyle of those families in which the wife works outside the home and those in which she does not are of interest in their own right. However, they are of further importance because, in Canada, throughout the last few decades there has been a steady increase in the proportion of wives who work, reaching 33.9% in 1972 (see Reference 15. Ramu, page 345). Thus the second type of marital relationship, in which both partners are employed outside the home, is becoming more and more prevalent. Should this trend continue, it could become the dominant form of the relationship in Canada.

Sociologists find it difficult to predict if trends such as these will accelerate or even continue. One possible approach is to examine the views and intentions of young women and compare them to those of women at later stages in the life cycle. While there are limitations on the extent to which the cross-sectional data can be used to examine trends, these data can give admittedly rough estimates of social change across generations. In the balance of this paper we present data of this type with a view to answering the following questions:

1) Is there evidence of changes in the proportion of women who are likely to work after marriage?
2) Is there evidence of any shift on the part of young women away from those occupations traditionally defined as "women's work"?

With respect to the first question, one might anticipate an acceleration of the trend toward increased female labour-force participation as a result of the women's movement and its various repercussions. It was with this expectation that our study was designed. Similarly, in terms of the second question, we anticipated evidence of a substantial movement away from traditional sex-typed occupations.

Data Collection and Fieldwork Procedures

Data were collected from a sample of 400 families living in the Hamilton area. The criteria for inclusion were that there be a child, born in 1957, living at home with both parents.[9] Interviews were conducted with the teenagers (201 males, 199 females) and questionnaires administered to their parents. Thus we have data from two generations of respondents, with the advantage of being able to link the child-parent responses into family units.

The fieldwork was conducted in 1975 by a team of professional interviewers from the Field Survey Unit at McMaster University. An area-clustered sample was drawn from the Regional Assessment lists of the City of Hamilton. The 400 completed interviews constituted 87% of those contacted, an unusually high completion rate for a metropolitan sample. Of these cases, we have data from 87% of the fathers and 88% of the mothers.

The focus in the data-gathering instruments was on the teenager's occupational choice and factors which may be seen as relevant to this choice. For the purposes of this analysis, the crucial questions are those which deal with the views of the female teenager concerning her intention to work at various stages in the life cycle and the type of work that she expects to do. Related questions were asked for both parents, and similar data from the male teenagers allow us to ascertain the extent to which sex-typing of occupations appears to be a factor in occupational choice.

The balance of the paper falls into two sections. The first deals with an examination of the evidence of changes in the proportion of women who are likely to work after marriage. The second focusses on the type of job the teenager elects to do.

Intentions to Work

In order to examine whether or not our data support the idea of an increasing tendency for women to enter the labour force, a first consideration is the pattern of employment followed by the mothers in the sample. The mothers were asked whether they had worked (and if so, whether full-time or part-time) at various stages in their life. The responses are given in Table 6.1.

While marriage affected the employment of some of the respondents (91% had a job before marriage, whereas 76% had one after marriage but before having children), the major factor is not marriage but the presence of children, particularly very young children. Only about a third of the respondents (37%) reported that they worked when they had pre-school-age children. The maternal role apparently has more of an impact on employment than the marital role. In fact, if we examine the mothers' attitudes to women working at various stages we see that an even smaller percentage (12%) favour working when one has a pre-schooler. (See the second panel of Table 6.1). There is less reluctance shown in either attitude or behaviour about working at later stages of the life cycle. In terms of working when one's children are all in school, approximately equal percentages of the mothers say it is a good idea and, in fact, themselves worked during this stage (56% and 59% respectively). With respect to the post-childrearing period, when all the children have left home, 81% of the mothers see working at this stage as a good idea, and 60% themselves intend to work when they reach this stage.

The information on the mothers' attitudes, rather than behaviour, gives the better base line for comparison, when we examine the teenager's responses, because these necessarily reflect intentions rather than behaviour. While the mothers were asked whether they defined a woman working at a particular stage as a good or bad idea, the teenagers were asked how likely they were to work. Their answers are presented in Table 6.2.

Table 6.1

Work Experience and Work Attitudes of the Mothers,
According to Life Cycle Stage (%)

Did you work?	Before marriage	After marriage, before children	With pre-schoolers	After children are in school
			Life Cycle Stage	
Yes, full-time	86.3%	69.0%	18.0%	29.1%
Yes, part-time	4.5	7.2	18.9	29.8
No	9.3	23.9	63.2	41.1*
N	335	335	334	302
Do you think it's a good idea for a woman to work?				
Good idea	99.4%**	95.5	11.9	55.8
Bad idea	.0	.9	66.1	21.8
N	336	336	336	335

*There were 27 mothers who still had pre-schoolers; eleven of these (41%) indicated that they probably or definitely would not work once the children were in school.

**The percentages do not add to 100% in the second section of the Table because the category "neither a good nor a bad idea" is included in the calculations but omitted from the Table.

Note: Mothers of the sons as well as the daughters are included in the above table. Excluding them makes essentially no difference in the results.

Table 6.2
Attitude of Daughters to Working At Various Stages
in the Life Cycle

Life Cycle Stage	Attitude to Working (%)				
	Definitely would work	Probably would work	Probably would not work	Definitely would not work	N*
Before marriage	89.7%	8.2%	1.6%	.5%	184
After marriage, before any children**	65.1	32.3	1.5	1.0	185
With pre-schoolers	4.1	8.2	22.4	65.3	196
With children in school	42.1	46.2	10.8	1.0	195
After children have left home	54.9	37.8	4.1	3.1	193

*The N's differ because of variations in the "don't know" and "no answer" rates.
**The actual question in the interview did not specify "before any children" but relied on the placement of the question to connote this. The estimate of 65.1 percent may, then, be an overestimate.

First of all, it is relevant to note that these questions presupposed that all would marry and have children. It was anticipated that some respondents would actively reject this definition, and interviewers were instructed to note if this happened. The field experience did not bear this out. There was no evidence that any of the teenage respondents rejected the assumption that they would marry and have children. This was the first clue that the shift away from traditional sex roles might be less than we had anticipated.

Looking at the specific responses given, we see that almost all the female teenagers anticipated working before marriage. After marriage but before there were children, 65% felt that they definitely would work and 32% that they probably would work.* Answers to supplementary questions about their work immediately after marriage indicated a considerable commitment to this idea. When asked whether they would work even if they did not need the money, 55% said they definitely would and an additional 30% said "yes," with some qualification. Even in the face of possible objections from the husband, the majority indicated that they would work. The question was: "If your husband disapproved of your working, would you quit?" In response, 17% said they definitely would not quit, 35% said they probably would not, 5% indicated they would not marry anyone who disapproved of their working. Only 11% said they would definitely quit under these circumstances.

Again, it is the presence of young children that appears to be the critical factor in a woman's intention to work. The proportion intending to work shifts drastically when the childrearing segment of the life cycle is under consideration. Even when, in a follow-up question, it was specified that there would be "adequate day care

---

*In a nation-wide study of high school students in 1965, Raymond Breton asked teenage girls if they intended to work full-time after they finished their schooling. He found that 47.8% of the English Canadians reported that they planned to work full-time both before and after marriage (see Reference 4, page 281). Some additional percentage, not given, apparently reported that they planned to work only before marriage. The nearest equivalent statistic from our study, the 65 percentage saying they definitely planned to work after marriage but before having children, would suggest a trend from 1965 to 1975, but as the two populations, English Canada and Hamilton are not comparable and as the Breton study specified only full-time work, not too much should be made of the difference.

facilities," only 27% of the teenagers felt that they would probably or definitely work (data not shown). With this period past and the children in school, the vast majority once again stated that they were likely to work.

Table 6.3
Comparison of the Attitudes of
Mothers and Daughters, by Life Cycle Stage

Life Cycle Stage	Percentage of teenagers saying they definitely or probably would work	Percentage of mothers who state it is a "good idea" for women to work	Percentage of mothers who actually worked
Before marriage	97.9%	99.4%	90.8%
After marriage, before children	97.4	95.5	76.2
With pre-schoolers	12.3	11.9	36.9
After children are in school	88.3	55.8	59.0
After children have left home	92.7	80.5	——*

*By virtue of the definition of the population no mothers were yet in this stage. 60.1 percent reported that they planned to work when they did enter this stage.

Table 6.3 repeats the crucial data from the earlier tables so that mothers and daughters may be compared. When it comes to attitudes toward women working in the first three stages, the mothers and daughters differ little. Both favour work before there are pre-schoolers and oppose it when they arrive. The major difference appears when one considers the later stages of the life cycle. While these questions deal with a time in the fairly distant future for the teenagers, the suggestion is that more of them intend to work than would be true if they held the same views as their mothers' generation—or if they followed their mothers' example. Close to 90% of the teenagers intend to work once their children are in school, as compared to 59% of the mothers who did work and 56% who saw it as a good idea. While more of the mothers (81%) see working once the children have left home as a good idea, 93% of the teenagers define this in sufficiently positive terms to anticipate working when they reach this stage of life.

Another point of information contained in Table 6.3 which could be relevant to anticipated changes is the discrepancy between the mother's report of her attitude to women working and her own behaviour. One might anticipate some shift in the mother's attitude over time, in the direction of becoming more liberal. This could explain the discrepancy with respect to the pre-child marital stage (96% say working is a good idea; 76% report working). The more striking discrepancy is found when one examines the responses dealing with the pre-schooler stage, where substantially more reported that they worked than reported that it was a "good idea." One could presume that economic necessity was a factor in producing this pattern. The relative affluence of our society, were it to continue, might allow more women than ever to withdraw when they have pre-schoolers. The pattern one can anticipate, if the preferences of the teenagers are realized, is a nearly complete withdrawal of women from the labour force early in their life cycle, followed by a return later to the labour force by a larger proportion of married women than in previous years.

In the previous tables the daughters as a group are compared to their mothers. We can go beyond this and compare the attitude of each daughter to the attitude and behaviour of her own mother. It seems reasonable to expect that the teenager's attitude to working would be strongly influenced by the example set by her mother. But such is not the case. Whether the mother is currently working has surprisingly little influence on the daughter's attitude to working. In ten questions relating to whether the teenager expects to work at different stages in the life cycle and under different conditions, only one shows a statistically significant relationship to whether the mother is working (data not shown). When asked if they would work when their children were in school, 47% of those with working mothers said they definitely would, 33% of those with non-working mothers said they definitely would. That is, the mother's current behaviour has influence only upon the daughter's intentions for the same stage in the life cycle. This suggests that the mother's behaviour in earlier stages may influence the daughter's attitude toward working during that stage. But this does not prove significant either. The effectiveness of the mother as a role model is very limited. Only her current behaviour matters and it matters only to the daughter's intentions for the same stage in the life cycle.

If the role model set by the mother appears to have limited influence, the parents' attitudes, rather than behaviour, might be the key factor. To see whether this is the case, correlation coefficients between the daughter's intention to work after marriage and the perceived and actual attitudes of the parents are presented in Table 6.4.

Table 6.4
Intercorrelations of Daughter's Plan to Work After Marriage
with Actual and Perceived Attitudes of Father and Mother

	Teenager's perception of father's attitude	Teenager's perception of mother's attitude	Father's attitude	Mother's attitude
Teen's intention to work	.32* (194)	.39* (195)	.15** (160)	.10 (164)
Teen's perception of father's attitude		.70* (195)	.10 (160)	.13 (164)
Teen's perception of mother's attitude			–.04 (161)	.14 (165)
Father's attitude				.12 (154)

*significant at .001 level
**significant at .05 level

The links between the attitudes of the parents and that of the daughter are weak. Only the cross-sexed link, between the attitude of the father and that of the daughter, achieves statistical significance and it remains small ($r=.15$). At the perceptual level, however, the relationships are significant and strong. The attitudes of the daughter are closely related to what she reports as the attitudes of the parents. There are major discrepancies between these reported attitudes and those actually held by the parents; the daughter's perception of the mother's attitude and the mother's actual attitudes are not significantly related and the correlation is small (r-.14). Probably what we have found is that the daughters project their own attitudes upon the parents, although it is possible that the parents are giving different cues from what they are aware of.

Part of the failure of Table 6.4 to show strong relationships between the attitudes of the parents and the daughter is that the questions omit the idea of life-cycle stage. When more specific questions are asked, dealing with the intentions to work at specific stages in the life cycle, significant relationships emerge. The data are given in Table 6.5. While the relationships are not significant in the earliest stages, as soon as children are mentioned, the attitudes of the daughter show the influence of the parents, slightly more so of the father than of the mother. The family does appear to play a role, albeit a weak one, in the formation of attitudes relating to how well a career and childbearing can be mixed.

Table 6.5
Relationship Between Daughter's Plan to Work
and Parent's Attitude, by Life Cycle Stage

Life Cycle Stage	Mother's attitude to work at this stage		Mother's report of father's attitude	
	r	N	r	N
Before marriage	−.06	156	−.01	156
After marriage, before children	−.02	166	−.04	166
With pre-schoolers	.16*	166	.19**	167
With children in school	.14	167	.22**	163
After children have left home	.14	164	.11	161

*statistically significant, .05 level
**statistically significant, .01 level

In summary, the data suggest a shift in female attitudes to work, but one much less dramatic than was anticipated. This would lead us to predict that an increase in the proportion of women working will occur only gradually and that there may even be some reversal during the childbearing years. The recent reassessments of the role of women in society appear to have had little impact as yet upon the expectations of the teenagers in our sample with respect to women working. It would follow that changes in the marital lifestyle associated with working wives will also occur only gradually.

Sex-Typing of Occupations and Sex Differences in Occupation Choice

The second issue which we wish to address is whether there is evidence in our survey of a shift away from traditional female sex-typed occupations on the part of the female teenagers.

To begin, our study contains two questions which deal directly with this issue: a) whether or not the respondent would consider working at a traditionally male occupation; and b) how comfortable she would feel in such an occupation. Parallel questions dealing with traditionally female occupations were asked of the male respondents. This allows not only a basis of comparison for the female responses, but also reveals the current attitudes of young males. Any increase in congruence between the male and female attitudes is relevant to future marital relationships. Data from both sons and daughters are contained in Table 6.6. On both questions the females appear appreciably less influenced by sex-typing of occupations than are the males. While 33.7% of the females say that they would definitely consider entering a traditionally male occupation, only 7% of the males say that they would definitely consider entering a traditionally female one. Over 30% of the females report that they would be quite comfortable in such an occupation, while only 14.1% of the males report that they would be quite comfortable in a female ocupation.*

---

*In research dealing with sex-typing the gender of the interviewer may be a factor. All our interviewers were female. Presumably, however, males might be most likely to disguise anti-feminine attitudes when speaking to a female and so the results of Table 6.6 would be stronger using interviewers of both sexes.

Table 6.6
Attitudes of the Teenagers to Entering
an Occupation Traditionally Identified with the Other Sex

Would you consider going into a traditionally female/male occupation?	Sons	Daughters
Definitely would	7.0%	33.7%
Probably would	29.9	37.8
Probably would not	28.9	16.8
Definitely would not	34.3	11.7
N	201	196

Statistically significant, .001 level, chi-square test

How comfortable would you feel (in such an occupation)?	Sons	Daughters
Quite comfortable	14.1%	31.1%
Moderately comfortable	32.8	33.2
Moderately uncomfortable	20.2	12.8
Quite uncomfortable	18.2	8.7
N	198	196

Statistically significant, .001 level, chi-square test

*Percentages do not add to 100% because the category "neither comfortable not uncomfortable" is included in the calculations but is omitted from the table.

Unfortunately we do not have comparable data from the parents to allow cross-generational comparisions. However, it is clear that, as one might anticipate, any shift in attitudes appears to have occurred mostly among the female respondents. The vast majority of females see entering a traditionally male occupation as something that they would consider. Any prediction of changes in the sex-typing of jobs, then, would be in the direction of more females entering male-dominated spheres, but few males taking to the traditional female occupations.

An alternate approach to this same matter involved asking the teenagers if they would like to have the same occupation as their father or their mother. Table 6.7 shows the results. The idea of taking up the same occupation as either the father or the mother was generally rejected as a "bad idea." But more sons rejected the idea of following the mother's lead (85%) than daughters rejected the idea of following the father's (77%). When sons were asked about the father's job or daughters about the mother's, roughly two-thirds rejected it as a possibility in both cases. The socio-economic status of the occupations is not a factor. In a sample of this size, one could have some degree of sampling fluctuation producing discrepancies in the status of the mothers of sons and the mothers of daughters. This particular sample is free of this difficulty, however. The fathers of sons and daughters were 34.1% and 33.7% in the white-collar sector, respectively. The mothers of sons and of daughters were 71.2% and 69.1%, respectively.

Additional data allow us to examine some of the underlying attitudes which could lead male and female teenagers to choose different occupations. Three questions were included in the study as measures of preferred working conditions. The questions dealt with preferences as to: closeness of supervision; whether the work was with people, data, or things; and the amount of self-reliance the job required.* There was no statistically significant difference between the male and female teenagers' preferences concerning closeness of supervision. But there was a substantial tendency for more sons than daughters to report that they would prefer an occupation which required a great deal of self-reliance (44% versus 31%). This difference might have the effect of steering the daughters away from the higher status occupations, because it is those that are said to require higher levels of self-reliance.

On the last of these three questions the sex difference was even more substantial. The sons reported a preference for working with "the hands" much more than the daughters (56% versus 19%). In contrast, working "with people" was much more frequently chosen by the daughters (74% versus 34%). This latter difference appears to reflect the traditional male dominance of the manual occupations and the female dominance of the service-oriented occupations.

---

*These three questions were based upon concepts developed by Melvin Kohn[8] in his research on class differences in values.

Table 6.7

Attitude of the Teenagers Toward the Idea of Entering
the Same Occupation as the Mother or the Father

Would you like your parent's job?	Father's Job			Mother's Job**		
	Sons	Daughters	%(M-F) Difference	Sons	Daughters	%(M-F) Difference
Good idea	23%	10%	13%	8%	14%	-6%
	(46)	(20)		(14)	(26)	
Bad idea	59%	77%	-18%	85%	67%	18%
	(119)	(152)		(153)	(123)	
N*	202	198		181	183	

*The N's are larger than the numbers given in the cells because the category "neither a good nor a bad idea" is part of the total N but is not reported in the body of the table.

**The question related to the mother's current job, or if she were not currently working, then the most recent job she had that lasted seven months or more.

The magnitude of the difference between the sons and daughters is an indication that the sexual division of labour remains a strong element in the process of occupational choice. This again becomes evident when the actual occupations that the teenagers expect to enter are examined. The teenagers were asked: "What job do you realistically expect to go into after you have completed all your formal education and training?" Their answers are given in Table 6.8, coded into broad occupational categories. Despite the evidence presented earlier of the daughters' willingness to consider entering a traditionally male occupation, the actual choices they give seem to be governed almost completely by the traditional sexual division of labour. Thus almost none of the daughters chose occupations falling into the skilled, semi-skilled, or unskilled manual categories. Rather, the vast majority chose jobs in the semi-professional and the clerical categories—the traditional "women's jobs" of teacher, nurse, secretary, and office worker. The sons, on the other hand, avoided jobs falling into the clerical group and chose manual work quite frequently (42%) as well as semi-professional, managerial, and professional. With, perhaps, the exception that more daughters are choosing managerial and professional work than formerly, the choices represented in Table 6.8 do not show evidence of a shift away from traditional occupations.

It might be said, on the basis of Table 6.8, that the daughters show higher aspirations than do the sons, because they almost all aspire to white-collar occupations. We suspect, however, that this is a result of the classification system used. If, as has been suggested,[13] the clerical occupations are distinguished by the level of skill required, the choices of the daughters appear to represent slightly lower rather than higher levels of aspiration. Some 21% of the daughters aspire to clerical jobs that would be classified as only semi-skilled or unskilled. Coded in a similar manner, only 15% of the sons chose jobs with this low a degree of skill content.

The job preferences, as well as the realistic expectations of the teenagers, were also solicited. The preferences show a similar pattern. While there is no sex difference at the highest managerial level, more females than males prefer semi-professional and related occupations (34% as compared to 27%). These differences produce a chi-square significant at the .05 level. Some females would prefer to have high-status jobs, but fewer realistically expect to attain them.

The teenagers were also asked: "What kind of job would you *not* want to go into?" The most striking finding to come from analysis of the responses is that a substantial number of the females, some 25%, singled out high-status occupations, in the top two categories, as jobs they would not want. This question, then, identifies a further group of females who do not feel that they would wish to pursue a high-status occupation. In all, the preferences, expectations, and aversions of the females present a more complicated picture than do those of the males. There is a lack of consensus, or perhaps it is ambivalence, shown in the answers from the female teenagers. Factors besides the status of the occupation may be more strongly influencing them. In general, the results suggest that the females tend to restrict their occupational choice to those areas traditionally associated with their sex, and their status ambitions tend to be moderate compared to their male peers.

Table 6.8
Vocational Expectations of Sons and Daughters

	Occupational categories*	Vocational Expectations (in %)	
		Sons	Daughters
White Collar	Managerial, professional	30.2%	25.6%
	Low-level managerial, semi-professional, technical, supervisory	21.2	33.9
	Clerical-sales-service	6.1	38.3
Blue Collar	Skilled manual, foremen	31.8	1.7
	Semi-skilled and unskilled manual	10.6	0.6
	N	179	180

X^2 significant at .001 level

*Based on Pineo, Porter, and McRoberts.[13]

Conclusions

A substantial research tradition exists which examines the question of how much and in what way marital relationships are altered when the wife takes on paid employment outside the home. While the results are sometimes inconsistent and are not fully synthesized, it seems reasonable to conclude that the marriage is influenced, in both positive and negative ways, when both partners work. We also suspect that the nature of the influences are different depending upon what type of occupation the wife enters. For these reasons, in order to understand the changes which may be occurring in marital relations, it is important to assess the magnitude of two trends in contemporary society:

1) The rate at which married women will be entering the labour force; and
2) The extent to which women will begin to enter occupations not formerly considered "women's work."

Data from our sample of teenage Canadians allow us to make crude estimates of the magnitude of these trends. The anticipated sharp changes, resulting from the recent reassessments of women's role in our society, were not found. Rather there was evidence of a continuing gradual increase in the proportion of women intending to work after marriage, with the exception of the possibly larger proportion of women who are likely to withdraw from the labour force during early childbearing years and later re-enter.*

Responses to the questions about the type of occupation women plan to enter suggested very little shift in the nature of the sexual division of labour. The data present us with the apparent paradox that, while the attitudes examined showed evidence of some change, the daughters nonetheless anticipate acting in fairly traditional ways.

---

*If the participation of married women in the labour force takes the form we anticipate, that is, almost all withdrawing when the children are very young, there are practical problems that must be dealt with. In particular, as the women re-enter the labour force, the problems of obsolescence of skills and the need for retraining will be encountered. Further, as pay scales more and more become associated with seniority, those following a discontinuous career-pattern will be penalized for the balance of their careers by lower incomes.

Underlying their surprisingly traditional expectations, there appears to be a flexibility in the kinds of work women, more so than men, are willing to do.

There are a number of possible explanations as to why the anticipated relatively strong shifts in attitudes were not found among our respondents. First, they are young enough that their attitudes may yet be modified, especially among those who will be exposed to the possibly liberalizing effect of university experience. Insofar as the university is the principal source, it would follow that only the minority who attend would ultimately change their attitudes, and this in turn would restrict the newer viewpoints to a small segment of the population, just as it is the more highly educated females who appear to be at the forefront of the women's movement to date. A second possible explanation is that we have merely discovered once again that social change is most often a gradual process, especially where deepseated attitudes are involved. A third, more remote possibility, is that the particular age cohort that we studied is the first of a new, more conservative and technically oriented generation of young people. We note that this group is the same age as those who are now showing a preference for continuing their education in community colleges rather than in the universities.

With respect, then, to the nature of the marital relationship, the styles of spousal interaction that are characteristic of marriages in which the wife works will become more common. The more complex adaptations that might be expected to occur, if large numbers of women undertake less traditional kinds of occupations, are yet to come.

References

1. Baum, Martha. "Love, Marriage and the Division of Labor," in Hans Peter Dreitzel, ed. *Family, Marriage and the Struggle of the Sexes.* Recent Sociology No. 4. New York: The Macmillan Company, 1972, pp. 83-106.
2. Blood, Robert O., Jr., and Wolfe, Donald M. *Husbands and Wives: the Dynamics of Married Living.* New York: The Free Press, 1960.
3. Booth, Alan. "Wife's Employment and Husband's Stress: a Replication and Refutation." *Journal of Marriage and the Family* 39, No. 4 (November 1977), pp. 654-650.
4. Breton, Raymond. *Social and Academic Factors in the Career Decisions of*

Canadian Youth. Ottawa: Dept. of Manpower and Immigration, 1972.

5. Burke, Ronald J., and Weir, Tamara. "Relationship of Wives' Employment Status to Husband, Wife and Pair Satisfaction and Performance." *Journal of Marriage and the Family* 38, No. 2 (May 1976), pp. 279-287.

6. Gillespie, Dair L. "Who Has the Power? The Marital Struggle," in Hans Peter Dreitzel, ed. *Family, Marriage, and the Struggle of the Sexes.* Recent Sociology, No. 4. New York: The Macmillan Company, 1972, pp. 121-150.

7. Heer, David M. "Dominance and the Working Wife." *Social Forces* 36, No. 4 (May 1958) pp. 341-347.

8. Kohn, Melvin L. *Class and Conformity: A Study in Values.* Homewood, Illinois: The Dorsey Press, 1969.

9. Looker, E. Dianne. "The Role of Value Elements in the Intergenerational Transmission of Social Status." Unpublished Ph.D. dissertation, Dept. of Sociology, McMaster University, 1977.

10. Martin, Thomas W., Berry, Kenneth J., and Jacobsen, R. Brooke. "The Impact of Dual-Career Marriages on Female Professional Careers: An Empirical Test of *a Parsonian Hypothesis." Journal of Marriage and the Family* 37, No. 4 (November 1975), pp. 734-742.

11. Nye, Ivan. "Maternal Employment and the Adjustment of Adolescent Children." *Marriage and Family Living* 21, No. 3 (August 1959) pp. 240-244.

12. Orden, Susan R., and Bradburn, Norman M., "Working Wives and Marital Happiness." *American Journal of Sociology* 74, No. 4 (January 1969), pp. 392-407.

13. Pineo, Peter C., Porter, John, and McRoberts, Hugh A. "The 1971 Census and the Socio-economic Classification of Occupations." *Canadian Review of Sociology and Anthropology* 14, No. 1 (1977) pp. 91-102.

14. Propper, Alice Marcella. "The Relationship of Maternal Employment to Adolescent Roles, Activities, and Parental Relationships." *Journal of Marriage and the Family* 34, No. 3 (August 1972), pp. 417-421.

15. Ramu, G.N. "The Family and Marriage in Canada," in G.N. Ramu and Stuart D. Johnson, eds. *Introduction to Canadian Society: Sociological Analysis.* Toronto: The Macmillan Company of Canada Limited, 1976, pp. 295-348.

16. Rapoport, Rhona, and Rapoport, David. *Dual-Career Families.* London: Penguin Books, Ltd., 1971.

17. Stolzenberg, Ross M., and Waite, Linda J. "Age, Fertility Expectations and Plans for Employment." *American Sociological Review* 42 (October 1977), pp. 769-783.

18. Vincent, Clark E. "Familia Spongia: the Adaptive Function." *Journal of Marriage and the Family* 28, No. 1 (February 1966), pp. 29-36.

19. Waite, Linda J., and Stolzenberg, Ross M. "Intended Childbearing and Labor Force Participation of Young Women: Insights from Non-Recursive Models." *American Sociological Review* 41 (April 1976), pp. 235-252.

7/Marital Stability and Marital Commitment in a Rural Dutch-Canadian Community

K. Ishwaran and
Kwok B. Chan

In our earlier writings on the Holland Marsh Community[3/4/5] we have made references to the strikingly high level of marital and familial stability and commitment of the Dutch families indexed by only a few isolated cases of family disruptions and marital breakdowns since the inception of the community in the 1930's. Our recent field data, indeed, indicate that there were reports of only two divorces and five cases of separation. Contrastingly, our analysis of the temporal trends of divorce in Canada based on 1975 Vital Statistics indicates that, over a 50-year period, the Canadian divorce rate increased 35 times, from a rate of 6.4 per 100 000 persons in 1926, to 54.8 in 1968 to 222.0 per 100 000 in 1975. Altogether there were 50 611 divorces in 1975 in Canada, which is a 12.4 percent increase over the previous year, compared with an annual increase of at least 9% since 1972.[7] Given the increasingly astounding rate of divorce in Canadian society in the past 50 years, the task of identifying and characterizing factors associated with marital stability and marital commitment in the Holland Marsh community has taken on considerable theoretical and practical significance.

While it is the primary intent of this paper to identify and discuss factors associated with marital stability and commitment, our theoretical and empirical analysis operates on familial, community, and institutional levels. Our discussion focusses first on the resources and power differentials in the husband-wife dyad, and then assesses their cumulative impact on the process and outcome of decision-making within the family, by relating them to patterns of sex-role allocation and development. We then proceed to determine the relative contributions of such factors as religion, kinship, and community to marital stability and commitment on the community and institutional levels.

Though we have attempted a more detailed account of the ecology, the social structure, the cultural system including religious ideology, and the economy of the Dutch-immigrant community in the Marsh in our earlier writings, it is necessary to provide a brief discussion of these aspects as a backdrop to the arguments and empirical analysis presented in this paper.

Holland Marsh is located on both sides of Highway 400 and is about 40 miles to the northwest of Toronto. The Dutch immigration started here in the 1930's, and from then onwards it took place in at least three phases. Beginning with the pioneers, the immigrants have been involved in a process of ecological transformation and community-building. Also, the community has been subjected to pressures for change and "modernization" exerted by the surrounding North American socio-cultural environment. The economic structure of the community has moved from a primitive agrarian system to one that has become highly mechanized and commercialized.[4]

In any consideration of the dynamics of community development in the Marsh, an important role should be assigned to the original Dutch social and cultural system based on the Calvinist ideology that the immigrants had brought with them to their new homes in Canada. In fact, the development of the community may best be seen as a process of modification of the original Dutch system for adaptation to the changing physical and socio-cultural environment in Canada. It has also implied a tension between commitment to the old system and the pragmatic utility of adaptation to a new and changing situation. As a result, there has emerged an overall pattern in which some of the old Dutch values and normative practices such as the pre-eminence of the church, the community, and the family in regulating individual and interpersonal behaviour, the close functional and affective ties between the family and kin networks, and the overall subordination of individuality to collectivism, have not yet lost their significance and importance. Other values, such as Calvinist ideologies underlying childrearing practices and marital relationships, in the context of increasing exposure to values prevailing in Canadian society at large, have been undergoing marginal changes, at least at the time of this study. In this connection, we suggest that any attempt to arrive at a comprehensive understanding of the Holland Marsh community in respect to marital relationships, in particular, is possible only when it is cast within a context of the dynamics of the community undergoing the tension between tradition and change.

Resources Theory as Conceptual Framework

In its theoretical interpretation of the data, this study has drawn on the resources theory,[7/2] a variant and a historical offshoot of the exchange theory.[1] The conceptual framework employed in this study considers marital relationships as exchange relationships insofar as they presuppose a pattern of systematic exchange of rewards and benefits between persons within a social structure. Such rewards and benefits may be intrinsic as in the case of a love relationship, or extrinsic as in the case of material transactions. Marital relationships involve both kinds of exchange, which means that the husband-wife relationships revolve around both intangible, psychological satisfactions and the more tangible material satisfactions. The two types of exchange reinforce each other and, in fact, they together constitute a single continuum of exchange relationships. Further, these exchange relationships may be asymmetrical or symmetrical, in the sense that the parties involved in the exchange relationship derive equal or differential benefits. In the specific context of marital relationships, either the husband or the wife enjoys a position of superiority leading to a pattern of control and dominance.

Wolfe[7] suggests that asymmetrical patterns of relationships in the husband-wife dyad rest on an unequal access to resources. More particularly, it is rooted in a system of differential access to the financial resources available within the family structure. Such a situation has significant consequences for the operation of the family system. On the other hand, if there is a symmetrical pattern in which the husband and wife have approximately equal access to financial resources, this would have an altogether different set of consequences. We hypothesize that in the case of what may be called a structure of unequal exchange, there is a higher probability of marital stability insofar as the dominance/dependence pattern functions to decrease conflicts. The partners involved are more likely to balance each other's demands. The superior partner is not likely to exercise the full potential of the available dominance since he or she would not push the other partner to a point where the system collapses. As a result, both partners soon tend to generate a pattern of relationships based on a high degree of commitment to the marriage relationship, which, in turn, leads to a relatively stable marital situation. In the more symmetrical pattern, the tendency to stabilize and routinize conflict increases in response to the fact that both the husband and wife have very nearly equal access to resources. The result is that marital commitment and marital stability turn out to be problematic.

Of course, husband-wife relationships do not exist in a socio-psychological vacuum and, therefore, need to be related to variables located outside the immediate context of the family. Such variables include the religious ideology of the community, its normative system, its wider economic, social, and cultural links with the external environment, and the technological changes in the community life.

Within the conceptual framework employed here, marital commitment is defined as the commitment of the marital partners to the marital arrangements of which they are parties. This commitment becomes manifest in their *beliefs* in the value of the marriage relationship and their *perception* of the overall, mutual usefulness of the marital system. Marital stability may be quantified in terms of the durability of the marriages, and may become manifest in the low frequency of breakdowns in marital relationships leading to divorce and separation. With the concepts of marital commitment and marital stability defined as such, the former corresponds to the ideological and attitudinal dimensions of the marital system, while the latter corresponds to the overtly behavioural dimensions.

The data to be reported in this paper came from a larger pool of information on the family life of the rural Dutch in the Holland Marsh gathered at different times between 1965 and 1978. One of us had done some informal intensive interviews with the married adults in the community and successfully administered questionnaires to a total of 155 parents between 1965 and 1971, with the gathered data resulting in a community study monograph.[3] Between October 1977, and March 1978, we interviewed husbands and wives from a total of 25 households in the evening in their homes, each interview lasting between two and three hours. While these interviews were intended to be intensive, in-depth, and semistructured, as a two-man research team one of us could concentrate on making detailed and comprehensive notes of the dialogues, while the other posed questions to the respondents, established rapport, and maintained the continuity of the interview. Since we did not adhere visibly to a set of preconceived questions, the resultant flexibility and ease of the interview situations were conducive to pursuing issues and concerns which were deemed interesting and important on particular occasions. In general, we started an interview with basic questions eliciting demographic and socio-economic data, then went on to questions on marital stability and commitment, and on attitudes, values, and patterns of behaviour of the adolescents in the community, and ended with a discussion of the conceptions of time and space of rural Dutch Canadians.*

Roughly 60% of the inhabitants in the Marsh are Dutch and live closely with each other, spatially and socially. The Dutch inhabitants who profess Calvinism would like to describe the Marsh as an integrated, multiethnic community, though our field data indicate that they are highly segregated from other local ethnic groups primarily composed of Polish, Hungarians, Ukrainians, Germans, Chinese, and Japanese. Socio-culturally, the Dutch express a strong sense of in-group solidarity and manifest considerable loyalty to the institutions of the community, especially the church, the school, and the family. The social organization of the Dutch people is very much centred around these institutions, which serve as strong barriers against others wishing to make entrance into the community. Socially and structurally speaking, the community of the Marsh bears striking resemblance to other better known religious communities such as those of the Hutterites and the Mennonites.

Familial Decision-Making and Male Dominance

The model of marital relationships based on resources control that we have formulated in the above material is empirically and conceptually related to the power structure within the family and the consequent power relations between husband and wife. In the Marsh community, the power structure within the family is based on the ideology and reality of male dominance, as manifested in the superior status and authority of the husband/father. This is reflected systematically in the

---

*Data on the socialization of rural Dutch-Canadian adolescents and on conceptions of time and space of rural Dutch Canadians are reported in two separate papers by us.[4/5]

patterns of decision-making in the family and, more specifically, underlies the system of financial control and management. Financial control has taken on considerable significance as an aspect of family life, because the Holland Marsh Dutch community is a farming community with near-total literacy and high standards of accounting, involving precise recording of income and expenditure. When 16 housewives were interviewed in regard to financial management and control within the family, it was found that only two of them were entrusted with the responsibility of bookkeeping. Besides, the details of these two exceptional cases were common knowledge in the community. In one case, the husband's physical illness prevented him from doing the work. In the other case, it was a personality factor: the concerned wife being well-known for her domineering behaviour. A more detailed analysis of our data showed that about 48% of husbands were exclusively handling accounts, while only 8% of the wives did this. In about 32% of the cases, something approaching joint management appeared. However, joint management proved, on more intensive investigation, to be based on the subordinate role of the wife. In regard to another critical area of North American family life, the question of who drives the car and thus controls a major means of need-satisfaction, the same pattern of male dominance was found. We found that about 34% of husbands as against 2% of wives in our sample drove the car. About 46% of the cases showed that both partners drove the car by turn. Even when both partners possessed licences, it was found that, in as many as 71% cases among such couples, the husband drove the car.

It was also found that in an overwhelming number of cases, whatever the superficial impression was, the husband constituted the final authority in decisions to purchase expensive items for the family. These items included car, real estate, or a travel plan. The so-called "family discussion" was no more than a ritual. Decisions regarding "holiday expenditure" was taken by 11% of husbands only, 2% of wives only, and 75% of husband-and-wife. Also, 22% of husbands, as against 4% of wives, took decisions regarding purchase of costly items; in 67% of the cases, both husbands and wives jointly took the decision. The data showed unequivocally that in most major economic and financial decisions, whether in the immediate internal context of the family or in relation of the family to the outside universe, the husband was the deciding person. In other words, male dominance was an unquestionable reality in the power structure of the family, even though it was somewhat softened on occasions by the countervailing role of the wife. The wife's role as mother, for instance, did enable her to exercise an important role in the child-socialization process in such areas as administration of punishment and control of monthly allowances. But this was less a power role than a role of psychological management in an interpersonal context. It is important to note that such marginal, ritualistic, and symbolic concessions made by the husband to the wife tend to diffuse protest and, consequently, further reinforce male dominance.

The authoritarian and asymmetrical domestic power structure is finally related to the fact that the husband remains the breadwinner, and the wife has neither opportunity nor motivation to become involved in any gainful employment.* Our evidence seems to point to the possibility that the wife has been socialized and culturally conditioned to accept her secondary and subordinate role *willingly*. However, it is also possible to interpret the willingness, however generated, as a consequence of a perception on the part of both parties of a functional differentiation of roles within the family structure: the wife has her role and its functional correlates, and the husband has his. The inequality and the differential status, then, become functionally legitimized and validated. In other words, the husband's dominance in the latter context is sociologically construed by both marital partners as deriving from a perception of functional necessity, not from any express need for exploitation or control. Though it is very difficult to accept either of the interpretations in an exclusive form, our impression is that the empirical reality is a good deal more complicated than the picture indicated by either of these two interpretations. We suggest that potentially both aspects co-exist, and this provides enough room for a variety of subjective equations between the marital partners. In other words, what happens is that, while there is a quantitatively unequal exchange based on differential access to resources, there is also a qualitative and symbolic exchange relationship which tends to nullify or mitigate the former aspect. It is, in fact, a structure of

---

*Our informant estimated that only five mothers actually took up full-time employment outside the Marsh.

balanced contradiction in which both parties are related on the basis of a mutually accepted imbalance.

The empirical data point, in fact, to the existence of such a complex situation of interesting patterns of interrelationship between the husband and the wife. In the first place, the field data clearly show that the husband is the "boss." One male respondent not only claimed to be the boss, but related this to his own parental tradition:

> In my family the final decisions come from me. In Dad's family, he was the boss. He never let anybody drive the car. In my family, it goes the same way.

A few other husbands made similar observations:

> In most situations of decision-making, the man has made a choice and the woman is too pleased to go along with it ... that's the way how it works in the Marsh.

> I am basically uncomfortable riding in a car which is not driven by myself. In terms of decision-making, farm-related activities were most often made by Daddy.

> There is very little economic rivalry between husband and wife. He will do things but not talk with wives. She will always talk with him before. Somebody had to be a boss in the household.

> When the male is the breadwinner, he then holds the authority in the family. The male is the authoritarian voice in this community. When we come to big decisions, I will talk to Diane. Mind you, if she does not like the decision, I'll still go ahead to do it my way.

We also have two female respondents' perceptions which capture succinctly the two basic aspects of the situation—economic basis of husband dominance and its functional acceptance by the wife.

> In the Marsh, man is the breadwinner. Here woman has willingly taken on the role of maintaining well-being of the family, leaving all major decisions to be made by the man.

> We have been talking about getting a tape-recorder for years. But we together finally decided to have a swimming pool built. When it comes to big decisions on the farm, he's the party who makes the final decisions. And that's his business too.

Two male respondents explicitly link male dominance in economic realms to marital stability:

> So long as there is no economic rivalry, the marriage remains stable.

> When there is competition between husband and wife for control over economic resources, the marriage is likely to be in trouble. When the wife works outside, the family is definitely in trouble. In the Marsh, it is the husband who controls.

Some of the responses from the wives show that they were perfectly aware of the situation of unequal exchange but did not seem to show manifest feelings of bitterness or resentment. The following response from a housewife underlines the fact that the husbands occasionally attempt to accept their wives' suggestions on such secondary issues as holidaying:

> My husband decides our holidays. A year ago he went to Holland with his sister. He had not seen his country for 50 years and wanted to see all his relatives. He thoroughly enjoyed his visit. The same year my neighbouring family was going to the Caribbean Islands for holiday and I liked the idea. I asked my husband if I should go. He approved the idea and paid for the trip.

The dominant marital situation in the Marsh community is one of potential and accepted male dominance neutralized in practice on occasions by symbolic and marginal gestures on the part of the husband to put up an appearance of equality and democracy with the family.

Our data also indicate that a utilitarian consideration was involved in the wife's acceptance of her position. One wife respondent said this implicitly:

> Single girls work but stop as soon as they get married. No mothers with small children work outside home for money.

While this response by no means constitutes a clear-cut statement, it can be argued that it shows that the wife saw the necessary connection between the role of being a mother and the need for giving up employment.

We have also examples in which the wife rationalizes her plight by seeing virtues in the husband being the decision-maker. One of them, a rich farmer's wife, argued:

> If I go on spending, he puts his foot down. We were brought up amidst poverty through the thirties. We know how difficult it is to earn, so we keep within our limits and run a happy, stable life.

In this case, the wife sees the husband's function as a necessary one in running what she calls "a happy, stable life."

Our analysis of patterns of familial decision-making within the traditional framework of male domination and female subordination points out that though unequal exchange and differential access to resources within the husband-wife dyad are real, there also exist countervailing practices, admittedly marginal or symbolic, by which husband dominance is made to appear less than it happens to be. The same phenomenon is subjectively perceived by the respondents as contributing to material stability in a positive way.

Religion and Cultural Conformity

From a sociological standpoint, the concept of resources cannot be limited to only material resources such as income or employment. The concept has to be broadened to account for the way in which cultural and ideological factors are utilized by individuals to justify and support their superior and dominant roles. In this sense, religious-cultural values and ideology may be defined as socio-cultural resources which individuals and groups in a given social system may use to bolster up and legitimize the existing patterns of unequal exchange and differential resources control. In other words, the material inequality in the hands of persons of power and superior status is further articulated in such a way that it is reinforced by ideological and cultural forces leading to a complicated structure of balanced contradiction.

Nevertheless, religious ideology functions in institutional terms and, therefore, its impact becomes highly structured through both overt regulation and internalized disposition towards religious conformity. This comes out not only through an objective assessment but also through the subjective perception and attitudes of the respondents. It is clear that the Marsh people themselves see the connection between marriage and religion to be a significant one. The following remarks illustrate how the Marsh people attach the significance of religion to marriage:

Religion keeps the marriage intact.

The church regulates marriages.

Religion is a big thing in marriage.

I think the Dutch people in this community are religiously conservative. Because of the influence of religion, our lifestyle is basically conservative about a lot of values, marital fidelity being one.

If the couples really believe in God, they pray together and stay together. If you have lived 25 years with a woman, then why should you separate from her? Why on earth?

Thus marital stability is connected with, and accounted for by the religious ideology and the supporting institutional system. The role of religion in the maintenance of a stable family system is construed as a subjectively experienced fact:

Christian ideology and commitment is a very strong force in integrating the family.

Marriages in Springdale are basically good, and it's so because of religious convictions. That's the way things should be. A common Christian faith resolves differences between husband and wife. A Christian belief spells out a basic discrepancy between man and woman, and allows the man to become the head of the household.

Our family has strived to live up to high Christian standards, to maintain a Christian atmosphere at all times. There is this commitment to Christ, and it has been there since we were married. Our children like home life. They don't have to seek fellowship from outside the home. Christian discussions have always happened among family members in the household.

We have this family devotion to the Bible and prayers and this desire to worship, sing, and pray together. Our children read the Bible before they go to bed. We know each other by talking among the family. One's spiritual life could die without sharing among each other one's communication with God.

Our respondents refer to marital commitment as an "old value," and the community claiming to strongly adhere to it is, in general, a tradition-loving, conventional one. Associated with this value is the specifically religious concept of marriage:

> We marry in the Lord and stay united. We live according to the will of the Lord.

A local minister whom we interviewed explained the marital situation this way:

> There are certain forces which have brought about this situation of marriage. Firstly, the Church enjoins one to marry till death. Secondly, there is the strong hold of the community traditions on the people. Ours is a closed community.

This analysis draws attention to two institutional dimensions relevant to the situation—the role of the church and the hold of tradition. They both tend to reinforce behaviour involving marital commitment and marital stability. Upon close examination of the nature of the institutional pressure exerted by religion on the marital situation, one would see the crucial role of the minister. Formally a spiritual figure, he naturally generates decisive moral influence on the community. However, an important point to note is that he can do this precisely because the community backs him up. In other words, he should be regarded less as a regulator of community marital ethics and behaviour than as spokesman for community values and norms. His role in the marital field is multifaceted. He not only assists officially in the wedding ceremony, but also examines and evaluates the eligibility of marriage partners in advance. In practice, he screens out individuals who appear to be poor candidates for a stable married life. Further, he also acts as a marriage counsellor, steering the marital ship clear of the perils and pitfalls that are likely to wreck it. A minister in Springdale explained his role in the following response:

> I do premarital counselling. I stress permanence of marriage, the promise of love and intimacy in marital life, and also talk about birth control in my counselling. I provide them with literature, extolling marriage from the point of view of the Church, and I discuss the moral philosophy of marriage in two or three sessions.

He underlined the religious basis of marital stability when he asserted:

> I will never consecrate a marriage between a Dutch believer and a non-believer.

He also linked the authoritarian power structure in the family to the religious factor:

> My members in the consistory are the representatives of authority in the Church. We don't wonder that their authoritarianism is reflected in their family life.

The minister in Ansnorveldt, the first one of the two settlements (the other being Springdale) in point of community chronology, set forth his role in the following words:

> As a Minister, it is my business to work with the community to bring the problem families to accept the Biblical view of marriage. Common law marriage is not the right way of living. To me it is an abnormal phenomenon. A healthy society cannot function morally when such marriages increase.

We find here a categorical rejection of a marriage not in conformity with the precepts of the Bible. In fact, the religious idea of marriage is equated with a moral view of marriage. He also stated that he exercised genuine control over the marriage process in which he officiated as a priest. He explained his functioning thus:

> When a couple want to get married, they would need the Minister. But I have made it known to the community that I will not perform the marriage ceremony of anybody unless I have met them over four to six sessions, which I call 'pre-marriage counselling about marriage.' I discuss with them the very purpose of marriage, and give my final approval only when I am satisfied.

The above statement points to the controlling role of the religious functionary in the fostering of marriages. He rounded off this formidable picture of religious regulation of the marriage system as follows:

> I have refused performing marriages of non-believers. Last year, a girl who never showed up at the Church phoned me up and

requested for a wedding date. I advised her to meet me with her fiancé. I asked her about the difference between a Christian marriage and a non-Christian marriage. They could not answer. Clearly, they did not like my questioning and got married by a Baptist Minister outside the Marsh. I never saw her again in the Church after that. I understand that she is working in Toronto.

What emerges thus far from the foregoing analysis is a marital system that shows a high degree of marital commitment not only because the marital partners find themselves in a very limited arena of conflict based on unequal exchange relationships and differential resource control, but also because the asymmetrical power structure in the marital dyad is supplemented and strengthened by a religious ideology which glorifies and legitimizes the value of marital commitment and marital stability as Christian values. Further, we find that the ideology is systematically enforced by a formal religious agency and its functionaries, namely, the church and its ministers. Thus the material basis of the asymmetrical marital relationship is reinforced by religious institutions and ideology.

Kinship Intervention and Community Regulations

The religious system does not directly generate the familistic values of the Marsh Dutch community; it functions rather as a mediating force.

The modified extended family occupies a dominant position in the value system of the community and, therefore, finds itself embodied in the institutional arrangements of the community. The fact that this is, even today, a predominantly closed society from which there is only a marginal population flow into the outside world, tends to strengthen the traditional familistic values. Most of the new generations tend to get married and take up residence in the Marsh. Within the kin context of the extended family, individual persons in general, and those who are married in particular, enjoy a substantial degree of material as well as psychological security and satisfaction. This in turn provides an appropriate setting for a stable and strongly committed marital relationship. The role of the kinsmen becomes strategically significant in maintaining and strengthening this marital and familial bond. When there are problems between the marital partners, the kinsmen take an active part in helping to bring about speedy settlement of disputes. Relatives arrange for informal negotiations leading to solutions and compromises which very often save many marriages. The following case, reproduced here in the words of a respondent, illustrates this process:

> Not long ago, someone beat up his wife and broke her ribs. The children were naturally very upset. The eldest child ran to their uncle and aunt, and reported the fight between the father and mother. The uncle and aunt gave refuge to the children, and later initiated the process of mediation. The interesting thing about this case was that it concerned an interfaith marriage. The kinsmen were able to manage the situation and help patch it up. The couple in question are still together. Finally, the husband moved to the wife's church, thus removing a source of tension and misunderstanding.

This pacifying and tension-management role of the kinsmen, based on strong familistic values, has contributed considerably to the prevention of the breakdown of many a marriage in the Marsh, and should then be reckoned as an important source of continuing marital commitment and marital stability in the community.

The ethic of reciprocity and mutuality within the systems of marital relationships should also be seen in the wider context of the nature of the overall community and its values. That the two are essentially interconnected aspects is borne out by some of our respondents. One of our respondents summed up the interdependence of community values and marital ethics cogently:

> Our community sense is another factor. Here the Marsh people want to belong to each other. They wouldn't accept the divorced couple and would keep them out of their social world. In their view, the Christian concept of marriage must be preserved and then life would be conducted accordingly.

Community disapproval and rejection of divorce as unchristian play an important role in the creation of a climate favourable to the continued maintenance of marital commitment and marital stability. The same point was made by another respondent in terms of conformity and community regulation of deviant behaviour:

> This is basically a conservative, familistic, and protective environment. Deviants won't last long here. They move out.

The Marsh society has clearly rejected the individualistic ethic of the fiercely aggressive, competitive, and violent society which surrounds it geographically. The mechanism of gossip and whispered discussions which would eventually convert problematic marital cases into public matter necessitating public intervention make it difficult for couples heading for marital breakdown to safeguard personal privacy. The representatives of the church soon get to know of such cases and begin to work for maximum mutual accommodation and adjustment. Several respondents made incisive observations about the role of community in regulating marriages by ensuring community norms and values:

> When a marriage is in trouble and caught in the early stage of breakdown, quite a few different parties are involved in doing something about it.

> There is an enormous amount of helping and help-seeking in the community.

> Given negative reactions to social partying, residents in the Marsh do talk among each other about partying. Gossiping is a bad thing in the Marsh; it's destructive, not constructive criticism, especially in a small community where everybody knows everybody else. People here enjoy gossiping, saying lots of bad things about other people. Very rarely do they say good things about others.

> People in the Marsh are worried about what other people say. Each one is watching on others' personal lives.

> Marriages that are not working properly will eventually become a public matter; this will induce people to continue to work things out. Normally, however, couples in marital troubles keep to themselves until the matter gets out of hand and becomes public information.

The community norms function as powerful brakes on "deviant" behaviour. Despite the absence of a formal procedure, there is an overall community pressure, all the more effective for being indirect, which isolates the deviant individual. One respondent summarized the community regulatory mechanisms as follows:

> If someone does wrong, he or she is first warned, then ostracized

and finally made an outcast, making it difficult for him or her to live in the community.

Symptoms of Marital and Familial Strain

While our portrayal of the Holland Marsh community dynamics and processes of husband-wife relationships in the Marsh denotes a high level of marital stability and harmony, and points to the operation of a set of well-articulated and well-integrated social norms regulating individual behaviour, marriages in the Marsh are not entirely immune to problems. When asked to identify and describe "deviant" cases of marital difficulties or breakdowns, the minister of Springdale recalled the following:

> I wouldn't say that ours is a community free from marital problems. In one case, I received a phone call from someone saying that his wife had left home and he didn't know where she was. I went and talked with him. The next day I got a call from his wife to tell me that she felt so desperate that she left home for her mother's place. Two elders and myself visited the families concerned and talked with both of them. After a discussion we persuaded them to meet together in my house. On the whole, it worked out though there were occasional sparks during the meeting. After a couple of such sessions, the couple started to live together again. I can't say that there is a hundred per cent stable marriage but it certainly seemed better.

What is worth noting is not only the actual high or low frequency of the occurrence of marital problems, but also the traditionally institutionalized means by which the community intervenes in marital affairs, which is usually started with the minister playing the role of initiating the process of reconciliation or peace-making, and mobilizing accessible community resources to bear on the problem.

Persons of divorced and separated status live in the Marsh under community censure. They are invariably marked out for reference both as families and as individuals living in shame and sin. Our interview data indicates that there were no divorces and separations in the Marsh until 1970, although we did hear reports about interfaith marriages running into problems of maladjustment. The recent occurrence of divorce and separation can perhaps be related to increasing relaxation in traditional ethics and behaviour in the face of increasing economic prosperity in the community. One informant put it this way:

> Divorce is a social disease. It is creeping into the Marsh. When immigrants come here, they come with the one desire to improve their lot. They have made it in the Marsh. They now enjoy leisure on two days in a week. This gives them a chance to socialize at drinking parties and thus they get mixed up.

There are also other isolated cases of "marital instability" or "deviant families," and our informants cited a few "causes": increasing moral relaxation toward divorce, gradual secularization of lifestyles and beliefs, transition from collectivism to individualism, tendency to derive satisfaction from extrafamilial activities, poor financial management among younger marriages, and increasing use of alcohol in social drinking parties (which has always been frowned upon by the more traditional elements of the community):

> Divorce does not upset them as it did 50 years ago.

> Marital stability is really going downhill, probably due to looser and freer lifestyles, and too much stress on individual freedom.

> Marriages are changing, not really for the better. There have been a few marital break-ups. People nowadays don't seem to have as much satisfaction from within the family as from without.

> There were a few odd cases of marriage breakdown. The younger marriages have problems; most of them have something to do with money. Maybe because they want too much out of life—buy a home, and can't afford to upkeep and go ahead to finance. Young people nowadays expect more from life.

> This one marriage I know really well. The husband is a good friend of mine, and I knew him when we were both very young. Drinking parties started to happen very early in his marriage. I personally know of a few extramarital affairs with people outside the Marsh. Marital breakdowns start from the drinking parties which are usually held outside the Marsh.

> Usually some social parties go on before the onset of problems in the family and marriage.

Alcoholism is increasing among both adults and teenagers (perhaps only for social drinking). Secularism is increasing, too.

We do things now that were wrong to do in the old days, e.g., dancing, movies, and changes in styles, etc. The children love to dance though their parents don't like it.

These reported symptoms of change in marital relationships can be traced back to more general changes in the relationship between the Marsh community and the external environment. Two such types of community-environment relationship changes seem relevant to our understanding of the changes in the marital relationships. The first is the increased opening up of the community as a system in the physical, economic, and socio-cultural sense leading to greater exposure to the secular values in Canadian society. The second, which makes physically possible the first type of change, is the substantial improvement in the transportation and communication facilities. The increased physical mobility enables the younger people to experience more frequent contacts with the larger society. The increased access to mass media provides greater opportunities for exposure to the values and behavioural norms of the external environment. The older generation, which has the foresight to sense the danger in instability inherent in the mass media, were opposed to the movies and the TV. In fact, up until the early 1950's, movies and the TV were successfully kept out of reach of the community. One Marsh resident explained the situation in this manner:

I was always against movies, though my grand-daughter goes to the movies. I don't like it. However, she grabs the car and goes to Aurora. Movies have an impact on the growing-up of these girls now.

The above statement accurately points to the link between better transport and exposure to mass media. Perhaps, one immediate consequence of greater exposure to secular values in Canadian society on the part of the younger generation lies in the development and maintenance of more permissive attitudes toward common-law and interfaith marriages and, also, marriages with people from outside the Marsh community.

One estimate suggests that there have been about 20 instances of interfaith marriages in the Marsh in the last 15 years. Other sources indicate that there are increasingly more young people dating and marrying persons from outside the Marsh. To the inherent difficulties of such marriages must be added the community disapproval of such marital alliances.

The tension between tradition and change, the increasing secularization of values and norms, and the gradual emergence of discomfort with, and disapproval of community traditionalism are, perhaps, most vividly exemplified in the inquisitive and critical positions adopted by some women and children regarding the existing patterns of husband-wife and parent-children relationships.

> I personally know of cases where both the grandfather and father are very authoritarian, and the grandchildren are beginning to react and rebel against this authoritarianism and traditionalism. With the Women's Liberation Movement slowly coming to the Church, some women become very hostile against the authoritarian personality of their husbands. The grandchildren are becoming progressive and reactive.

> Children will rebel and reject many of the things that their parents stand for. Their parents, in making adjustments to difficult immigrant life in a strange country, gave up labour and political activities as they did in Holland. They hang on to the Church and the education system and choose to isolate themselves from the external society. This "green-house mentality" of preserving what they have got cannot be maintained nowadays, especially when education is supposed to involve the individual in the society, to be open to a diversity of values and ideas.

> Many conflicts within the family stem from young people questioning values of their old folks. More and more teenagers are reaching out to the outside world. There seems to be a gradual evasion of the traditional system of the Dutch community. Quite a number of them work outside the Marsh.

> In Holland Marsh, the home is gradually losing ground. Parents preach some important things but children tend to see some phoniness in them, e.g., "Love thy neighbour as Thyself."

> Nowadays children are more critical of values, and do a lot more

thinking. They like to test ideas and values out by actually living through them. They then finally come to some position of their own—either acceptance or rejection.

That the forces of change have not made the impact they could have made, resulting only in some marginal aberrations in the overall level of marital commitment and marital stability, is attributable to the existence of factors and forces identified in the earlier sections of this paper which exert counterpressures against change. In a highly tradition-bound immigrant community such as the Marsh, the built-in resistance to any change is very strong. In the process of preserving tradition and counteracting change, the Dutch ideology, the religious culture, the church, and the familistic values, all play an important role. The cumulative consequence of these ideological and institutional forces and pressures is that the Marsh Dutch community at the time of our investigations remained very much a traditional community highly resistant to change. It is in this total context that one has to understand the high degree of marital commitment and marital stability that prevailed at the time.

Conclusion

The high degree of marital commitment and marital stability that we were able to record in our fieldwork requires a complex interpretation. In the first place, we have related the marital situation to cumulative and contextual forces and factors, which include community traditionalism and values, religious ideology and its institutional manifestation through the church, and differential access to resources between marital partners. Each one of these factors by itself might not have brought about the kind of situation we encountered. But together they converged and continued to strengthen the traditional community system and its values and, within this context, created an overall sociocultural climate pressing toward the maintenance of a high degree of marital commitment and marital stability. It is a moot question, perhaps unresolvable, whether community tradition continues because of the marital situation or whether, because of the community traditionalism, we find marital commitment and marital stability. What is indisputable is that they reinforce each other to create the kind of marital situation that presently exists. While it is likely that the balance of forces in the Marsh community may increasingly shift toward change and away from tradition in the years to come and might very well have launched the community into a phase of transition and strain, that such a shift will encounter formidable counteracting institutional barriers embedded in the socio-cultural norms of the community, calls for serious consideration. In the process of containing change, marital commitment and stability, based on unequal exchange and differential power distribution and sustained by community religious ideology and institutions, may well play an important role.

References

1. Blau, P. *Exchange and Power in Social Life.* New York: John Wiley, 1964.
2. Blood, R.O. Jr., and Wolfe, D.M. *Husbands and Wives: The Dynamics of Married Living.* Glencoe, Ill.: Free Press, 1960.
3. Ishwaran, K. *Family, Kinship and Community: A Study of Dutch Canadians.* Toronto: McGraw-Hill Ryerson, 1977.
4. Ishwaran, K., and Chan, Kwok B. "The Socialization of Rural Adolescents," in K. Ishwaran, ed. *Childhood and Adolescence in Canada.* Toronto: McGraw-Hill Ryerson, 1979, pp. 96-118.
5. _____. "Social Time, Social Space and Family Relationships among the Dutch-Canadians," in K. Ishwaran, ed. *Canadian Families: Ethnic Variations.* Toronto: McGraw-Hill Ryerson, 1980.
6. Statistics Canada. *Vital statistics,* Vol. II, Marriages and Divorce, 1975.
7. Wolfe, D.M. "Power and Authority in the Family," in D. Cartwright, ed. *Studies in Social Power.* Ann Arbor: University of Michigan, Institute for Social Research, 1959.

Part III
Interethnic Marriages

There are three papers in this section, which are explicitly concerned with the problem of interethnic marriage or intermarriage in the multi-ethnic and multicultural society of Canada. Given the immigrant's strong desire to preserve original identity in a new environment, it is to be expected that interethnic marriages would not have an easy or smooth course in Canada. By the same token, the modernizing forces in the developing Canadian society tend to counter the dominance of parochial-ethnic exlusiveness of the different groups. In short, we have an interplay of two opposed processes—on the one hand, the process of consolidating ethnic identity and, on the other, the process of interethnic fusion.

Using the hypothesis that ethnic assimilation would register an upswing in the period 1961-1971 but that there would be significant variations in the extent of assimilation between the different major ethnic groups, Kalbach attempts to test this proposition by measuring "propensity for intermarriage." He assumes that propensity for intermarriage could be used as an index to the decline in ethnicity. Therefore, propensity for intermarriage served as a measure of assimilation. Kalbach conceptualizes propensity for intermarriage in quantitative terms as "the rate of 'actual' to 'possible' proportions of families having native-born heads with wives of a different ethnic origin." Kalbach points out that his concept is a departure from the earlier concept based on rates of "actual" to "expected" proportions of interethnic marriages. He notes a difference in propensity between groups characterized by recent and large-scale immigration and those lacking this feature. Kalbach demonstrates a relationship between ethnicity, residence, and propensity for intermarriage. He suggests that the data do not provide any basis for generalization. He argues that, in the context of the observed association between ethnicity and religious affiliation, recent increase in intermarriage requires further probing.

Leo Driedger's paper examines the phenomenon of intermarriage from a different and more specific perspective, that of student dating and mating. Taking as his starting point Farber's perception of the family system of an ethnic group as a microcosm of its overall social structure, Driedger distinguishes between relatively closed and open ethnic family systems. The former is oriented toward a systematic preservation of ethnic values through the mechanism of adaptive, minimal change, while the latter is oriented toward greater receptivity and flexibility, more capable of accommodating intermarriages. He suggests that a rural context is favourable to the closed model and the urban milieu more conducive to the open model. Just as the ethnic group as a whole may continue its traditional value system through systematic socialization, the ethnic family may find it more easy to preserve its religious-cultural identity if dating and mating are confined strictly within the ingroup. In his study of University of Manitoba students, Driedger found that, in general, the open model was the preferred model, as far as attitudes went. But their practice departed considerably from their articulated attitudes. He found that this attitude-practice gap existed in different degrees in the different ethnic groups. He found evidence that the Jewish group showed the greatest commitment to the closed model, implying an orderly, traditional, and minimal change. The Scandinavian group, on the contrary, was relatively more committed to the open model. Driedger suggests that the sex differences are not accidental but reflect the general nature of the overall social system of the concerned ethnic group. The Jews, for instance, had strong ethnic-religious identity leading to a greater social distance between them and the other groups.

Peter Chimbos' paper shifts the focus from the children to their parents. Making a comparative, cross-ethnic analysis of the immigrants' attitudes towards their children's interethnic marriages, based on 130 Dutch, 150 Greek, and 170 Slovak samples, Chimbos demonstrates significant interethnic variations in parental attitudes to ethnic exogamy. His data suggests that the Dutch were the least opposed to intermarriages of their offspring. Of the other two, the Greek and the Slovak, the Greek immigrant parents showed a greater degree of resistance and hostility toward their children's marriages outside the ethnic fold. Chimbos finds that interethnic marriages were disapproved on the ground that they affected adversely the prospects of preserving ethnic identity and religious culture. Going deeper into the causal structure of such attitudes, he arrives at the proposition that ethnic exclusiveness and commitments were themselves dependent on other variables, such as educational level, rural/urban background in the home country, sex, and the age at which immigration was effected. Chimbos feels that his data generated hypotheses which need further testing through research.

8/Propensities for Intermarriage in Canada, as Reflected in the Ethnic Origins of Husbands and Their Wives: 1961-1971*

Warren E. Kalbach

At the beginning of the twentieth century, the population of Canada was reported as being 57% British in origin, 31% French in origin, and 12% other ethnic in origin. Seventy years later, the distribution was 45%, 29%, and 26%, respectively. The historical dominance of the two "founding races" in relation to the other combined ethnic populations has eroded considerably as a result of changes in patterns of fertility and immigration. Until recently, the French Canadians have managed to maintain their relative proportion of the national total through high fertility, while the population of British origins has had to rely primarily on favourable immigration.

The picture has been changing, and there has been an increasing interest in the relative positions of the "founding races" with respect to those of other origins, and the processes which have affected the balance between them. This is particularly true of a government which gives emphasis to the co-existence of the Anglophone and Francophone societies with freedom for the other ethnic populations to integrate with the society of their choice. Whether or not this will suffice to preserve the bicultural nature of Canada remains to be seen. In the meantime, Canada will continue to be shaped, as it has been in the past, by the volume and character of its immigration, differences in group fertility, changes in marital behaviour, and the distribution of the population across the land under the forces of continuing urbanization and industrialization. Developments in modern society have made it difficult for groups to remain regionally and culturally

*This is a revised version of a paper presented at the 1974 annual meeting of the Canadian Sociology and Anthropology Association, at Toronto, Canada. The author wishes to express his appreciation to Madeline Richard, Research Assistant, Erindale College, for her assistance in the preparation of this manuscript and to Erindale College for its continuing support of population research.

isolated. Increased mobility, rapid growth, and social change in general, have brought diverse cultural groups into increasing contact within the larger regional and national systems. Under modern conditions, it becomes increasingly difficult to maintain strong ethnic identities because of different cultural experiences. Educational opportunities and experience have become increasingly standardized throughout the country, and the effects of mass production and distribution, as well as the mass media, have contributed to an increasing similarity of lifestyles from one end of the country to the other. Rapid urbanization and increased social mobility have increased the amount of interaction between all segments of the population and the probability of intermarriage between diverse ethnic and socio-economic groups. Intermarriage itself may be both cause and effect of this homogenization of society and, for this reason, has been frequently used as a measure of assimilation. As an index of assimilation, it is not without faults. As Marcson has pointed out, intermarriage is not necessary for assimilation to occur within ethnic families.[10] Yet, it would be difficult to imagine that behavioural changes would not occur in individuals who chose to marry across racial, ethnic, or cultural lines, in such a way as to blur ethnic differences either between husband and wife, or between parent and child. While intermarriage might not be required for some assimilation to occur, it would be difficult to imagine total assimilation without some intermarriage.

The analogy might be a poor one, but, following Marcson's reasoning, one would have to also argue that measures of residential dispersion (for ethnic populations) would not be useful as an index of assimilation, since assimilation can occur to some degree within highly segregated, residential, ethnic ghettos. However, residential dispersion, like intermarriage, serves to increase the families' interaction with members of other ethnic and cultural groups and serves as a catalyst for the assimilation process. The ultimate test would be to determine whether those ethnic groups with high rates of intermarriage, and low residential segregation, are more similar to the general population with respect to certain social, economic, and psychological characteristics than those which exhibit low levels of intermarriage and high residential segregation. For the purpose of this chapter, it matters little whether one assumes that intermarriage operates to blur ethnic differences more rapidly than if strict endogamy was the rule, or whether one assumes that intermarriage is a consequence of increasing similarities between the various ethnic groups because of assimilation.

Table 8.1

Percentage of Endogamous Marriages for Males of
Selected Ethnic Origins, by Geographical and Linguistic Groupings,
Canada: 1921, 1931, 1941, 1961 and 1971.

Ethnic Origin	1921[a]	1931[a]	1941[a]	1961[b]	1971[b]
British	92.0	—[d]	—[d]	81.2	80.9
French	84.9	95.0	93.4	88.3	86.2
German	75.2	72.5	58.6	52.0	49.2
Netherlands	47.0	54.6	51.1	54.9	52.5
Scandinavian	57.3	46.0	33.4	31.2	26.9
Hungarian	85.6	89.9	66.9	62.8	53.3
Polish	80.0	78.0	51.8	49.0	43.2
Russian	77.2	70.6	56.1	47.7	43.1
Ukrainian	92.5	90.2	79.3	61.8	54.0
Italian	80.7	77.0	55.2	76.6	76.5
Jewish	95.8	97.0	95.1	91.1	91.2
Asiatic	90.5	—[d]	—[d]	79.9	80.5
Total	88.4	—[d]	—[d]	77.7	76.4
Geographical Grouping:					
Northwestern European	66.7	62.2	47.2	48.3	45.7
South, Central, and					
Eastern European	83.8	81.6	63.8	65.7[c]	65.1[c]
Linguistic Grouping:					
Scandinavian	57.3	45.8	24.8	31.2	26.9
Germanic	70.8	68.0	55.4	52.8	50.0
Latin and Greek	77.8	74.1	52.4	—[d]	—[d]
Slavic	85.2	82.4	65.9	—[d]	—[d]

[a]Based on the parentage of children born in Canada in 1931 and 1941 and in the Registration area (Canada exclusive of Quebec) in 1921, as reported in the following sources: Hurd, W.B., *Origin, Birthplace, Nationality, and Language of the Canadian People*, Census monograph, 1921 Census of Canada, Dominion Bureau of Statistics, Ottawa: The King's Printer, 1929, Table 59, p. 117; *Racial Origins and Nativity of the Canadian People*, Census

monograph, 1931 Census of Canada, Vol. XIII. Dominion Bureau of Statistics, Ottawa: The King's Printer, 1942, Table XLVI; and *Ethnic Origin and Nativity of the Canadian People*, Census monograph, 1941 Census of Canada, Dominion Bureau of Statistics, Ottawa: The Queen's Printer, Table XLV.

[b]Based on reported ethnic origins of spouses in normal husband-wife families from special census tabulation provided by Statistics Canada.

[c]Includes only the major ethnic-origin groups. Other geographical and linguistic categories are approximately equivalent with respect to numbers of origin groups.

[d]Not available.

Ethnic Intermarriage in Canadian Society

Perhaps the foremost scholar of ethnic intermarriage in Canadian society betwen 1921 and 1941 was W. Burton Hurd, Professor of Economics at McMaster University. He published three major census monographs dealing with the ethnic and racial composition of the Canadian population, the last monograph being published posthumously about ten years ago.[7]

The treatment of intermarriage in the three monographs provides a consistent set of analyses covering a 20-year period. However, as in most historical studies based on secondary data sources, Professor Hurd had to make do with somewhat less than adequate data. Lacking direct information on the ethnic character of the total population of husbands and wives, Professor Hurd made use of data providing ethnicity of parents of children born during census years. Notwithstanding the limitations of his data, i.e., underestimation of older families, and less fertile ethnic combinations, he presents a fair amount of evidence in support of increasing intermarriage, and significant differences between ethnic origin groups.

Table 8.1 presents a summary of Professor Hurd's data, in geographical and linguistic groupings, for the years 1921, 1931, and 1941.* From these, he concludes that intermarriage has increased materially for all groupings, but much more markedly for the more recent immigrants between 1931 and 1941, and particularly for those

---

*These are weighted averages based on the number of intermarriages between specific ethnic groups, e.g., German, Dutch, etc.

from South, Central, and Eastern European countries. In 1941, it may be noted, that the intermarriage rate for Northwestern Europeans was only 1.5 times that for the South, Central, and Eastern Europeans, compared to a level two and a half times as great in 1921. In the explanation of his findings, Professor Hurd states,

> Reared and educated in Canada, and unusually mobile because of economic pressures associated with business fluctuations during the decade 1931-41, and war conditions towards its close, these young adults not only mixed more freely than their parents with persons of different origins, but inevitably intermarried to a much greater extent.... Clearly, during the decade there was a great breaking down of the social barriers separating the different ethnic groups from one another.[7]

Data are available from the 1961 and 1971 censuses showing ethnic origin of husband and wife for normal families, i.e., families with both spouses present. While these data are more of the type desired by Hurd, they are, of course, not directly comparable with his data for the period 1921-41. However, where it was possible to reconstitute roughly comparable groups, the percentages appear to approximate the levels reported in the 1941 Census; and the proportionate declines between 1961 and 1971 are of nearly the same magnitude as those between 1921 and 1931. The "very clear" trend of decreasing endogamy, reported by Hurd, while less clear during the 1961-1971 period, appears to be consistent with his earlier analyses.

However, his explanation for the rapid change during the Depression decade needs additional comment. Hurd properly calls attention to the fact that immigration virtually ceased during this period and that "length of residence" consequently was much greater for the foreign-born population at that time than is normally the case. On the other hand, he failed to recognize its full significance when he attributed the decline in endogamy to the changing attitudes of the second and later generations. The same effect could have been produced even if the second and later generations had shown no increase in exogamous behaviour over prior levels. What appears to have produced this reduction in endogamous marriages was the absence of arriving immigrants, large proportions of whom are already married at the time of their arrival in Canada; and, not surprisingly, tend to have spouses of the same ethnic origin.* Thus, with the virtual cessation of immigration during the depression years, the absence of arriving (and married) immigrants would automatically produce a much lower level of endogamous marriages, particularly among the more recently established ethnic populations in Canada.

Ethnic Intermarriage, 1961-1971

Data presented in Table 8.2 provide a basis for comparing estimates of endogamous marriages for all families, and for those with native-born heads reported in the national censuses of 1961 and 1971. Estimates of ethnic intermarriage for all families provide a measure more consistent with Professor Hurd's insofar as it includes both native and foreign-born heads of families. On the other hand, estimates only for families with native-born heads would reflect more clearly the extent of ethnic or cultural constraints influencing the choice of spouses among second and later generations. For this reason, intermarriage rates for second- and subsequent-generation Canadians of differing origins provide a more valid index of ethnic assimilation. Again, as Marcson has already reminded us, absence of intermarriage in itself does not necessarily indicate the lack of assimilation to the dominant culture's values and attitudes, etc. On the other hand, the willingness of individuals to cross ethnic boundaries for marriage does suggest that ethnic differences have to be regarded as relatively unimportant, or that they will become less significant as a result of intermarriage.

Hurd's estimates for the 12 selected ethnic origins in 1921 show generally high levels of endogamy, ranging from 96% for Jewish fathers to a low of 47% for those of Netherlands origin. By 1971, the range had widened and had shifted downward to a high of 91% for Jewish heads of families and a low of 27% for the Scandinavians. The proportion of endogamous marriages for the combined 12 groups, a weighted average, had declined from 88% to 76% over the 50-year period. The significance of this decline is difficult to assess, because it is

---

*Between 1933 and 1961, excepting the immediate post-war year of 1946, the average percentage-married for arriving immigrants, varied between 50% and 60%. See W.E. Kalbach, *The Impact of Immigration on Canada's Population*, 1961 Census monograph, Dominion Bureau of Statistics, Ottawa: The Queen's Printer, 1970, Chart 2.20, p. 64.

based on total families, including foreign-born immigrants who were married prior to their arrival in Canada, and hence quite sensitive to fluctuations in numbers of immigrant arrivals.

Table 8.2
Percentage of Family Heads with Wives of Same
Ethnic Origin for Selected Origins of Total and Native-born
Family Heads, Canada: 1961 and 1971.

Ethnic Origin of Family	Total Family Heads		Native-born Family Heads	
	1961	1971	1961	1971
British Isles	81.2	80.9	79.9	79.7
French	88.3	86.2	88.6	86.5
German	52.0	49.2	37.9	38.3
Netherlands	54.9	52.5	29.5	26.9
Scandinavian	31.2	26.9	18.0	19.1
Hungarian	62.8	53.3	22.8	25.8
Polish	49.0	43.2	25.5	24.1
Russian	47.7	43.1	44.7	41.0
Ukrainian	61.8	54.0	50.5	45.0
Italian	76.6	76.5	27.2	30.1
Jewish	91.1	91.2	87.5	89.8
Asiatic	79.9	80.5	67.7	63.8
Total[a]	77.7	76.4	76.9	75.6

[a]Total for the 12 combined groups only.
Source: Statistics Canada special census tabulations.

With respect to the rank ordering of these ethnic groups in terms of their proportions of endogamous marriages, those of Jewish origins have consistently been in first place, followed closely by those of French, British, and Asiatic origins. At the other extreme are the Scandinavians for whom most ethnic boundaries appear to offer little resistance, insofar as intermarriage is concerned. The rank ordering of the 12 selected ethnic groups changed little between 1961 and 1971, with only the Hungarians and Ukrainians exchanging adjacent ranks during the decade.

Calculating the proportions of endogamous unions for native-born family heads drops the levels of in-group marriages for all ethnic groups rather significantly, the exceptions being those of British, French, and Jewish origins. One of the largest changes in both the 1961 and 1971 data occurred for family heads of Italian origin. In 1971, their proportion of endogamous unions was either 76.5 or 30.1%, depending upon whether the calculations were based on total family heads or just the native born. Clearly, if the research is concerned with intermarriage patterns which reflect preferences and opportunities in Canada, the latter are the only appropriate data to use.

Neither set of data shows a significant decline in the overall level of endogamous unions, the decrease being just 1.3 percentage points for the weighted average for the 12 ethnic groups in 1961 and 1971. This is, of course, a reflection of the disproportionately large size of the British- and French-origin populations, and the fact that the greatest declines occurred in the smaller ethnic populations. Nevertheless, 7 of the 12 groups showed declines ranging from -0.2 to -5.5 percentage points.

Of interest here, in a corroborative sense, is the work of David Heer.[3] His historical analysis of interfaith marriages has shown an increase on the part of Protestants, Catholics, and Jews in Canada from 1927 to 1957. In 1927, 5.8% of all brides and grooms married spouses of a different faith; and, by 1957, this proportion had increased to 11.5%.[3] Since ethnic origin and religion tend to be related, Heer's and Hurd's analyses would seem to be logically consistent with each other. However, in a recent updating of the "interfaith" analysis, the proportion of interfaith marriages was shown to have almost doubled between 1957 and 1972 reaching 21.5% during this 15-year period.[4] This is in considerable contrast to the small increase reported for the 12 ethnic-origin groups analysed for this study for the period 1961-1971, when the proportion of interethnic marriages increased from 23.1% to 24.4%. The implications of this are interesting, but unfortunately the available data preclude their pursuit.

Intermarriage with British and French Origin Populations

Professor Hurd emphasized the importance of intermarriage between the minority ethnic groups and the dominant British and French groups as a means of facilitating assimilation into Canadian society; and, through his analyses, showed that Northwestern Europeans were much

Table 8.3

Proportions of Exogamous Husband-Wife Families by Origin of Wife for Selected Origins of Native-Born Husbands, Canada: 1961 & 1971.

Ethnic Origin of Husband	Ethnic Origin of Wife							
	1961				1971			
	British	French	N.W. European	Other	British	French	N.W. European	Other
British	—	31.9	41.5	23.0	—	34.1	39.0	26.9
French	73.1	—	5.3	21.6	73.1	—	12.2	14.7
German	68.4	9.4	8.1	14.1	67.6	10.7	7.8	13.9
Netherlands	73.0	7.0	12.0	8.0	69.0	7.6	14.1	9.3
Scandinavian	65.8	7.9	13.1	13.2	64.3	7.1	14.1	14.5
Hungarian	46.1	8.0	20.8	25.1	49.0	8.0	20.3	22.7
Polish	38.7	9.1	14.1	38.1	44.3	9.4	16.5	29.8
Russian	39.0	5.5	19.6	35.9	49.0	6.3	22.3	22.4
Ukrainian	43.8	9.7	17.3	29.2	49.8	9.9	19.1	21.2
Italian	50.3	27.3	8.4	14.0	52.6	26.9	8.4	12.1
Jewish	45.8	15.1	8.9	30.2	61.1	13.0	10.3	15.6
Asiatic	53.4	21.6	10.2	14.8	54.9	19.1	12.4	13.6

Note: The manner in which the above table should be interpreted may be illustrated by reference to the native-born heads of families of German origin. Of all the husbands who married outside their own ethnic origin, i.e., exogamous marriages, 68.4% had wives of British origins, 9.4% had wives of French origin, 8.1% had wives of Northwestern origins (other than German), and the remaining 14.1% of the wives were of other origins in 1961.

Source: Statistics Canada special census tabulations.

more likely to intermarry with those of British origins, than those who were of South, Central, or Eastern European origin.[7]

Ethnic choices of native-born heads of families who married outside their own ethnic-origin groups are presented in Table 8.3 to show whether or not the patterns described by Hurd still have validity for the 1961-1971 decade. It is clearly evident, from a cursory examination of the data, that significantly larger proportions of native-born husbands of Northwestern European origins acquire wives of British origin when they marry outside their own ethnic group, than is the case for the other ethnic origins shown. The data also show that the proportions of Northwestern Europeans marrying British-origin women have declined somewhat, while the proportions for the remaining origins have all shown relatively large gains. This would seem to indicate that both distributional and socio-cultural factors have become more conducive to social interaction with the latter ethnic populations and less so with the former. It is worth noting that this pattern of relative change observed for the 1961-1971 decade is very similar to that observed and reported by Hurd for the 1931-1941 decade.

The relative sizes of the ethnic populations from which wives are selected would lead us to expect that a large percentage of exogamous marriages would be with persons of British and French origins, all other things—including geographical distribution—being equal. However, in the case of the British-origin males who chose from the pool of non-British wives, those of French origin would appear to be significantly underrepresented. For example, in 1961, women of French origin constituted 54% of the non-British female population 15 years of age and over; and comprised 66% of the population of non-British wives. By contrast, only 32% of the British males marrying non-British wives, married women of French origin. Most of the under-representation in this case might be traced to the excessive concentration of French-origin population in two of Canada's provinces.* A

---

*That this is partly the case may be seen in the analysis of similar data for Quebec in 1971. Wives of French origin are still underrepresented among wives of British males who entered exogamous unions, but the degree of underrepresentation is not great. For example, in Quebec the French-origin wives comprise 95.1% of all non-British wives. However, of those British males who married outside their own origin group, only 83.3% married French wives.

similar analysis of wives of French-origin males who married outside their own ethnic population shows only a slight, and probably not significant, overrepresentation of British-origin wives. British wives comprise 73% of all non-French wives reported as living in normal husband-wife families at the time of the 1961 Census. Its significance, of course, depends upon whether this percentage is compared to the fact that British women constitute 65% of all non-French women 15 years of age and older, or to the fact that 72% of all non-French wives are of British origin.*

It becomes quite clear that measures of intermarriage, to be useful in the understanding of ethnic relations, must provide some control for disparities in the size of ethnic populations, their geographical distributions, and generational composition.

Propensities for Ethnic Intermarriage

A review and updating of Hurd's analyses has provided a rough indication of historical trends for intermarriage between Canada's major ethnic-origin populations. In 1971, almost one in four husband-wife families represented an interethnic marriage. Variation between ethnic groups in the amount of intermarriage was considerable. On the one hand, only 9% of all Jewish family heads had non-Jewish wives, while 73% of all Scandinavian husbands had non-Scandinavian wives. All in all, this represented little change from the situation reflected in the 1961 Census.

Roughly the same picture may be seen in the data for native-born heads of families. Again, there is relatively little change from 1961 to 1971, but the range in variation is somewhat wider, running from a minimum of 10% intermarriage for native-born heads of Jewish origin to 81% for Scandinavians. The most significant difference, however, is that the levels of intermarriage are considerably higher for most of those of non-British and non-French origin.

---

*The percentages are identical for Canada in 1971. For Quebec, the data indicate a slight preference for British wives above what might be expected on the basis of the numerical distribution alone. While British wives, in this case, comprise 70% of all non-French wives in Quebec, 73% of the wives of French males who married non-French wives were of British origins.

Table 8.4

Propensities for Intermarriage Expressed as Ratios of "Actual" to "Possible" Proportions of
Ethnic Intermarriages for Native-born Heads of Selected Origins: Canada and Regions, 1961 and 1971

Ethnic Origin of Family Head	Canada		Atlantic Provinces		Quebec		Ontario		Prairie Provinces		British Columbia	
	1961	1971	1961	1971	1961	1971	1961	1971	1961	1971	1961	1971
British	0.33	0.34	0.40	0.38	0.44	0.54	0.47	0.48	0.46	0.48	0.55	0.55
French	0.21	0.24	0.39	0.42	0.25	0.31	0.55	0.57	0.65	0.70	0.85	0.84
German	0.81	0.76	0.79	0.79	0.94	0.92	0.78	0.80	0.71	0.69	0.87	0.82
Netherlands	0.86	0.86	0.90	0.92	0.98	0.92	0.93	0.92	0.64	0.74	0.84	0.87
Scandinavian	0.91	0.90	0.94	0.94	0.96	0.94	0.96	0.94	0.88	0.88	0.92	0.91
Hungarian	0.88	0.86	0.98	0.92	0.91	0.75	0.89	0.85	0.85	0.85	0.93	0.90
Polish	0.86	0.86	0.94	0.92	0.85	0.82	0.83	0.84	0.86	0.86	0.95	0.93
Russian	0.71	0.74	0.89	0.97	0.74	0.92	0.83	0.93	0.71	0.78	0.58	0.61
Ukrainian	0.66	0.70	0.95	0.94	0.81	0.80	0.78	0.80	0.57	0.62	0.83	0.84
Italian	0.83	0.81	0.97	0.95	0.79	0.78	0.80	0.78	0.94	0.91	0.91	0.90
Jewish	0.18	0.16	0.39	0.37	0.14	0.09	0.18	0.17	0.19	0.23	0.38	0.43
Asiatic	0.45	0.52	0.83	0.84	0.60	0.59	0.46	0.54	0.53	0.39	0.21	0.35

Source: Special Tabulation provided by Statistics Canada.

It is quite clear that ethnic intermarriage can contribute to changes in the ethnic composition depending upon the particular pattern of ethnic intermarriage, and to the consequences for fertility and the ethnic identity of the children of such unions. Of more importance to this analysis is the fact that the existing ethnic composition of the population can itself set limits to the amount of ethnic intermarriage that can occur. Hence, variations in the proportions of endogamous marriages by ethnic origin are difficult to interpret unless some control over the effects of differences in the sizes of the various ethnic populations can be achieved.

Professor Hurd had already noted the importance of size for explaining intermarriage variance in his multiple-correlation analyses of the 1921, 1931, and 1941 census data. Barron,[1] Thomas,[11] and Locke,[9] all pointed out the inverse relationship between group size and intermarriage rates. In 1965, Besanceney emphasized the mathematical necessity for this generalization and advised the following procedure used by Glick in his analysis of intermarriage and fertility patterns.[2] The procedure for calculating propensities towards intermarriage, also illustrated by Yinger in his research note on interfaith marriages, involves the calculation of a ration of "actual" to "expected" intermarriage rates based on random pairing.[12] While the "actual" to "expected" intermarriage ratios have been the ones most commonly reported in the literature, they present some difficulties in interpretation because of a variable upper limit for those ethnic-origin groups which comprise over 50% of the population. Theoretically, these groups are not able to achieve a condition of total intermarriage. The solution to this was suggested to Yinger by Hewitt in the form of a modified-propensity measure which utilized the ration of "actual" to "possible" proportions of intermarriage, rather than the ration of "actual" to "expected" proportions.[12]

This modified index has the advantage of producing an index with constant limits of 0 and 1, regardless of the size of the groups involved, and makes the index directly comparable across all groups. Both types of indexes were calculated, but only the indexes based on "actual" to "possible" proportions of intermarriages have been presented in Table 8.4.

The ratios for Canada as a whole still show a surprising range of propensities for intermarriage on the part of the major ethnic origin groups included in this analysis. As with the data using proportions of intermarried only, native-born males of Jewish origins showed the least propensity to intermarry, while those of Scandinavian origins exhibited the greatest tendency to cross ethnic boundaries.*

The rank ordering of these groups changed little during the 1961-1971 decade (rho = 0.98), and the partial controlling for disparities in size by use of the intermarriage ratios likewise produced no significant changes in their rank ordering regardless of which propensity measure was utilized.

Of the 12 ethnic groups considered, the propensities for intermarriage increased slightly for five groups, declined in five others, with two remaining constant during the decade. The unweighted means of the propensity indexes for the 12 groups remained virtually the same in 1971 as in 1961 (0.65 versus 0.64). All things considered, there is little evidence to indicate any significant change in the overall level of ethnic intermarriage during this period.**

Of the individual groups, those of Asiatic origins showed the largest relative increase in propensity ratios from 0.45 to 0.52; while the largest relative decline was observed for those of Jewish origins, from 0.18 to 0.16. The groups are listed in Table 8.5 for Canada as a

---

*The Scandinavians would appear to be the least restricted by socio-cultural impediments to crossing ethnic boundaries. However, this should not be interpreted to mean that they have minimal ethnic preferences. Closer examination of the data revealed that of those who did cross ethnic lines, 64% married women of British origin, and 14% married women of either German or Netherlands origin.

**One way to examine the data in Table 8.4 in relation to the general hypothesis of an increase in intermarriage rates for the 1961-1971 decade in Canada would be to examine the data in relation to the null hypothesis of no change, using each of the 12 ethnic groups in each of the five regions as one of a total of 60 observations. If the changes from 1961 to 1971 were purely random in nature, one would expect to find something representing a random distribution of increases and decreases. In actual fact, the data for the five regions shown in Table 8.4 show 25 instances where the intermarriage ratios increased, 29 instances where they declined, and 6 cases showing no change. This outcome would scarcely be considered as sufficient evidence to warrant rejecting a null-type hypothesis. Even if the difference between the 25 cases of increases and 35 showing no change or declines was considered large enough to warrant rejecting the null hypothesis of no change, it would be in the wrong direction from the hypothesized increase in ethnic intermarriage.

whole, showing their rank orders for 1961 and 1971, their propensity ratios ("actual" to "possible"), and the relative change for the decade.

Table 8.5
Ethnic Intermarriage Propensity Ratios for Selected Ethnic Origins,
Showing Rank Orders and Percentage Change, 1961 to 1971, Canada.

Ethnic Origin of Native-born Family Head	Rank Order		Propensity Ratios		Percentage Change
	1961	1971	1961	1971	1961 to 1971
Jewish	1	1	0.18	0.16	−11.1
French	2	2	0.21	0.24	14.3
British	3	3	0.33	0.34	3.0
Asiatic	4	4	0.45	0.52	15.6
Ukrainian	5	7	0.66	0.70	6.1
Russian	6	5	0.71	0.74	4.2
German	7	6	0.81	0.76	−6.2
Italian	8	8	0.83	0.81	−2.4
Netherlands	9.5	10	0.86	0.86	0.0
Polish	9.5	10	0.86	0.86	0.0
Hungarian	11	10	0.88	0.86	−2.3
Scandinavian	12	12	0.91	0.90	−1.1

Source: Table 8.4.

Since the various ethnic populations are not uniformly distributed across Canada, there are significant regional ethnic concentrations that would essentially alter the propensities for intermarriage for specific regions. Economic areas within provinces might provide the best approximation of "interactional" areas within which individuals carry out their social, political, and economic lives, and whose contextual characteristics would most influence the nature of the individuals' opportunity structure. However, lacking data for such areas, Canada's five major regions were selected as the next most feasible set of areas for analysis, and propensity ratios for these areas are also presented in Table 8.4.

Examination of these indexes will provide some indication of the significance of regional variations in ethnic populations arising from historical factors which affected the timing and settlement of subsequent waves of immigrants arriving in Canada. A case in point is that of the French Canadians. Their propensity for intermarriage is least in the cultural stronghold of Quebec. It increases significantly in either direction as one moves away from the province, and is highest in the province of British Columbia. The Asiatic cultural and settlement gradient, which runs from west to east, is similarly reflected in their propensities for intermarriage, which increase steadily as one proceeds from British Columbia eastward to the Atlantic Provinces. Intermarriage propensities are lowest for the British origins in their region of highest concentration, i.e., the Atlantic Provinces. As a result of early migration patterns, the Ukrainian settlements in the Prairie Provinces provide the core of Ukrainian cultural influence in Canada and this is likewise reflected in their low-intermarriage propensities for this area. Ukrainians outside this original area of settlement and concentration all show higher propensities for ethnic intermarriage. Native-born Italian males have a surprisingly high propensity for intermarriage considering the recency of their settlement in Canada. Yet, the influence of their concentrations in Montreal and Toronto is reflected in the somewhat lower ratios found in Quebec and Ontario than in the other regions. It would appear that while the relative number involved tend to set the limits for the extent of possible ethnic interaction, there is some "critical" size necessary for the emergence and maintenance of ethnic and cultural identity. However, the limiting effects of small numbers can be overcome by high concentration in urban areas, as is the case for both Jewish and Asiatic origins, or in rural areas, as might be expected for the Hutterites if data were available for this group.

Obviously, the analysis of ethnic intermarriage cannot stop here. There is a need to explore the nature of ethnic choices when individuals do choose to marry exogamously to see to what extent such choices reflect the prevailing patterns of ethnic preferences of the dominant British origin group. There is also a need to explore more precisely the possible implications of Heer's findings regarding a rapid increase in interfaith marriages in Canada during the period subsequent to the 1961 Census, when little change seems to have occurred in the propensity for interethnic marriage. More detailed cross-tabulations are required to explore the extent of interfaith marriage within the ethnic-origin groups, as compared to interethnic marriages within the larger religious denominations. The findings would have considerable significance in determining the relative importance of ethnicity and religion in the structuring of Canadian society. At this point, the present analysis combined with Heer's findings would suggest that the triple melting-pot model developed in the United States has little validity for Canada. Furthermore, research is also needed to explicate the characteristics of those who intermarry, to determine the extent to which ethnic intermarriage actually modifies or alters socio-cultural attitudes and behaviours, and to see how it is affected by patterns of residential segregation and occupational concentration which is characteristic of Canadian ethnic urban populations. Some of these problems and others, amenable to study by means of the data provided in the 1971 Census Public Use Sample Tapes, are currently under investigation.

References

1. Barron, M.L. *People Who Intermarry: Intermarriage in a New England Industrial Community*. Syracuse, N.Y.: Syracuse University Press, 1946.
2. Besanceney, P.H. "On Reporting Rates of Intermarriage." *The American Journal of Sociology* 70 (May 1965), pp. 718-719.
3. Heer, D.M., "The Trend of Interfaith Marriages in Canada: 1922-1957." *American Sociological Review* 27, No. 2 (April 1962), pp. 245-250.
4. Heer, D.M., and Hubay, C.A., Jr. "The Trend of Interfaith Marriages in Canada: 1922-1972," in S. Parvez Wakil, ed. *Marriage, Family, and Society*. Toronto: Butterworth & Co., Ltd., 1975.
4. Hurd, W. Burton. *Origin, Birthplace, Nationality and Languages of the Canadian People*. Ottawa: The King's Printer, 1929.
6. Hurd, W. Burton. *Racial Origins and Nativity of the Canadian People*. 1931 Census of Canada, Vol. XIII. Ottawa: The King's Printer, 1942.
7. Hurd, W. Burton. *Ethnic Origin and Nativity of the Canadian People*. 1941 Census of Canada. Ottawa: Queen's Printer, Circa 1964.
8. Kalbach, W.E. *The Impact of Immigration on Canada's Population*. 1961 Census monograph. Ottawa: The Queen's Printer, 1970.
9. Locke, H.J., Sabagh, C., and Thomas, N.M. "Interfaith Marriages." *Social Problems* 4 (1957), pp. 331ff.
10. Marcson, Simon. "A Theory of Intermarriage and Assimilation." *Social Forces* 29, No. 1 (October 1950).
11. Thomas, J.L. "The Factor of Religion in the Selection of Marriage Mates." *American Sociological Review* 16 (August 1951), pp. 489ff.
12. Yinger, M.J. "A Research Note on Interfaith Statistics." *Journal for the Scientific Study of Religion* 7 (Spring 1968), pp. 98-99.

9/Ethnic Intermarriage: Student Dating and Mating*

Leo Driedger

Farber has suggested that families may be relatively open or closed social systems depending on how concerned they are with the orderly replacement of values and norms which they wish to perpetuate (see Reference 9, pages 29-35). Jewish or Roman Catholic families may wish to perpetuate religious values which can be passed on effectively if their offspring date and marry persons of their own kind. French or Ukrainian Canadians may wish to perpetuate their language or other cultural norms by passing their values on to their offspring.

Bernard Farber[9] suggests that the modern family is changing from traditional orderly replacement in rural settings (a closed system) to universal availability in more urban, industrial cities (open system). The traditional rural community, which is more isolated ecologically, institutionally, and socially, provides greater opportunity for controlled continuity. Thus, rural families can often be sustained by orderly replacement with relatively little change.

The urban environment, in contrast to the rural, controlled family setting, opens individuals to universal permanent availability for marriage to many others.[8] Industrialization and urbanization tend to expose the family increasingly to outside influences which change the traditional family structure and behavioural patterns. Marriage becomes a personal, rather than a kinship or community arrangement. Orderly replacement and universal permanent availability are two popular types, which may seldom be found in a pure form, because of other factors which modify these rural and urban tendencies.

In this paper we contend that ethnicity is one of the factors that greatly modifies these urbanization and universal-permanent-availability trends. Even in the city there will be some ethnic and religious

*This research was made possible by a grant from the Canada Council (S69-1445) whose support is gratefully acknowledged.

groups such as the Jews, French Roman Catholics, and others who sustain forms of traditional orderly ethnic replacement by in-group marriage. Farber (see Reference 9, page 55) suggests that culture is an important factor which creates variations of orderly replacement. He says, "The norms and values which people hold regarding courtship, marriage, kinship identity and obligation, socialization, residence, and household maintenance are the elements of family culture." Ramu and Johnson[12] also claim that ethnicity, especially in Canada, is an important factor in mate selection and intermarriage.

The task in this paper is to compare university students of seven different ethnic groups (British, French, German, Ukrainian, Polish, Scandinavian, and Jewish) to see what their attitudes toward interethnic dating and intermarriage may be. We will also see what the actual interethnic dating and intermarriage behavioural patterns are. Many of these ethnic groups established rural enclaves in Manitoba, which were almost exclusively French, Ukrainian, Icelandic, German Mennonite, and the like. Many individuals from these rural communities are moving into the city and they are maintaining distinctly ethnic urban enclaves, similar to Gans' urban villagers.[10] It is expected that such urban ethnic enclaves, often reinforced by rural migration, will tend to slow the trend toward universal permanent availability for dating and marriage in Winnipeg.

Methodology

A sample of 1560 questionnaires, collected from randomly selected classes at the University of Manitoba, represented 15% of the undergraduate enrolment on the campus in 1971. Seventy-six of the 95 classes participated in the study, with a total enrollment of 3697. Nineteen classes did not participate because professors would not consent to have the questionnaire administered during class time; refusals were not confined to any one faculty nor limited to any particular size of class. The sample was diminished further by a less than full class attendance and an 8% student refusal rate.

The following seven groups were sufficiently represented (50 or more) for the purpose of group comparison: British (157), French (86), German (160), Jewish (112), Polish (56), Scandinavian (61), and Ukrainian (188). The many other groups represented in the sample were not included in the study.

Over 90% of the students at the University of Manitoba come from Manitoba. Over half (51%) of the population in the province lives in Winnipeg and well over half of the students in the sample were from Winnipeg.

The 20-page, seven-part questionnaire included Likert-type questions on dating and marriage, as well as on cultural identity. It also included social-distance questions and questions on dating and marriage behaviour. The questionnaire was administered in the classroom during regularly scheduled 50-minute class periods.

Selection of Mates

The first part of our analysis of the data on mate selection will focus on the attitudes of university students toward interethnic dating and intermarriage. In the second part we will explore to what extent members of their families have intermarried. We expect that the university, as a relatively open social system, will provide many opportunities for interethnic dating and intermarriage. Whatever in-group dating and in-group marriage we find will be attributed to a counter social system, possibly an ethnic group that may have a substantial influence.

Interethnic Dating

Dating is of major concern to single university students because it plays an important role in the continuity of the life of an individual and his or her family. With the pressures of dating and mate selection, we might expect that concerns for ethnic continuity would take second place in finding a compatible mate.

Table 9.1 shows that three-fourths of the entire student sample (72%) did not think that it made any difference whether they dated within or without their ethnic group. However, only one-third (37%) of the Jewish students could agree to such liberal interethnic dating. Well over half of the Jews (55%) disagreed with such liberal interethnic dating. About one-third of the German students were Mennonites and they too could not agree to much interethnic dating, which reduced the German percentage (64%) below the average.

The influence of parents should be a social-control factor which would retard interethnic dating. Three-fourths (75.7%) of the students agreed that parental interference would be a disservice. Again, only

Table 9.1

Attitudes of University of Manitoba Students toward Interethnic Dating

Statements with which Students Agreed	By Ethnic Groups (Percentages)								
	Jewish (N = 112)	German (160)	Ukrainian (188)	Polish (56)	French (86)	British (157)	Scandinavian (61)	Total (820)
It makes no difference to what ethnic group the person I date belongs.	36.9	63.5	80.0	78.3	81.3	83.1	83.6	72.1
Parents who discourage interethnic dating do a disservice to their children.	33.3	67.5	82.4	87.5	79.1	88.5	83.0	75.7

one-third (32.3%) of the Jewish students agreed with the rest, and one-third (31%) disagreed that parents who discouraged interethnic dating did a disservice to their children. Jewish children especially seem to sense a connection between continuity of the Jewish family and control over interethnic dating.

Turning to actual interethnic dating, we found, as expected, that other factors such as the ethnic community, ethnic institutions, social interaction, and the ethnic cultural environment seemed to create much more in-group dating than the attitudes of the students might suggest.

As shown in Table 9.2, one-fourth (26.5%) of the total student sample had never dated outside its ethnic group; in fact, three-fourths (71.1%) had not dated outside the in-group to speak of. Only one-fourth (28.9%) had engaged in interethnic dating three or more times. Actual interethnic dating behaviour was much less than the liberal attitudes toward interethnic dating would suggest.

The amount of interethnic dating varied by ethnic group. About one-third of the Scandinavian, Ukrainian, Polish, and German students had dated someone from an out-group three or more times. Jewish students especially were very minimally engaged in any form of interethnic dating; half had never dated outside their own group.

Our data would seem to show that although attitudes of university students toward interethnic dating are very liberal, not many do in fact date outside their own in-group. Jewish students especially tend to frown on interethnic dating, and very few are actually engaged in dating outside the Jewish group.

Ethnic Intermarriage

Ramu and Johnson (see Reference 12, page 331) suggest that "Endogamy should be viewed as an indication of stability and structural differentiation, while intermarriage should be interpreted as moves toward individual freedom and secularization in marital choice." Thus, individuals who have more permissive attitudes toward ethnic intermarriage would also likely be more prone to intermarriage, or come from families where intermarriage was permissible. When ethnic culture, religion, and community control are more in operation, we would expect that students would be less permissive and more selective in their potential marriage partners.

Table 9.2
Interethnic Dating of University of Manitoba Students by Ethnic Groups

Frequency	By Ethnic Groups (Percentages)								
	Jewish	German	French	British	Polish	Ukrainian	Scandin-avian	Total
Never	49.1	36.3	25.9	21.9	18.4	15.3	12.5	26.5
Once or Twice	41.7	31.8	44.4	51.7	49.0	48.6	50.0	44.6
Three or More Times	9.3	31.8	29.6	26.5	33.7	36.1	36.1	28.9
	100.	100.	100.	100.	100.	100.	100.	100.
	(N = 108)	(157)	(81)	(151)	(49)	(183)	(56)	(785)

Table 9.3
Attitudes of University of Manitoba Students toward Ethnic Intermarriage

Statements to which Students Agreed	By Ethnic Groups (Percentages)								
	Jewish	German	Ukrainian	Polish	French	British	Scandin-avian	Total
Members of my ethnic group may marry outside my own ethnic group.	53.2	81.1	88.3	89.1	94.0	93.4	100.	84.5
Persons of my ethnic group should not have unfavourable attitudes toward those who marry outside my group.	80.4	92.5	96.3	94.6	97.7	96.8	95.1	93.8

In Table 9.3 we see that university-student attitudes toward ethnic intermarriage are permissive, with the exception of Jewish students. Only about half of the Jewish students (53%) agreed that members of their ethnic group may marry non-Jews, while one-fourth (25%) said that they should not. More than four out of five of the other ethnic students agreed that members of their group were permitted to marry outside their group. Certainly university-student attitudes would not greatly hinder ethnic intermarriage.

The second question indicates that most of the students agreed that members of their own group should not react unfavourably toward those who do intermarry. This would seem to say that in-group pressures should not be brought to bear on those who do intermarry. In the past such in-group pressures tended to bring more conformity, which in the future will not be as strong.

Actual intermarriage within the families of these university students is much less frequent than their attitudes would suggest. We would expect that other factors such as ethnic culture, the ethnic community, ethnic institutions, religious beliefs, and other values and norms would result in much lower intermarriage rates. The data in Table 9.4 show that 70% of the students reported that none of their parents, or brothers and sisters had married outside their ethnic group. A majority of students of all ethnic groups reported no intermarriage. Jewish endogamy (91.3%) was very high.

The attitudes of university students toward ethnic intermarriage are very permissive, although actual intermarriage reported is still quite low for most of the groups. It is very likely that the permissive attitudes will slowly erode endogamy and will result in more intermarriage in the future. That may not be the case for the Jews and some other groups.

Ethnic Factors Which Influence Mate Selection

Our analysis of the interethnic dating and intermarriage patterns of university students shows that they vary considerably. Jewish students especially demonstrated attitudes that would support the orderly replacement of traditional Jewish values and norms, and their in-group dating and marriage patterns were especially strong. We would expect that such support must be "grounded in cultural values" as Lewin[11] put it, which Farber,[9] Ramu and Johnson,[12] and Driedger[6] would

Table 9.4

Exogamy of Parents, Brothers, and Sisters of University of Manitoba
Students by Seven Ethnic Groups

Number of Exogamous Marriages	By Ethnic Groups (Percentages)						
	Jewish	Ukrainian	British	French	German	Scandin- avian	Polish	Total
None	91.3	75.6	72.0	65.4	62.8	57.1	53.2	70.3
One or More	8.7	24.4	28.0	34.6	37.2	42.9	46.8	29.7
	100.	100.	100.	100.	100.	100.	100.	100.
	(N = 103)	(156)	(143)	(81)	(154)	(49)	(47)	(735)

support. Furthermore, we expect that ethnic institutions also would play an important part. Breton[1] and Driedger and Church[6] found that the ethnic institutional completeness of the Jews in Winnipeg was high.

On the other hand, our analysis shows that the attitudes toward interethnic dating and intermarriage, and the dating and marriage behaviour of the Scandinavians especially, is very permissive. We would expect that the in-group cultural and institutional support of Scandinavian students would be very low. In other words, their ethnic social system is undeveloped, and this is reflected in Scandinavian universal permanent availability in dating and marriage. Support for orderly replacement of traditional Scandinavian values through the family is minimal.

First we shall explore interethnic social distance, followed by evidence of ethnic institutional completeness and ethnic cultural identity.

Mate Selection and Social Distance

The data on dating and marriage seem to show that university students are very open to dating across ethnic lines, but that actual ethnic intermarriage is less frequent. They seem to differentiate between willingness to marry outside their group and willingness to be a close friend of a person of another group.

Using Bogardus' social-distance data, we found that indeed the same students differentiated between marriage and friendships. In Table 9.5 we see that whether students are more willing to marry or be a close friend is differentiated by group origin. Generally students were more willing to marry into European-origin groups, who would also be mostly Caucasian and of Christian heritage. Only one-fifth or one-fourth were willing to marry into non-European groups, who would be Mongoloid or Negroid racially and probably of non-Christian religious heritage. These findings would seem to suggest that marriage is perceived as an important means of continuity of their ethnic and religious background, so that they are reluctant to marry someone who is different racially, culturally, or socially.

For those who suspect that unwillingness to marry is an indicator of prejudice, we find in Table 9.5 that most of those who are not willing to marry into out-groups are, however, willing to be close friends of the same people. Three-fourths or more of the students were willing either to marry or be a close friend of a member of the 20 ethnic groups listed. This may throw further light on our earlier findings, i.e., that attitudes toward interethnic dating were more liberal than toward intermarriage.

It would seem that marriage is perceived as a means to maintain ethnic or religious identity. Therefore, some choose to forego ethnic intermarriage. However, there are great pressures in society to include all people as potential friends, so students are willing to do this by interethnic dating. Since so few respondents wished to debar, or have others as visitors only, it is doubtful that prejudice is as important a factor as the desire to maintain family continuity through in-group marriage. We need to examine whether those who indicate high ethnic identity indicate, indeed, higher social distance from others.

Driedger and Peters[7] and Driedger[5] found that there is a high correlation between ethnic cultural identity and social distance from others. As Simmel[13] predicted, in-group identification seems to preoccupy and sustain the individual so that he or she creates more social distance between self and others as personal identification with the in-group increases. Social distance discourages interethnic dating and intermarriage.

Mate Selection and Institutional Completeness

Breton[1] argues that "The direction of the immigrants' integration will to a large extent result from the forces of attraction (positive and negative) stemming from three communities: the community of his ethnicity, the native (receiving) community, and the other ethnic communities." These forces are generated by the social organization of ethnic communities and their capacity to attract and hold members within their social boundaries. Integration into their own ethnic community, supported by the institutional completeness of their group, would reinforce solidarity.

The rationale for institutional completeness is that when a minority can develop a social system of its own with control over its institutions, then the social interaction patterns of the group will take place largely within the system. Breton[1] suggests that religious, educational, and welfare institutions are crucial. Vallee[14] confirmed Breton's claim by summarizing the need for organization of group structures and institutions which influence socialization and ethnic-community decision-making. Driedger and Church[6] found the same.

Table 9.5

The Degree of Social Distance that University Students Would Prefer to Maintain
Between Themselves and Twenty Groups of European and Non-European Origin

Ethnic Groups	Social Distance Scale (Bogardus)						
	1 Willingness to marry	2 Willingness to have as close friend	3 Willingness to have as neighbour	4 Willingness to work with on job	5 Willingness to have as acquaintance	6 Willingness to have as visitor only	7 Would *debar* from nation
				(percentage)			
European Origin							
British	79.7	14.1	2.8	3.1	1.2	.8	.3
American	77.5	12.9	2.8	2.1	2.8	.6	1.2
Scandinavian	66.3	23.3	5.7	2.5	1.6	.7	.0
Dutch	65.7	22.3	7.0	2.3	1.6	.8	.3
German	63.9	22.9	6.7	2.3	3.1	.4	.6
French	62.1	23.5	6.8	2.3	2.9	.9	1.6

Ukrainian	59.8	27.4	6.4	2.7	2.5	.9	.4
Polish	54.5	28.3	9.0	3.4	3.3	1.2	.4
Russian	51.0	28.6	8.0	4.2	4.6	2.5	1.5
Italian	47.8	32.6	7.9	4.0	4.9	1.8	.9
Jewish	42.2	35.6	10.0	3.9	5.4	1.9	.9

Non-European Origin

Mexican	28.4	44.5	13.2	6.0	6.4	1.2	.4
Negro	27.4	53.4	12.2	4.0	2.1	.8	.1
Japanese	26.9	49.6	13.6	3.5	4.4	1.7	.3
West Indian	26.6	47.6	12.8	5.8	5.5	1.4	.3
Filipino	25.6	46.7	14.1	6.5	5.0	2.0	.3
Canadian Indian	24.3	46.9	11.6	7.8	7.2	.9	1.3
East Indian	23.4	48.0	14.8	5.6	5.2	2.5	.4
Chinese	22.9	50.9	13.3	3.8	5.8	2.3	.8
Inuit	20.3	52.4	13.8	5.9	5.8	2.1	.3

In our studies we also found, as illustrated in Table 9.6, that Jewish institutional completeness was high, while Scandinavian institutions were undeveloped.[6] The Jews maintained eight synagogues, four parochial schools, and more than a score of Jewish volunteer organizations. While some of the other groups also maintained many institutions, the Scandinavians especially provided only a token number of institutions. We found that Jewish institutions are strong in all areas of religion, education, and volunteer organization. Compared to the other ethnic groups in Winnipeg their institutions are as complete as any of the other ethnic groups, and more complete than most. These institutions should provide additional opportunity for interaction with in-group members, which in turn should boost in-group dating and endogamy.

Mate Selection and Cultural Identity

We began by saying that in-group dating and endogamy would be strongest within those groups who provided ethnic cultural support for their members. Farber's[9] ethnic family continuity would take place effectively within an ethnic subculture sustained by institutional support.

In Table 9.7 we see that endogamy leads the list of six cultural identity variables which are important to cultural identification. Endogamy is the most important of the two associational factors; choice of friends is important for about half of the groups, but not very important for some. Attendance at parochial schools is the most important of three ethnic institutional forms of participation. Regular participation in religious services was important for some groups, while few students participated in ethnic volunteer organizations. A majority of French students spoke French at home, but for the other students ethnic language use was of less importance.

We found that Jewish student attitudes toward in-group dating and endogamy were conservative and that they reported extensive in-group dating and high endogamy within their families. Table 9.5 shows that extensive Jewish attendance at parochial schools (74%), extensive choice of in-group friends (62.5%), and more support of ethnic organizations (28.6) than the other students seems to go hand in hand with extensive in-group dating (90.8%), and high endogamy (91.3%).

Table 9.6

A Comparison of Institutional Completeness (Religion, Parochial Education, Volunteer Associations) by Ethnic Groups

Ethnic Groups (Population, 1961 Census)	Social Institutions									
	Religion				Education				Associations	
	Members per capita	(No.)	Churches/ Synagogues per 1000 population	(No.)	Students per 1000 population	(No.)	Schools per 1000 population	(No.)	Per 1000 population	(No.)
Jewish (19 376)	.36	(7 000)	.42	(8)	.70	(1365)	.20	(4)	1.18	(23)
French (39 777)	.27	(10 700)	.22	(9)	1.08	(4300)	.25	(10)	.56	(22)
Ukrainian (53 918)	.23	(12 500)	.50	(27)	.04	(200)	.04	(2)	.58	(31)
German (50 206)	.26	(13 200)	.68	(34)	.18	(900)	.10	(5)	.18	(9)
Polish (24 904)	.16	(4 000)	.12	(3)	.00	(0)	.00	(0)	.24	(6)
Scandinavian (17 834)	.04	(800)	.11	(2)	.00	(0)	.00	(0)	.39	(7)

Table 9.7

Comparison of Ethnic Group Behavioural Rankings by Six Identity Factors
(Endogamy, Education, Religion, Friends, Language, Organizations)

	Composite Mean Behavioural Identity Rank	Behavioural Identity Factors (Percentages)					
		Endogamy	Parochial Education	Religious Participation	Choice of Friends	Language Use	Participation In Ethnic Organizations
1. French (F)	55.0	91.3(J)	79.1(F)	55.6(G)	62.5(J)	60.5(F)	28.6(J)
2. Jewish (J)	44.2	75.6(U)	74.0(J)	53.5(F)	48.8(F)	29.4(G)	22.9(U)
3. German (G)	40.8	72.0(B)	57.1(P)	46.4(P)	44.6(B)	21.8(U)	22.6(F)
4. Ukrainian (U)	36.8	65.4(F)	44.3(G)	43.6(U)	36.3(G)	14.3(P)	16.3(G)
5. Polish (P)	31.5	62.8(G)	41.1(U)	22.9(B)	15.9(U)	1.8(J)	12.7(P)
6. British (B)	29.3	57.1(S)	27.4(B)	14.7(S)	5.4(P)	0.0(S)	10.0(B)
7. Scandinavian (S)	16.4	53.2(P)	24.5(S)	7.2(J)	0.0(S)	0.0(B)	2.0(S)

French students reported high parochial school attendance (79.1%), French-language use (60.5%), religious participation (53.5%), and choice of in-group friends (48.8%). The Jewish and French students both showed high cultural identification. However, Jewish student attitudes toward out-group dating and intermarriage were negative, whereas French-student attitudes were much more open. Jewish participation in out-group dating and intermarriage was also minimal, while French students participated much more. Many students of both groups had attended parochial schools. However, Jewish students ranked high on endogamy and choice of in-group friends, while French students were much more involved in in-group language use and religious participation. Jewish students seemed to participate in associational activities more, of which dating and endogamy are much more an integral part. Jewish family support appears to be an important factor.

Driedger[5] found a direct correlation between ethnic cultural identity and willingness to marry into out-groups. When he measured degree of identification on his Ethnic Cultural Behavioral Identity (ECBI) index, he found that as identity went up, willingness to intermarry declined. Those who scored low on ethnic identity were also much more willing to intermarry. This would seem to show that identification with an ethnic culture is important for in-group dating and marriage as Lewin[11] suggested.

Conclusions

We began by saying with Farber[9] that the ethnic family as a mini-social system might continue the orderly replacement of the ethnic tradition by promoting in-group dating and marriage, or that it might open up to more universal permanent availability by increased interethnic dating and intermarriage. The first would operate more as a closed system, and the second as a more open family system.

We found that, in general, students tended to follow the open-availability model in their attitudes toward intergroup mate selection, but in practice they tended to follow the more closed orderly replacement pattern. In Canadian society it is not popular to make many distinctions in our selection of friends or potential dates. However, the culture, institutions, and values of ethnic tradition, even in the more assimilated groups, seem to retard extensive interethnic dating and intermarriage.

We also found that mate selection varied by ethnic group. Jewish students tended to follow a more closed, traditional, orderly replacement system, while Scandinavian students followed the more open universal-availability model. Jewish student attitudes indicated reluctance to date interethnically, and intermarriage was minimal. Scandinavian students dated freely across ethnic lines and they were open to considerable intermarriage, which in fact took place more and more. Students of other ethnic groups ranged between these two types, but they tended to support the open-availability model more.

We sought to explain these variations in dating and marriage patterns by arguing that attitudes and activity in dating and marriage take place within social systems. When the ethnic social system has strong in-group institutions; when its members identify with an ethnic counter-culture; and when they place greater social distance between themselves and others, then interethnic dating and intermarriage will be less frequent, because they are committed to the traditional orderly replacement of the family to perpetuate their in-group. We found that this was the case for the Jews. On the other hand, when such an ethnic counter-culture is minimal and the social system is not maintained, then the norms and values of the larger society will lead to universal permanent availability in dating and marriage. Scandinavian students followed this pattern.

We conclude that the extent of interethnic dating and intermarriage will depend on how well an ethnic group can keep its members committed to a strong ethnic social system. Traditional orderly replacement of the family is possible in the city as well as the country, as the Jews in Winnipeg have shown.

References

1. Breton, Raymond. "Institutional Completeness of Ethnic Communities and Personal Relations to Immigrants." *American Journal of Sociology* 70 (1964), pp. 193-205.
2. Comeau, Larry, and Driedger, Leo. "Opening and Closing in an Open Society." *Social Forces* 57 (1978).
3. Driedger, Leo. "In Search of Cultural Identity Factors: A Comparison of Ethnic Students." *Canadian Review of Sociology and Anthropology* 12 (1975), pp. 50-162.
4. Driedger, Leo. "Ethnic Self-Identity: A Comparison of In-group Evaluation." *Sociometry* 39 (1976), pp. 131-141.
5. Driedger, Leo. "Attitudes of Students Toward Immigrants of European and Non-European Origin," in Gurbachen Paul and S.M.A. Hameed, eds. *Multiculturalism in Canada: Third World Perspective.* Scarborough, Ontario: Prentice-Hall of Canada, 1978.
6. Driedger, Leo, and Church, Glenn. "Residential Segregation and Institutional Completeness: A Comparison of Ethnic Minorities." *Canadian Review of Sociology and Anthropology* 11 (1974), pp. 30-52.
7. Driedger, Leo, and Peters, Jacob. "Ethnic Identity and Social Distance: Toward Understanding Simmel's 'The Stranger.'" *Canadian Review of Sociology and Anthropology* 14 (1974), pp. 158-173.
8. Eshleman, J. Ross. *The Family: An Introduction.* Boston: Allyn and Bacon, Inc., 1974.
9. Farber, Bernard. *Family: Organization and Interaction.* San Francisco: Chandler Publishing Company, 1964.
10. Gans, Herbert J. *The Urban Dwellers: Group and Class in the Life of Italian Americans.* New York: Free Press of Glencoe, 1962.
11. Lewin, Kurt. *Resolving Social Conflicts.* New York: Harper and Brothers, 1948.
12. Ramu, G.N. and Johnson, Stuart D. *Introduction to Canadian Society: Sociological Analysis.* Toronto: Macmillan of Canada, 1976.
13. Simmel, Georg. *Conflict.* Trans. Kurt Wolff. Glencoe, Illinois: Free Press, 1955.
14. Vallee, Frank G. "Regionalism and Ethnicity: The French-Canadian Case," in Card, ed. *Perspectives on Regions and Regionalism.* Edmonton: University of Alberta, 1969, pp. 19-25.

10/Immigrants' Attitudes Toward their Children's Interethnic Marriages*

Peter D. Chimbos

Many articles and books have been written about the Dutch, Greek, and Czechoslovakian minorities in Canada, but the families of these groups, as such, have not been subject to study.[1] A review of the literature of ethnic groups in Canada indicates that the studies and writings on these three ethnic minorities have focussed primarily on their demographic problems and historical backgrounds,[2] but are limited as to the problems and other aspects of their family life. Although some studies have been done in the family life of other ethnic minorities[3] in Canada, we should not assume that what applies to one ethnic group applies equally well to all ethnic groups. The present study deals primarily with Dutch, Greek, and Slovak parental attitudes toward their children's ethnic exogamy. A comparative study of this kind can lead to further sociological research in the family life of Canadian minorities.

The Problem

Although there are no adequate data available on exogamous marriages, interethnic marriages among Canadians seem to be increasingly common especially on the part of the second generation. However, many immigrant parents do object to their children's marriages with someone outside their ethnic group and this usually results in a familial conflict. The objection to interethnic marriages by the immigrant parent is, perhaps, one of the characteristics of the prejudice he or she shows against the out-groups in the adopted

*Reprinted from *International Migration Review*, Vol. 5 (Spring 1971) by permission of the author and publisher. The data on which this paper is based are part of a larger study conducted by the author in "Ontario City." The study was supported by Canada Council research grants and carried on from June 1968 to July 1969. The author wishes to thank Dr. Anita Chen and Professor Victor Wightman for their advice and criticisms, and Randal Montgomery for editorial assistance.

country. But the parent may also be aware of the problems that mixed marriages will probably face during their life cycles. The preponderance of data that social scientists have suggests that interethnic marriages are often faced with peculiar obstacles, in addition to those that all marriages face.[4]

In this survey, the attitudes of the immigrants of three minority groups toward their children's interethnic marriages* were studied comparatively. The survey was confined to the Dutch, Greek, and Slovak immigrants of "Ontario City," Ontario.** Because of religious, linguistic, and historical distinctiveness of the three cultures that the immigrant parents represented, their attitudes toward their children's interethnic marriages were expected to differ along ethnic lines. It was also expected that the immigrants' attitudes toward interethnic marriages would be affected by such factors as their sex, their educational background, and whether they came from urban or rural areas in their native countries. In all known cultures men and women are assigned different roles and are expected to differ in their general outlook. The belief that education serves as a liberalizing influence was another factor in the formulation of our hypothesis. The immigrant's place in the continuum from urban to rural residence in the old country was also expected to relate to the degree of ease of adaptation to a new culture, inasmuch as urbanization tends to have many features in common throughout the Western world. The general hypothesis therefore was that: Dutch, Greek, and Slovak immigrants*** differ in their attitudes toward their children's interethnic marriages. It was also expected that the degree of positive or negative attitudes toward the interethnic marriage would be related to the immigrant's sex,

---

*In this study interethnic marriage refers to the marriage of the children of an immigrant to someone outside their own ethnic group.

**Fictitious Name. In 1969 "Ontario City" had approximately 100 000 inhabitants. Among these were approximately 80 Dutch families, 90 Greek families, and 240 Slovakian families.

***"Dutch immigrant" refers to the individual who was born in Holland and later emigrated to Canada. "Greek immigrant" refers to the individual who was born in Greece and later emigrated to Canada. "Slovakian immigrant" is a person who was born in the eastern part of Czechoslovakia and later emigrated to Canada. This part of the country which previously has been called Slovakia has a distinctive culture from the rest of Czechoslovakia.

educational attainment in the home country, and his or her rural-urban regional origin.

The Sample and Methodology

The sample for this survey was drawn from the following directories which contained most of the immigrant families in "Ontario City": (a) the Greek Orthodox community, (b) the membership list of the "Slovak League" and the membership list of St. Peter's Slovak Church, and (c) the Vice-Consulate of the Netherlands and the membership list of the Bethlehem Christian Reformed Church, which contained Dutch family names. The names of those immigrants who were not members of the ethnic community's social or religious organizations were obtained from the immigrant community leaders and other immigrants who knew the whereabouts of such persons in "Ontario City." Subjects were also located through their residence in neighbourhoods believed to be occupied by members of the three minority groups. The sampling units included both husband and wife because sex of the respondent was expected to be an important independent variable. The total number of married immigrant interviewees consisted of 130 Dutch, 150 Greeks, and 170 Slovaks.

The data for this study were obtained from personal interviews with Dutch, Greek, and Slovak immigrants of "Ontario City." The interview questions sought to elicit specific facts concerning the immigrant parents' attitudes toward their children's marriage with someone outside their ethnic group. An attempt was made to interview the spouses separately without any time intervals between the interviews. This was done to prevent any discussion of interviews by the spouses which could influence their answers.

Findings

The attitudes toward interethnic marriages were obtained by asking the immigrants to indicate if they would like their children to marry someone outside their ethnic group. Three questions attempted to ascertain the attitudes of the Dutch, Greek, and Slovak immigrants toward interethnic marriages. The first question was intended to ascertain the attitudes of the Dutch, Greek, and Slovak immigrants toward interethnic marriages. The first question was stated as follows: "If you had an unmarried, grown-up son would you be in favour of his marrying someone outside your ethnic group?" As Table 10.1 indicates, 2 (1.3%) of the 150 Greeks, 6 (3.5%) of the 170 Slovaks, and 39 (30.0%) of the 130 Dutch who answered this question would be "definitely" in favour of a son marrying outside the ethnic group. Also, a higher percentage of Dutch than Slovaks or Greeks stated that they "might" like their children marrying someone outside their ethnicity.

Table 10.1
Immigrants' Attitudes toward Their Son's Interethnic Marriage

	Dutch		Greeks		Slovak	
	%	No.	%	No.	%	No.
Definitely favoured interethnic marriage	30.0	(39)	1.3	(2)	3.5	(6)
Definitely objected to interethnic marriage	10.8	(14)	72.7	(109)	51.8	(88)
Stated that they "might" favour interethnic marriage	57.7	(75)	25.3	(38)	41.2	(70)
Don't know	1.5	(2)	0.7	(1)	3.5	(6)
Total	100	(130)	100	(150)	100	(170)

Generally speaking, the Dutch immigrants showed more favourable attitudes toward intermarriage than did the Slovaks or the Greeks. This suggests that perhaps the Dutch immigrants identify their culture more closely with the "dominant Anglo-Saxon" culture of Canada. However, the highest rate of objection was found among the Greeks. For example, from the Greek, 109 (72.7%) were "definitely" opposed to their son's intermarriage as compared to 88 (51.8%) of the Slovak, and 14 (10.8%) of the Dutch groups "definitely" opposing such a marriage. The high degree of objection found among the Greek respondents might be caused by either the relatively stronger identification with their native-Greek culture that Greek immigrants usually have in terms of such cultural values as patriotism and strong family ties,* or to the relatively greater cultural distance of Greek culture from the dominant "Anglo-Saxon" Canadian culture. This latter alternative might apply equally well to the Slovak immigrants. The reasons for their objection given by the 14 Dutch, 109 Greeks, and 88 Slovaks are stated in Table 10.2.

Table 10.2
Reasons Given by the Immigrants for Objecting to
Children's Interethnic Marriage*

	Dutch	Greeks	Slovak
Desire to maintain immigrant culture and religion	30.0%	95.0%	81.0%
Felt that families would be more stable when spouses have the same values	69.0%	8.0%	22.7%
Felt that people from their own ethnic group would make better husbands and wives	0.0%	9.0%	10.2%
Other reasons	2.6%	4.5%	3.5%

*In this tabulation involving subjective-choice answers by respondents, the percentage adds up to more than 100% because two or more responses were proffered sometimes.

Immigrants from the three minority groups who favoured interethnic marriage gave certain reasons for their unbiassed attitudes. The most common were: (a) the child's wishes should be considered as more important than parental wishes, and (b) interethnic marriage promotes cultural mixture and there it is necessary.

In the second question, the immigrants were asked how they would feel about intermarriage if the person concerned were a daughter rather than a son. There were not any marked differences in any of the

*An analysis of Greek immigrants' identification with their ethnic group in two American communities is contained in the studies of J.M. Stycos, *The Spartan Greeks of Bridgetown: Community Cohesion*, Common Ground 8, 1948, pp. 24-34, and Peter Chimbos, *The Hellenes of Missoula, Montana: Social Adjustment*, (M.A. Thesis, University of Montana, 1963).

three minority groups. For example, the percentage of immigrants who would "definitely" favour their daughter's marriage with someone outside the ethnic group was found to be as follows: Dutch 28.1%, Greeks 2%, and Slovaks 3% of the total number answering the question.* The same reasons for favouring or objecting to interethnic marriages given by the immigrants to Question 1 were given to Question 2 also.

Although a number of immigrants definitely objected to their son's or daughter's interethnic marriage, it was also found that there were children who had gone against their parents' wishes by marrying someone outside their ethnic group. Six out of eight (75%) Dutch who already had a married child or children and who "definitely" objected to interethnic marriage, stated that at least one of the children had married outside the ethnic group. Fifteen out of thirty-two (46.9%) Greeks who already had a married child or children, and who also "definitely" objected to interethnic marriage, stated that at least one of the children had practised ethnic exogamy. The corresponding proportion for the Slovaks was 48 out of 58 (82.7%). These findings are not necessarily marked especially for the Dutch and Slovak groups, because these two minorities showed more favourable attitudes toward interethnic marriage when religious endogamy, as indicated below, was the alternative. For example, for the six Dutch immigrant parents who objected to their child's marriage outside their ethnicity, and who at the same time stated that at least one of their children had practised ethnic exogamy four (66.7%), would "definitely" favour the child's marriage with someone outside the ethnic group, but one who has the same religion. From the 48 Slovaks belonging to this category, 45 (93.7%) would "definitely" favour the child's ethnic exogamy with someone who had the same religion, where of the 15 Greek parents only two (13.3%) would do so. The data to determine the distinction between ethnic and religious exogamy among the second generation were not obtained in this study.

Because religion was given as an important reason for objecting to interethnic marriage, especially among Greeks and Slovaks, the

---

*See the corresponding percentage of immigrants who would "definitely" favour their son's interethnic marriage in Table 10.1.

immigrants were asked what their attitudes would be if the person their son or daughter desired to marry was outside the ethnic group, but had the same religion. The question was stated as follows: "If you had a grown-up son or daughter would you be in favour of his or her marrying outside your ethnic group but with one who has the same religion?" Table 10.3 indicates the marked differences of response especially between the Dutch and Slovak immigrants. In the Dutch group the favourable attitudes toward intermarriage increased from 30.0% to 60.8% and among the Slovaks from 3.5% to 90%, where in the Greek group they increased only from 1.3% to 4%. But to this question a higher percentage of Greeks answered "maybe" when it came to religious endogamy. This indicates the strong determination of the Greek immigrants to keep their culture alive in a foreign land, whereas religion seems to be the main concern for the other two minority groups.

Table 10.3

Attitudes Favouring Children's Intermarriage with Someone Outside the Nationality, But Who Has the Same Religion

	Dutch		Greeks		Slovak	
	%	No.	%	No.	%	No.
Definitely favoured interethnic marriages	60.8	(79)	4.0	(6)	90.0	(153)
Definitely objected to interethnic marriages	6.2	(8)	56.0	(84)	0.6	(1)
Stated that they "might" favour interethnic marriages	26.9	(35)	39.3	(59)	8.2	(14)
Don't know	6.1	(8)	0.7	(1)	1.2	(2)
Total	100	(130)	100	(150)	100	(170)

A breakdown of the overall results by sex of the respondent seemed to have some importance as Table 10.4 indicates. A higher percentage of husbands than wives expressed favourable attitudes toward their son's or daughter's interethnic marriage in all three minority groups. However, an ethnic endogamy was preferred by a much higher percentage of Greek than Dutch or Slovak wives. It must be noted that no marked differences were indicated in attitudes with respect to sex when the immigrants were asked to say how they would feel about interethnic marriage if the child was a daughter.

The immigrant's educational background in the home country was considered as a possible control variable in this study. Objection to intermarriage from those with elementary school education in the sample was found to be as follows: 2 (12.5%) Dutch, 78 (74.3%) Greeks, and 52 (55.3%) Slovaks. From those with secondary school education, the objections came from 7 (7.9%) Dutch, 25 (69.4%) Greeks, and 32 (51.6%) Slovaks. It was also noted that all four Greeks who belong to the 13- to 15-year educational level objected to interethnic marriage, but this should not be considered a significant finding as the number is too small for making generalizations. Objections to intermarriage from the 13- to 15-year educational level for the other two groups included 4 (16.7%) Dutch and 2 (28.6%) Slovaks. Note that the same rank order of ethnicity is maintained in each educational level. It seems therefore, that in this respect nationality rather than educational background is the important factor.

It was expected that the immigrants' attitudes toward interethnic marriages would differ with respect to their rural-urban residence in the home country. The immigrant was asked to indicate what type (size)* of community he or she lived in most of the time before coming to Canada. It was found among the Greeks and Slovaks that the larger the community they came from the higher the percentage of objection to interethnic marriages. It seems possible that immigrants who came from the culturally disadvantaged communities in their native country would be more amenable to ethnic exogamy (especially with native-born Canadians) as a means of achieving a "respectable" status within the Canadian community. A further investigation is needed to confirm or reject this hypothesis. There were no marked differences in attitudes among the Dutch with respect to rural-urban background. Table 10.5 indicates attitudes toward interethnic marriage by nationality and size of community in the home country.

---

*The size of the community was classified according to the population. For example, village (less than 3000), town (3000 - 10 000), city (10 000 and over).

Table 10.4
Attitudes toward Intermarriage by Sex of Respondent

	Males						Females					
	Dutch		Greek		Slovak		Dutch		Greek		Slovak	
	%	No.	%	No.	%	No.	%	No.	%	No.	%	No.
Definitely favoured interethnic marriage	32.9	(20)	1.4	(1)	3.8	(4)	24.6	(17)	1.3	(1)	3.1	(2)
Definitely objected to interethnic marriage	8.2	(5)	64.4	(47)	47.6	(50)	13.0	(9)	80.5	(62)	58.5	(38)
Stated that they "might" favour interethnic marriage	55.7	(34)	34.2	(25)	42.9	(45)	59.5	(41)	16.9	(13)	38.4	(25)
Don't know	3.2	(2)	0.0	(0)	5.7	(6)	2.9	(2)	1.3	(1)	0.0	(0)
Total	100	(61)	100	(73)	100	(105)	100	(69)	100	(77)	100	(65)

Table 10.5
Attitudes toward Interethnic Marriages by Nationality and Size of Community of Origin

	Village						Town						City					
	Dutch		Greek		Slovak		Dutch		Greek		Slovak		Dutch		Greek		Slovak	
	%	No.	%	No.	%	No.	%	No.	%	No.	%	No.	%	No.	%	No.	%	No.
Definitely favoured inter-ethnic marriage	30.2	(3)	1.0	(1)	2.9	(4)	14.3	(4)	4.5	(1)	12.5	(2)	35.6	(21)	0.0	(0)	0.0	(0)
Definitely objected to interethnic marriage	16.3	(7)	67.7	(67)	47.1	(65)	14.3	(4)	81.8	(18)	68.8	(11)	3.4	(2)	79.3	(23)	75.0	(12)
Stated that they "might" favour interethnic marriage	44.2	(19)	29.3	(29)	45.7	(63)	67.8	(19)	13.7	(3)	12.5	(2)	57.6	(34)	20.7	(6)	25.0	(4)
Don't know	9.3	(4)	2.0	(2)	4.3	(6)	3.6	(1)	0.0	(0)	6.2	(1)	3.4	(2)	0.0	(0)	0.0	(0)
Total	100	(43)	100	(99)	100	(138)	100	(28)	100	(22)	100	(16)	100	(59)	100	(29)	100	(16)

242 / Interethnic Marriages

The age of the immigrant at the time of immigration and attitudes toward intermarriage were also considered in this study. There seemed to be a general trend among the Greek and the Slovak groups which indicated that the younger the age at which the immigrants came to Canada, the lower the percentage objecting to their children's interethnic marriages. Among the Dutch the age group objecting to intermarriage did not show any marked association. However, these finds should not be considered as marked since the size of the sample of those very young at immigration was too small for generalizing.

The actual number of interethnic marriages of the samples in the three minority groups at the time of the study was also obtained from the immigrants. From the 130 Dutch, 27 (20.8%) were married outside their ethnic group. From the 170 Slovaks, 16 (9.4%) were married outside their ethnic group, whereas only 6 (4%) of the 150 Greeks acknowledged ethnic exogamy. Among the Greeks and the Slovaks the rate of interethnic marriage was higher among males, whereas among the Dutch the rate was a little higher among females. A comparative study with larger samples of ethnic exogamous marriages would be needed to get at the reasons for the differences in the sex ratio.

The immigrants were also asked to indicate if at least one of their children had married outside the ethnic group. Slovaks had a higher percentage of children married outside their ethnic group than the Dutch or Greeks. For example, 86 (50.6%) of the Slovaks stated that at least one of their children had married outside the ethnic group, whereas 32 (25%) of the Dutch and 17 (11.4%) of the Greeks stated that such a marriage had occurred. However, the differences of children's interethnic marriages between Slovaks and the other two minorities should not be considered as marked, for the reason that the Slovak immigrants were the older group of the three and therefore had more older married children than the Dutch or Greeks.

In this study an attempt was also made to find out how the immigrants who were married outside their ethnic group would feel about their children's interethnic marriages. It was found that although certain immigrants had married outside their ethnic group they would definitely object to their children's interethnic marriages or even to saying that they "might" favour such a marriage. For example, in the Dutch exogamous group consisting of 27 immigrants, 3 (11.1%)

"definitely" objected, 16 (59.3%) said that they "might," and 8 (29.6%) stated that they would favour such a marriage. From the 6 Greeks who were married outside their nationality, 2 (33.3%) "definitely" objected, 4 (66.7%) said that they "might," but none would "definitely" favour such a marriage. Among the 16 Slovaks who had married outside their nationality, 4 (25%) "definitely" objected, 11 (68.7%) said that they "might," one did not have an opinion, but none "definitely" favoured such a marriage. The number of immigrants who had married outside their ethnic group, and who "definitely" objected to their children's interethnic marriage, was too small for making generalizations as to the reasons for their objection. An exploratory study with larger samples of immigrants who have practised ethnic exogamy is needed in order to (a) make meaningful comparisons of the rates of positive and negative attitudes toward their children's interethnic marriages, (b) get at the reasons for their objection to such marriages, and (c) find out how the immigrant's attitudes toward children's interethnic marriages are related to certain social variables, such as gender, economic status, educational achievement, social relationships with the spouse, and age at immigration.

Summary

In this investigation, it was found that the highest percentage (30) of favourable responses toward children's interethnic marriages came from the Dutch ethnic group. Almost none of the Greek and Slovak respondents approved. Similarly, less than 11% of the Dutch definitely objected to their children's exogamy compared to 73% of the Greeks and 52% of the Slovaks. When asked to consider ethnic exogamy but within the same religion, the differences between Greeks and Slovaks become highly accentuated, although this alternative had little effect on Dutch responses.

The females, in all three groups, indicated a higher percentage of objection and reluctance toward their children's interethnic marriage than the males. The educational background was not an important factor among the Dutch, but among the Greeks and Slovaks the higher percentage of immmigrants objecting to intermarriage came from the lower educational levels. With respect to the immigrant's rural-urban background in the home country, it was found among the Greeks and Slovaks that the larger the community they came from, the higher the rate of objection to interethnic marriage. It was also found that some of the immigrants who already had practised exogamy definitely objected to their children marrying outside their ethnic group.

References

1. Elkin, Frederick. *The Family in Canada*. Canadian Conference on the Family, 1968, p. 59.
2. A few examples of these studies are: Peterson, William. *Planned Migration*. Berkeley: University of California Press, 1955; Thomas, Alan. "Differentials in the Integration Process of Dutch and Italian Immigrants in Edmonton," M.S.W. Thesis, University of Alberta, 1964; National Statistical Services of Greece. *Emigration from Greece in 1962*, in *International Labour Review*, 88, No. 5 (November 1963), pp. 518-521; Cuten, Constantine. *Slovaks in Slovakia and Canada*. Toronto: Canadian Slovak League, 1965; Kirschbaum, J.M. *Slovaks in Canada*. Canadian Ethnic Press Association of Ontario, 1967; Klymasz, Robert. "Canadianization of Slavic Surnames." M.A. Thesis, University of Manitoba, 1960; Vanderhil, B.G. *Pitt Polder: Dutch Enterprise on Canadian Soil*. Canadian Geographical Journal 65 (September 1962), pp. 94-99.
3. For example, such studies would include: Chiel, A. *The Jews in Manitoba*. Toronto: University of Toronto Press, 1961; Kosa, J. *Land of Choice, The Hungarians in Canada*, Toronto: University of Toronto Press, 1957; Lewis, Claudie. *Doukhobor Children and Family Life*, in H.B. Hawthorn, ed. *The Doukhobors of British Columbia*. Vancouver: University of British Columbia, 1952, pp. 97-121; Stefanow, M. "A Study of Inter-marriage of Ukrainians in Saskatchewan." Master's Thesis, University of Saskatchewan.
4. Berry, Brewton. *Race and Ethnic Relations*, 3rd ed. Boston: Houghton Mifflin Company, 1968, p. 294.

Part IV
Marital Conflicts
And Dissolution

In this section, marriage is examined as a problematic institution, whose functioning is beset with acute tensions and conflicts. These conflicts and tensions might lead to dissolution and divorce. How can one conceptualize this phenomenon? One may either perceive this as an aberration and a malfunctioning of an otherwise successful social institution or one may see in it symptoms of more radical social change, implying the emergence of new forms and structures performing the old functions in a new context. In short, one might conceptualize the situation as one of marital pathology or one of radical change. Neither view can be sustained without assembling relevant evidence.

Monica Boyd examines the sociological context of marital dissolution. She notes that, in this century, Canada has been recording a rise, both in the number and the rate of divorces. She asks the question: "How can one explain this rise?" She finds the explanation confined merely to the marital system itself as inadequate, and goes beyond it to identify large-scale causal processes, such as urbanization and industrialization as they affect the family, the social effects of World War II, and the changes in relevant law. She finds that divorce does not occur to the same extent in all groups in Canada. According to her, factors more favourable to divorce are: low age at marriage, low income, female participation in the work force, urban residence, being non-Roman Catholic, accelerated family building, and a broken family of origin. She looks at the 1971 Census data on separated as well as divorced and currently married Canadians, and finds that the modalities of terminating unworkable marriages differed in relation to such factors as education, religious affiliation, ethnic group, and mother tongue. She finds the relationship between social variables and the divorce rate to be mutual and reciprocal. She concludes that divorce results in female-headed families and reduced family income, which have an impact on the organization of the family and the welfare of the children.

Kwok Chan's paper of wife-beating or wife-battery is in the terrain of marital pathology. His study is based on 194 files relating to Women in Transition, a shelter residence for wives and children fleeing from husband/father violence. This institution is located in Toronto, first set up in 1974 to provide shelter for women facing two kinds of crisis—marital crisis and wife-beating. Thus, the paper is concerned with intrafamily violence, and its data reveal patterns and trends similar to those for wife-beating in the United States. Recognizing the unrepresentativeness of the data, Chan tries to salvage as much tentative theoretical insight as possible. The paper demonstrates a significant association between wife-battery and extreme poverty, and economic and socio-psychological dependence on the husband. Most of the samples scored very low on educational attainment, less than half going beyond Grade 10. This explains their economic dependence, as they could not readily be absorbed into the work force. Chan finds a hypothetical relationship between the variables of class, stress, and violence, but he is aware of the need for further research and testing in this regard. He also suggests that intrafamily violence may be related to the wider alienation in society, "an endemic feature and systematic product of our existing socio-economic structure." Finally, the paper draws attention to the paradoxical process of routinization and normalization of a pathology such as wife-battery. This explains why victims of wife-battery go back to their homes.

The ultimate victims of divorce are the children. Sally Palmer discusses the initial impact of divorce on children. Her study is based on data collected during interviews with these families conducted for the Official Guardian as part of divorce proceedings. Her finding is that the arrangements for children in these cases reflected more the convenience of the parents than the needs of the children. The aspects examined include custody, financial support, visiting with absent parents, and adjustment of children to the situation. She argues that children's needs are better served if the mother is made custodian. She finds that absent parents failed to visit children regularly. On the whole, the children were able to adjust themselves to the situation, and delinquency, an index of serious maladjustment, did not become a significant problem. The paper suggests that both courts and parents should do more than they have been doing to serve the needs of the children of the divorcing families.

An important question to be asked about marital breakdown is: "What are the factors underlying this phenomenon?" Whitehurst, Booth, and Hanif address themselves to this question in their collaborative paper. The authors investigate the role of such factors as changing sex roles, sexuality, careers, children, and division of household labour in the decisions to separate and divorce. They use for their sample 369 Ontario adults of whom 36% were male. The paper found that the wives involved complained that their husbands did not provide any support in household chores, made aggressive demands, behaved in a domineering way, and maltreated them verbally as well as physically. Wives also felt that they were allowed no participation in major decision-making. Husbands, in their turn, countercharged that wives failed to give tender solace and adequate sexual gratification. It was found that husbands either wanted wives to do both outside work and housework, thus being subject to "double-bind," or refused support to their wives in their career problems. This implied that changing sex roles was a critical factor in marital break-up for the sample studies. They found evidence that children were a significant deterrent factor in separation or divorce. Separation cases were associated with loneliness, social isolation, and companion deprivation. Women had greater economic problems than men. The authors conclude that as women become increasingly aware of their own capacities to do without men, husband dominance could end, at least for some groups.

11/The Social Demography of Divorce in Canada*

Monica Boyd

Imagine a society in which there are approximately 9 marriages and two divorces for every 1000 persons. Now imagine a society in which the divorce rate has increased 35 times during the past 50 years. In both cases, Canada has been described. The first set of figures implies that family formation rather than family dissolution predominates in Canada today. But, the second set of figures indicates that there are growing numbers of Canadians who experience marital dissolution.

This increase in divorce in Canada is paralleled by the increased attention paid to divorce by social scientists. Although marital dissolution is also pertinent to social work and law, much of the recent research utilizes either a demographic or sociological perspective. Demographers, or students of population, provide and analyse information on divorce which is collected either through the Vital Registration system or in the censuses. Most often they focus on rates of divorce, changes therein, and the relationship between divorce and population composition. Sociologists interested in marriage and divorce often investigate the association between divorce and social roles, or socio-economic and socio-psychological factors. They also may assess the impact of divorce on the institution of marriage and the family.

In reality, however, these distinctions between demographic and sociological investigation into divorce are often blurred by the commonality of questions asked in both disciplines: What are the trends in divorce and why? Who gets a divorce? What are the consequences of divorce? Thus, in answering these three questions, this paper will draw from both demographic and sociological materials. How-

*Data analysis reported in this paper was funded by the faculty computer grant of Carleton University. The author wishes to thank Mary Francis McKenna and Debby McLaughlin for their patience and assistance in the typing of background research materials. This paper was completed in October, 1977.

ever, it will adopt the social demographic framework. This perspective includes both demographic and social phenomena within its domain of inquiry.[19] But it emphasizes divorce as the dependent variable, or as that phenomenon to be explained, and focusses upon sociological phenomena only to the extent that they are independent variables affecting divorce. The focus of attention, therefore, will be on answering the first two questions: What are the trends in divorce and why? and Who gets a divorce? Only a cursory look is given to the third question, which inquires into the sociological consequences of divorce.

Divorce in Canada: Demographic Trends and Social Causes

What are the temporal trends of divorce in Canada? As noted earlier, over a 50-year period, the Canadian divorce rate increased 35 times, from a rate of 6.4 per 100 000 persons in 1926 to 222.0 per 100 000 in 1975 (the last year for which published data are available). This increase, however, is neither monotonic nor linear over time. The years immediately following World War II show a sharp upswing in the divorce rate, from 32 divorces per 100 000 persons in 1944 to 65.4 divorces per 100 000 persons in 1947. While the divorce rate never returned to the prewar level, it dipped to a low of 36 in 1961. Such fluctuations in the divorce rate, however, seem minor in comparison with changes in the late 1960's and early 1970's. In 1968 the divorce rate in Canada was 54.8 divorces per 100 000 persons; by 1975 the rate had skyrocketed to 222.0 divorces per 100 000 or more than a fourfold increase.[40]

Although changes in the crude divorce rate, defined as the number of divorces in a given year per 100 000 mid-year population, can reflect changes in the age composition of a population, it is clear that the temporal variations in divorce rates in Canada are due to social factors rather than demographic ones. A number of explanations may be given for the long-term upward movement of divorce rates in a society such as Canada (see Reference 13. Duberman, pages 181-185), but the prevalent sociological explanation sees industrialization and urbanization as underlying the increase in divorce rates.[13,22,25,26,42] The disruptive impact of industrialization and urbanization upon marriage may be mediated in several ways: by creating a companionship family structure which is more vulnerable to dissolution; by exposing individuals in marriages to a diversity of experiences which may strain the persistence of love throughout a marriage (see Reference 13. Duberman pages 181-183); and by requiring the restructuring of marital roles as a result of social change in general and female employment in particular.[22/26/42]

While marital stresses and strains resulting from industrialization and urbanization may underlie the overall upward trend in Canadian divorce rates, at least two specific events account for the upswings in 1946-1947 and after 1968: notably, World War II and changes in the Canadian divorce laws. Marriage rates rose briefly during the early part of World War II. How long the couples had known each other prior to marriage is uncertain, but popular images of this era suggest that some of these wartime marriages were hastily contracted. In addition, wartime separations appear to have caused adjustment problems.[42] As a result of these wartime conditions, the number of marital dissolutions rose after the war ended.

The increase in divorce after 1968 in Canada also is induced socially inasmuch as it reflects the liberalization of divorce laws in Canada.[29] Prior to 1968 most provinces had their own divorce legislation which specified conditions under which divorce might be obtained. Two provinces, Quebec and Newfoundland, had no divorce laws, but rather relied upon acts of Parliament to dissolve marriages.[4/27/29/44] Conditions for obtaining a divorce were stringent, and in many provinces the main ground was adultery. Fewer than 1000 divorces were granted each year prior to 1932; by 1967-1968 the number was only slightly more than 11 000 annually. The limited grounds for divorce coupled with social sanctions against family dissolution not only limited the number of divorces granted in Canada but also induced many Canadians to obtain divorces in the United States or Mexico.[4/29] As a result, the small numbers of divorces granted in Canada prior to 1969 must be regarded as severe underestimates of the number of couples either desiring divorce but failing to meet the legal requirements, or obtaining divorces outside the country.

On July 2, 1968 the more liberal federal Divorce Act 1968 was enacted; it took precedent over the previously existing provincial legislation. The response was immediate. Between 1967 and 1969 the number of divorces more than doubled, and by 1975 over 50 000 divorces were granted.[40] The crude divorce rate similarly increased, rising from a rate of 54.8 in 1968 to 222.0 in 1975. Since these increases clearly reflect the introduction of a new law rather than demographic changes in population composition, a closer examination of the 1968 Divorce Act and its impact on the incidence of divorce is warranted.

The 1968 Divorce Act and Divorce Trends, 1969-1975

In general, divorce legislation is based on one or more of the following principles: 1) the fault principle; 2) the failure principle; 3) divorce by consent; 4) divorce on demand.[17] In Canada, the Divorce Act of 1968 is based on both the fault principle and the failure principle. The fault principle upholds the right of a spouse to a divorce if his or her partner is guilty of a fundamental breach of marital obligations. As specified in Section III of the 1968 Divorce Act, four fault-related grounds for divorce are: 1) adultery; 2) sodomy, bestiality, rape, or a homosexual act; 3) entering into a form of marriage with another person; and 4) physical or mental cruelty of such a kind as to render continued co-habitation intolerable.[17/44] Provided that the husband and wife are living separate and apart, the failure principle embodied in Section IV of the 1968 Divorce Act permits a petition for divorce on the ground that there has been a permanent breakdown of marriage by reason of one or more of the following circumstances: 1) lengthy imprisonment of the respondent (spouse) for a period of at least three years preceding the petition for divorce; 2) gross addiction of the respondent for a period of not less than three years to alcohol or narcotics; 3) disappearance of the respondent with no knowledge or information by the petitioner as to his or her whereabouts for a period of not less than 3 years; 4) non-consummation of the marriage for a period of at least a year because of the refusal of the respondent; 5) living separate and apart for a period of (a) five years if the parting occurred by reason of the respondent's desertion of the petitioner, and (b) three years if the parting occurred for reasons other than desertion.[17/44]

The Divorce Act of 1968 thus introduced a variety of grounds for divorce which could be used either singly or in combination in a petition for divorce. That this Divorce Act greatly facilitated divorce is shown in the sharp rise of the divorce rates and numbers of divorces following 1968, and in changes of the grounds used in divorce petitions. The overall increase in national divorce rates between 1968 and 1975 is described above, but changes in provincial divorce rates also occurred. Between 1968 and 1975 the rates increased in all provinces with the two highest increases in the crude divorce rates occurring in Quebec and Newfoundland where there were no divorce courts prior to 1968, and where divorce was obtained only by an act of Parliament (See Reference 4. Basavarajappa, pages 48-49; also References 28 and 40).

The Divorce Act of 1968 also changed the grounds for divorce petitions. Prior to July 2, 1968, adultery was the primary ground for divorce in Canada, but in 1969 it accounted for only 21% of the divorces granted. Separation and desertion, based on the principle of marital breakdown rather than the fault principle, were the grounds for half of the divorces in 1969. The intensity of their use reveals that the principle of marital breakdown in the 1968 Divorce Act facilitated the legal dissolution of marriages which in fact had been inoperative for a number of years. The diminishing backlog of divorce cases held up by pre-1968 conditions in turn is partly responsible for some of the changes in divorce statistics between 1969 and 1975. Divorces based on the principle of marital failure or breakdown have decreased from 55% of all divorces in 1969 to 39% in 1977. Divorces using offenses under the fault principle have increased from 45% of all divorces in 1969 to 61% in 1975. Some, if not all, of this shift can be explained by the processing of long-duration marriages which were not dissolved prior to 1968, but which satisfied the conditions of separation and desertion as embodied in the marital breakdown principle. Since 1969, the median duration of marriages dissolved by divorce had declined from 14.9 years to 11.4 years in 1975. Despite these declines in mean duration, however, most marriages which are legally dissolved in Canada are not short-lived. Only one-eighth of the divorces in 1975 were granted to marriages lasting less than 5 years and over one-third of the legally dissolved marriages had lasted 15 years or longer (see Reference 40, Table 19).

What will occur in the future with respect to divorce trends in Canada is only speculation. Prior to 1968, Canada generally had much lower divorce rates than the United States or Western European Countries.[29/42] Since the 1968 Divorce Act, Canadian divorce rates have been approximately one-quarter of the United States divorce rates (see Reference 22. Larson, Table 2.2), but it is probably unreasonable to expect that Canadian rates will grow to equal those of the United States, given Canada's large Roman-Catholic population and the possibility of differences between the two countries with respect to attitudes towards marriage and divorce.[29] However, the upward trend of divorce since the 1968 Divorce Act suggests at least some continued increase in the numbers and rates of divorce in Canada. Any future liberalization of divorce legislation also might increase the incidence of divorce in Canada. Divorce legislation is undergoing review in the near future, and, in this regard, both the Advisory Council on the Status of Women[1] and Hahlo[17] writing in the Law Reform Commission Report on Divorce, 1975 recommend that marriage breakdown be the only ground for divorce. Divorce on demand is unlikely as it is considered to be "the most radical of all possible divorce reform" (see Reference 17. Hahlo, page 55), and hence the most controversial. Certainly public opinion is divided. An October 1975 Gallup Poll indicates that 49% of all adult Canadians and 54% of the non-Roman Catholic pollsters agreed with the idea of "no fault divorce" where only the needs of the concerned parties are assessed, and where no effort is made to assess guilt or innocence. Disapproval of the idea was voiced by 38% of those polled, with 48% of Roman Catholics disapproving compared to 31% of non-Roman Catholics.

Factors Affecting Divorce

Although divorce is a more frequent occurrence in Canada today than in the past, not every couple obtains a divorce. Rather, studies of divorce in North America show that divorce is a selective process. People with certain characteristics appear more prone to obtain a divorce than people without these characteristics.

What are the factors affecting divorce in Canada? Studies addressing this question are embarrassingly few in number[41] and generally adopt two approaches: 1) correlation of divorce rates with other information available from either vital statistics or census reports;[4/28/31] or 2) surveys of individuals which ascertain reasons for divorce.[27/33/34] From these studies as well as those conducted in the United States, the following factors are shown to have a negative impact on marital stability: early age at marriage;[8/11/16/27] low income,[10/11/12/16/18] non-Roman Catholic religion and interfaith marriage;[4/8/23/31] urban residence and size of city;[28/31] previous divorce;[23] brief duration of contact between partners prior to marriage;[15] premarital pregnancy, accelerated family building, childlessness, low fertility, and the presence of school-age children;[8/9/11/15/26] broken parental home;[8/24/30/33] dissatisfaction with the marital role;[11] and psychological factors.[33]

As noted earlier, not all of these factors have been studied in Canada with respect to divorce. Research to date shows a relationship between divorce and urban-rural residence, Roman Catholic religion, age at marriage, income, family-building patterns, broken family of origin, and socio-psychological factors. In their examination of the covariation of divorce rates with census data, Peters[28] and Roberts and Krishnan[31] find that provinces with high proportions of urban populations have higher divorce rates. The reasons for these findings are not given, although such results are compatible with the general theory that industrialization and urbanization exert a deleterious effect on family stability. Conversely the proportion of Roman Catholics in provincial populations is associated with lower divorce rates.[4/31] Here, the proscription of divorce by the Roman Catholic Church would appear to account for this relationship.

Throughout North American research, early age at marriage and low income emerge as two variables consistently associated with divorce. In her study of 291 Ontario couples who divorced between 1963 and 1965, Palmer[27] observes that the average age at marriage of these couples is much younger than that of married couples in Canada. Vital Statistics data show the persistence of this relationship. Of the Canadian divorces in 1975, 43% of the wives had been married before the age of 20 and 66% of the husbands married before age 25 (see Reference 40, Table 15). Young age at marriage is conducive to divorce, in part because it is associated with low income, low education, premarital pregnancy, and number of children, all of which are factors making for marital instability. However, since the relationship between age at marriage and divorce persists after controlling for these other variables,[8] it is likely that young age at marriage is conducive to divorce because it indicates the relative immaturity of the partners at the time of marriage.[27/33]

In addition to age at marriage, poverty is also a major factor in marital instability. Palmer[27] finds that the divorcing families in her

Ontario study were worse off economically than the general population because of the lower incomes of husbands and the resulting necessity of the wives to work. Low income is associated with marital breakdown because lack of income is related to high rates of unemployment, adverse living conditions, deteriorated neighbourhoods, poor health, lack of community resources, all of which tend to undermine the stability of families (see Reference 10. Chilman, page 57). Low incomes of the husband also create pressures for the wife to enter the labour force. Female employment outside the home in turn is a significant correlate of divorce rates in Canada,[31] perhaps because wives with income independent of their husband's earnings are less likely to be tied to their marriage.[23/18]

Income, of course, is but one indicator of socio-economic status. In her study of divorce in Ontario, Palmer[27] also finds that divorcing couples have low-education and low-occupational status. However, these variables in turn are associated with low income and with early age at marriage. Studies in the United States show that when the impact of age at marriage and other variables is taken into account, the relationship between low education and divorce disappears.[8] The relationship between low education, low occupational status, and separation or divorce also disappears when income is taken into account.[12]

Premarital pregnancy, number of children born, and timing of these births are additional factors affecting divorce. Palmer[27] finds that divorcing couples in Ontario were burdened with children sooner than the average couple, although no information is given as to how many of these might be premarital conceptions. United States studies suggest, but do not conclusively confirm, that both premarital pregnancy and rapid and frequent childbearing are conducive to divorce, because of the financial strains which they introduce into a marriage.[11/15]

Marriages may fail not only because of early age at marriage, low income, and financial stress exacerbated by early childbearing, but also because the propensity to divorce is transmitted across generations. In his study of 96 Ontario couples, Schlesinger[33] finds a tendency for divorce and separation to be a family pattern transmitted across generations. Although the evidence is not conclusive, other United States studies have also found support for the contention that offspring of a broken family are in turn more likely to experience marital instability than are offspring of an intact family. At least five reasons exist for the disruptive influence which broken parental marriages exert upon their children's marriages: 1) social or biological inheritance of personality problems; 2) lower economic status in the family of origin; 3) improper social control by the family of origin; 4) inculcation of permissive attitudes toward divorce; and 5) inappropriate sex-role socialization.[30]

In addition to young age at marriage, low income, reproductive behaviour, and transmission of marital instability across generations, a number of other factors affect divorce in Canada. In his study of 96 couples in Ontario, Schlesinger[33] asked the previously divorced to give their reasons for divorce. In order of frequency, the reasons were: emotional incompatibility; psychopathology such as neurosis, alcoholism, mental illness, physical violence, incompatibility in terms of lifestyle and life goals; infidelity; immaturity; irresponsibility; and inability to hold employment. The first and the last two reasons once again confirm the earlier observed association between divorce, age at marriage, and financial status.

Who Are the Divorced and Separated in Canada? Results of the 1971 Census

The increasing rates of divorce and the factors associated with divorce in Canada imply not only that the proportion and numbers of divorced Canadians are growing, but also that the divorced population differs from the currently married population with respect to socio-economic characteristics. As will be shown below, census data support both these contentions and in turn suggest some sociological consequences of divorce.

In Canada, the increases in divorce rates are parallelled by an increase in the population who are enumerated as divorced. Reflecting the social sanctions against divorce and the difficulty of obtaining one, only 661 Canadians were divorced in 1901 according to the census. By 1971, Canada's divorced population was officially enumerated at 175 115 persons or 1.2% of the population age 15 and over. The small population enumerated in census, however is misleading. Census data provide information on Canada's population at one point in time, and since divorced people may marry or die, a census will always underestimate the actual experience of divorce.

Partly reflecting the small numbers of the divorced at any one point in time, little attention has been directed to examining the socio-demographic characteristics of the divorced in Canada. But an equally important reason for the failure of social scientists to intensively examine data on the divorced in Canada is the absence of published data. For the first time in Canadian history, this situation is remedied by the release of Public Use sample tapes from the 1971 Census of Population. Using this data, it is possible to answer the question: Who are the divorced and separated in Canada? and How do they differ socio-economically from the currently married population?

In order to answer these questions, data are presented in Table 11.1 for the ever-married population excluding those of very young age (15-24) and the older ages (65 and older) where sample numbers become very small. Table 11.1 also presents data for separated people in Canada. The use of separation as a mechanism to dissolve marriage is a much-neglected topic in Canada, primarily because there is no vital registration system for collecting information on legal separations and no accurate way of assessing informal separations initiated by agreement or desertion. Data from the Public Use tape suggest that of the age group 25-64, separation is more common than divorce (Table 11.1, first line). However, it cannot be inferred that marriages are dissolved more by permanent separations than by legal divorce. Some of the separated persons in Table 11.1 may simply be fulfilling requirements of living apart in order to petition later for divorce on the marital-breakdown principle. Some of the previously divorced population may have remarried (an option not available to separated persons) by the time of the 1971 census, thus removing themselves from the enumerated divorced population.

Table 11.1
Characteristics by Marital Status and Sex,
Ever-Married Population, Age 25-64, Canada, 1971

Characteristics, Percent[a] and Means	Females			Males		
	Married	Separated	Divorced	Married	Separated	Divorced
Sample N	7375	334	195	7589	259	146
Age	100	100	100	100	100	100
25-34	32	29	29	29	30	22
35-44	29	29	32	28	28	25
45-54	25	29	21	25	24	35
55-64	14	12	18	17	18	18
Mean, Years	41.2	41.8	42.2	42.3	42.2	44.2
Age at First Marriage	100	100	100	100	100	100
Before 20	23	29	35	5	8	10
20-24	51	46	45	45	49	44
25+	25	25	21	50	43	46
Mean, Years	22.5	22.4	21.4	25.6	24.7	24.4

Place of 1971 Residence						
30 000+	58	73	75	58	69	66
Urban, < 30 000	19	16	14	20	16	17
Rural non-farm	16	11	8	16	14	13
Farm	7	—	2	6	1	4
Nativity						
Native Born	79	87	84	78	85	79
Foreign Born	21	13	16	22	15	21
Mother Tongue						
English	56	57	73	56	63	74
French	27	31	13	26	28	10
Other	17	11	14	18	9	16
Ethnicity						
British	44	45	55	43	46	57
French	28	32	16	27	33	13
German	7	6	10	7	5	7
Italian	4	3	1	5	1	3
Ukrainian	3	2	2	3	3	1
Scandinavian	2	1	3	2	2	3
Other	13	12	12	13	10	15

(Table 11.1 Cont'd)

Note: "100" totals appear at the head of each residence/nativity/mother tongue/ethnicity subgroup column.

Characteristics	Females			Males		
	Married	Separated	Divorced	Married	Separated	Divorced
Religion	100	100	100	100	100	100
Roman Catholic	45	49	32	45	47	31
Jew	1	1	2	1	—	3
Fundamentalist Protestant	5	4	6	5	4	4
Non-fundamentalist	39	36	49	38	35	45
Other	6	4	5	6	6	4
No religion	3	7	6	5	8	12
Education	100	100	100	100	100	100
Elementary	34	43	27	36	42	33
High School	58	51	61	50	48	48
University	8	6	12	14	10	19
Childless, Percentage	12	15	16	b	b	b
Mean Number of Children	2.9	2.9	2.3	b	b	b
Family membership	100	100	100	100	100	100
Head	—	52	48	99	19	17
Other relative	99	14	15	—	13	14
Non-family member	1	34	37	1	68	69

Main Source of 1970 Income						
No Income	51	6	4	1	3	10
Wage, Salary, Self Employment	39	56	69	95	88	80
Family Allowances	—	7	2	1	—	—
Other Government Income[c]	2	19	17	2	7	7
Other[d]	8	12	8	1	2	3
Labour-Force Status	100	100	100	100	100	100
In Labour Force	38	61	71	93	86	86
Not in Labour Force	62	39	29	7	14	14
1970 Earned Income[e] Mean	$2972	$3514	$3834	$7712	$6394	$6579
Total 1970 Income[f] Mean	$1513	$3186	$3800	$7734	$5863	$5940

(Each "Main Source of 1970 Income" column total = 100)

[a] Column percentages may not sum to 100 because of rounding.

[b] Data on number of live births are not collected for males.

[c] Includes all government transfer payments (excluding family and youth allowance and old age pensions, Canada and Quebec Pensions) from all levels of government funds, such as unemployment insurance, veterans pensions and allowances, welfare, mother's allowances, etc.

[d] Includes income from scholarships and alimony.

[e] 1970 wage, salary, and self-employment income for persons working in 1970.

[f] Income for everyone in 1970 whether or not they were in the labour force.

Source: Statistics Canada. 1971 Census Public Use Sample Tape of Individuals. One in Five (sub) sample.

Keeping in mind that census data provide a snapshot of the Canadian population at one point in time, Table 11.1 shows that, in 1971, the separated and divorced populations differ from the currently married populations, particularly with respect to those variables which previous research has shown to be associated with marital instability. There is a slight tendency for the divorced to be older than the separated and currently married populations. This would be expected, given the dissolution of marriages of long duration immediately after the 1968 Divorce Act. The data in Table 11.1 also show that separated and divorced men and women were married at younger ages than their currently married counterparts, a finding which is compatible with studies showing the association between early age at marriage and divorce. Compared to the currently married population, persons who were separated or divorced in Canada in 1971 are more likely to be residing in large urban areas of 30 000 population or greater[28/31] and are more likely to be native born.

Given the Roman Catholic proscription of divorce and the association of Roman Catholicism with French mother tongue and ethnicity, it is not surprising to find religious, linguistic, and ethnic differences between the separated and divorced population. Compared to the currently married and separated populations, divorced men and women in Canada in 1971 are more likely to be British in ethnicity, have an English mother tongue, and be non-fundamental Protestants. They are less likely to be French in ethnicity, have French as the mother tongue or to be Roman Catholic. The data thus suggest that in Canada the mechanism used to dissolve unsuccessful marriages varies with the ethno-religious affiliation of the person(s) involved.

Education also appears to be a variable affecting the mechanism used to dissolve a marriage. Divorced persons in Canada are less likely to have only elementary schooling and more likely to have university education, compared to the separated and currently married population. Conversely, separated men and women in Canada are most likely to have less than a high school education. These findings can be explained by the association of education with ethnicity and religion, which in turn appear related to mechanisms used to dissolve marriages. In addition, the less well educated may also lack the resources and familiarity with law to deal with the Canadian legal system in order to obtain a divorce.

Consequences of Divorce in Canada

Earlier studies showed that premarital pregnancy and rapid family building were factors precipitating divorce. Data in Table 11.1 do not address this issue, but rather show that childlessness is slightly higher for separated and divorced women. Similar results are found in the United States.[8] Reasons for these findings are complex. Childlessness may cause divorce, either directly, or more likely because the absence of children removes the pressures to keep an unhappy marriage intact.[23] On the other hand, separation and divorce often mean an intermittent sexual life with the result that the chances of conceiving a child are much lower than in marriage. As a result, divorce usually interrupts the childbearing of women, and suppresses their fertility. The lower average fertility of divorced women shown in Table 11.1 no doubt reflects this interruption, as well as the higher levels of education of these women (high education is also associated with reduced fertility and with childlessness).

The fertility of separated and divorced women is of interest to social scientists because the presence of a dependent child usually implies the existence of a female-headed family. The number of dependent children involved in divorces has been increasing in Canada partly because of the processing of many marital dissolutions which were of long duration and involved no dependent children, but which were prevented by pre-1968 legislation. In 1969 nearly 55% of all divorces had no dependent children compared to 42% in 1975. Since 1969, the number of dependent children involved in divorce cases has increased from 20 099 to over 58 000 in 1975, with the average number of children per divorce increasing from .92 in 1969, to 1.22 in 1974, and to 1.17 in 1975 (see Reference 38, page 234; Reference 39, Table 24; Reference 40, Table 20).

Since mothers are awarded custody of approximately three-fourths of dependent children in the divorce proceedings (see Reference 40, Table 22), the increase since 1969 of children involved in divorce means an increase in the number of female-headed families. Reflecting trends up to 1971, the 1971 Census shows over 9% of all Canadian families were single-parent families, with 378 065 female-headed families and 100 680 male-headed families. Between 1961 and 1971, the increase in one-parent families was almost twice that of husband-wife-headed families (38% versus 21%). Reflecting the maternal custody of children after divorce, Table 11.1 shows that approximately one-half of the separated and divorced women in Canada in 1971 are heads of families compared to less than one-fifth of the separated and divorced males.

If separation and divorce mean a change from a two-parent family to a one-parent family, they also imply a change of economic status. Downward economic movement for all parties may be experienced, but especially by the wife who no longer has access to all or part of the usually higher income of her ex-husband.[5/6] The economic vulnerability of separated and divorced men and women is shown in Table 11.1 by the percentage relying on other government income as a main source of 1970 income. This category includes such transfer payments as welfare, mother's allowance, and unemployment insurance benefits.

A reduced family income also induces many women to work, even when small children are present.[5] The data in Table 11. 1 show that separated and divorced women are far more likely to be in the labour force than are married women. Employment income is the main source of 1970 income for over half of the separated and divorced women, compared to less than two-fifths of the married women (over half of the latter received no earned income at all in 1970, evidently relying on other forms of income or on income earned by the husband and/or other family members).

Income data in Table 11.1 show that employed separated and divorced men and women earn on the average more than their married counterparts. However, for females, such differences reflect the longer working hours and weeks worked of the separated and divorced women, compared to married women.[5] Because most single-parent families are female-headed, the sex difference in income, whereby the average total male income is nearly halved for women, is more noteworthy. Minimally, it suggests considerable economic hardship for female-headed, single-parent families. In 1971 the average income of female-headed, single-parent families was $5401 compared to $9931 for male heads of families.[37]

The earlier discussion of the factors affecting divorce indicated that low income creates stress leading to marital instability. The evidence seemed equally clear that marital dissolution in turn creates economic hardship. One of the reasons for such hardship would appear to be the already low incomes prior to divorce and separation.[3] Nothing divided is still nothing. However, a six-year study on income in the United States has confirmed that marital disruption itself has a negative effect on income. Persons who divorced experienced less of an increase in their incomes in subsequent years than did intact families. And, divorced women fared much worse than men.[3/21]

Socio-demographic characteristics of the divorced and separated Canadian population in 1971 thus not only corroborate past research into the factors affecting divorce, but also suggest that divorce and separation mean the creation of single-parent families and a reduction in economic resources. Alteration in family structure and income are but two out of a multitude of consequences that divorce and separation have on family organization and behaviour, ranging from such topics as the emotional impact,[32/43] to the stigmatization of divorce,[6/32/35] the alteration of kinship ties,[2/36] and the impact on the authority structure within the home, the economic status in the community, and the impact on children.[6/7] But, single-parent families and economic need are two very important consequences of divorce which affect family life in general and the behaviour of children in particular. In the literature, children in female-headed families are cited as prone to juvenile delinquency, poor school performance, and psychological disorders. However, recent research suggests that methodological errors account for such results and that socio-economic hardships rather than single-parent status accounts for many of the observed effects of marital dissolution upon children.[3/7] If this is indeed the case, then the economic hardships which result from marital dissolution deserve greater scrutiny and ameliorative action.

Summary

In conclusion, marital dissolution in Canada must be understood within a sociological context. Demographically, twentieth-century Canada has experienced a rise in both the number and rate of divorces; yet the cause of this rise is social, reflecting the general impact of urbanization and industrialization upon family life, the impact of World War II, and, more recently, the liberalization in divorce legislation. That divorce is more characteristic of some Canadians than others also attests to the influence of social factors. Studies in Canada indicate that young age at marriage, low income, female labour-force participation, urban residence, non-Roman Catholic religion, accelerated family building, and a broken family of origin, are all factors which are conducive to divorce. The 1971 census data on the characteristics of the separated, as well as the divorced and currently married Canadian population, reveals that strategies to dissolve inoperative marriages vary by education, religion, ethnicity, and mother tongue. Although the analysis clearly shows the influence of social variables upon divorce, the data also show that the relationship between divorce and social variables is reciprocal. If social phenomena affect divorce in Canada, then it is equally true that divorce has social consequences for Canadian family life. Female-headed families and reduced income, particularly for women, are two consequences of divorce which in turn affect the family organization and the well-being of children.

References

1. Advisory Council on the Status of Women. *Divorce Law Reform: ACSW Recommendations.* 22 September, 1976.
2. Anspach, Donald F. "Kinship and Divorce." *Journal of Marriage and the Family* 38 (May 1976), pp 323-330.
3. Bane, Mary Jo. "Marital Disruption and the Lives of Children." *Journal of Social Issues* (Winter 1976), pp 103-116.
4. Basavarajappa, K.G. "Marital Status and Nuptiality in Canada." *Statistics Canada.* Unpublished paper, 1977.
5. Boyd, Monica. "The Forgotten Minority: The Socio-economic Status of Divorced and Separated Women," in Pat Marchak, ed. *The Working Sexes.* Vancouver: University of British Columbia Institute of Industrial Relations, 1977, pp. 47-69.
6. Brandwein, Ruth A., Brown, Carol A., and Fox, Elizabeth M. "Women and Children Last: The Social Situation of Divorced Mothers and Their Families" *Journal of Marriage and the Family,* 36 (1976), pp. 498-514.
7. Brown, Carol A., Feldberg, Roslyn, Fox, Elizabeth M., and Kohen, Janet. "Divorce: Chance of a New Lifetime." *Journal of Social Issues* 32 (Winter 1976), pp. 119-133.
8. Bumpass, Larry L., and Sweet, James A. "Differentials in Marital Instability: 1970." *American Sociological Review* 37 (December 1972), pp. 754-766.
9. Cherlin, Andrew. "The Effect of Children on Marital Dissolution." *Demography* 14 (August 1977), pp. 265-272.
10. Chilman, Catherine S. "Families and Poverty in the early 70s: Rates, Associated Factors, Some Implications." *Journal of Marriage and the Family* 37 (February 1975), pp. 49-60.

11. Coombs, Lotagne, and Zumeta, Zena. "Correlates of Marital Dissolution in a Prospective Fertility Study: A Research Note." *Social Problems* 18 (Summer 1970), pp. 92-101.
12. Cutright, Phillips. "Income and Family Events: Marital Stability." *Journal of Marriage and the Family* 33 (1971), pp. 291-306.
13. Duberman, Lucile. *Marriage and Other Alternatives.* New York: Praeger Publishers, 1977.
14. Duncan, Beverly, and Duncan, Otis Dudley. "Family Stability and Occupational Success." *Social Problems* 16 (1969), pp. 273-285.
15. Furstenberg, Frank F., Jr. "Premarital Pregnancy and Marital Instability." *Journal of Social Issues* 32 (Winter 1976), pp. 67-83.
16. Glick, Paul C. and Norton, Arthur J. "Frequency, duration, and probability of marriage and divorce." *Journal of Marriage and the Family* 33 (1971), pp. 307-317.
17. Hahlo, Herman R. "Reform of the Divorce Act, 1968," in Law Reform Commission of Canada, ed. *Studies on Divorce.* pp. 3-98. Ottawa: Information Canada, 1975.
18. Hannan, Michael T., Tuma, Nancy B., and Groeneveld, Lyle T. "Income and Marital Events: Evidence from an Income-Maintenance Experiment." *American Journal of Sociology* 82 (May 1977), pp. 1186-1211.
19. Hauser, Phillip M. "Demography in Relation to Sociology." *American Journal of Sociology* 65 (September 1959), pp. 169-171.
20. Heiss, Jerold. "On the Transmission of Marital Instability in Black Families." *American Sociological Review* 37 (February 1972),pp. 82-92.
21. Institute for Social Research. "Marriage, Divorce Crucial in Changes to Economic Fortunes, Eight-Year Study Shows." *ISR Newsletter 5* (Spring 1977), pp. 2-3.
22. Larson, Lyle E. *The Canadian Family in Comparative Perspective.* Scarborough, Ontario: Prentice Hall of Canada Ltd., 1976.
23. Levinger, George. "A Social Psychological Perspective on Marital Dissolution." *Journal of Social Issues* 32 (Winter 1976), pp. 21-44.
24. Mueller, Charles W., and Pope, Hallowell. "Marital Instability: A Study of its Transmission between Generations." *Journal of Marriage and the Family* 39 (February 1977), pp. 83-93.
25. Nett, Emily M. "The Changing Forms and Functions of the Canadian Family: A Demographic View," in K. Ishwaran, ed. *The Canadian Family,*Revised ed. Toronto: Holt, Rinehart and Winston of Canada, 1976, pp. 46-76.
26. Norton, Arthur J., and Glick, Paul C. "Marital Instability: Past, Present, and Future." *The Journal of Social Issues* 32 (Winter 1976), pp. 5-18.
27. Palmer, Sally E. "Reasons for Marriage Breakdown." *Journal of Comparative Family Studies* No. 2 (1971), pp. 251-262.
28. Peters, John F. "Divorce in Canada: A Demographic Profile." *Journal of Comparative Family Studies* 7 (Summer 1976), pp. 335-349.
29. Pike, Robert. "Legal access and incidence of divorce in Canada: A Socio-

Historical Analysis." *Canadian Review of Sociology and Anthropology* 12, No. 2 (1975), pp. 115-133.

30. Pope, Hallowell, and Mueller, Charles W. "The Intergenerational Transmission of Marital Instability: Comparisons by Race and Sex." *Journal of Social Issues* 32 (Winter 1976), pp. 49-64.

31. Roberts, Lance, and Krishnan, P. "Age-specific Incidence and Social Correlates of Divorce in Canada." Discussion Paper No. 2. Edmonton: Population Research Laboratory, University of Alberta, 1973.

32. Schlesinger, Benjamin. "The One-Parent Family in Perspective," in B. Schlesinger, ed. *The One-Parent Family.* Toronto: University of Toronto Press, 1969.

33. _____. "Women and Men in Second Marriages," in S. Parvez Wakil, ed. *Marriage, Family and Society.* Scarborough, Ontario: Butterworth, 1975, pp. 317-333.

34. _____. "Remarriage as Family Reorganization for Divorced Persons," in K. Ishwaran, ed. *The Canadian Family*, Revised ed. Toronto: Holt Rinehart & Winston of Canada, 1976, pp. 460-478.

35. Sprey, Jetse. "The Study of Single Parenthood: Some Methodological Considerations," in B. Schlessinger, ed. *The One-Parent Family.* Toronto: University of Toronto Press, 1969.

36. Spicer, Gerry W., and Hampe, Gary D. "Kinship Interaction after Divorce." *Journal of Marriage and the Family* 37 (February 1975), pp. 113-119.

37. Statistics Canada. *1971 Census of Canada, Population*, Volume II—Part 2, Tables 82, 83.

38. Statistics Canada. 1973 *Canada Yearbook.* Ottawa: Statistics Canada, 1973.

39. _____. *Vital Statistics.* Volume II. Marriage and Divorce. 1972. Ottawa: Statistics Canada, 1974.

40. _____. *Vital Statistics.* Volume II. Marriage and Divorce, 1975. Ottawa: Statistics Canada, 1977.

41. Wakil, S. Parvez. "Introduction: Life Style of the Family," in S.P. Wakil, ed. *Marriage, Family and Society.* Toronto: Butterworth and Company, 1975.

42. Wakil, S. Parvez, and Wakil, F.A. "Marriage and Family in Canada: A Demographic Cultural Profile," in K. Ishwaran, ed. *The Canadian Family*, Revised edition. Toronto: Holt, Rinehart & Winston of Canada, 1976, pp. 380-407.

43. Weiss, Robert S. "The Emotional Impact of Marital Separation." *Journal of Social Issues* 32 (Winter 1976), pp. 135-145.

44. Wuenster, T.J. "Canadian Law and Divorce," in S. Parvez Wakil, ed. *Marriage, Family and Society.* Scarborough, Ontario: Butterworth, 1975, pp. 295-316.

12/Wife-Beating: Some Substantive and Theoretical Issues*

Kwok B. Chan

In the summer of 1976, I came to Women In Transition, a residence shelter for mothers and their children during crisis circumstances, to solicit help in locating 20 to 30 battered wives as subjects for an ongoing research project on "wife-battery." The staff at Women In Transition then disclosed to me that two students had been hired under the auspices of the Department of the Secretary of State's Summer Student Community Programme to systematically organize hitherto accumulated files of women who had been admitted into the shelter since its inception in 1974. A preliminary inspection of statistical tables constructed from the 194 files seemed to reveal some interesting theoretical aspects of the problem of wife-beating in Metropolitan Toronto, and the desire to report on and interpret this specific set of data provides the major impetus of this paper.

Initiated on a Local Initiatives Programme Grant, Women In Transition was opened in February of 1974 at 374 St. George Street to provide temporary accommodation for mothers and their children at times of crisis, which include both "Marital Crises" and "Housing Crises." "Marital Crises," as distinguished from "Housing Crises," are defined by Women in Transition as those "in which a woman is suddenly homeless because of the breakdown of her current union." Often, this type of crisis has involved battery. Women who find themselves in this crisis are given priority at Women In Transition because 1) they are facing the problems of homelessness and single-support parenthood simultaneously, and 2) this type of crisis usually involves a great deal more emotional stress for the woman involved, thus she requires much support and counselling. Response from the

*My gratitude should be extended to Ann Cools, Director of Women in Transition, a women's shelter in Toronto, Ontario, Canada, for her generosity in making data accessible to us, and in giving opinions and insights throughout the whole research process.

community at large, social-service delivery quarters, and other interested individuals, was so enthusiastic and massive that there was little doubt of the urgent and immediate need of this kind of service. With successful appropriation of funds and allocations from United Community Fund and Metro Social Services, the relocation of the Women In Transition from St. George Street to 143 Spadina Road was made possible. The same relocation permitted increase in resident capacity, improvement of the physical condition of the quarters, and provision of more services.

While the primary goal of this women's shelter is to assist each individual woman in managing or coping with her distress, a number of standard services is being provided: food, shelter, counselling, referrals, daycare, crisis intervention, and support services. With very rare exceptions, only women with children were admitted. Prior to admission, one woman staff member is to carefully assess the urgency, exigency, and appropriateness of the need as claimed by the clientele. At least more than 90% of these women residents had been referred to Women In Transition by social agencies, such as Children's Aid Society, Welfare, Family Court, Police, Public Health Office, Ontario Housing Corporation, Family Services, Information Services, Hospitals, and Distress Centres, etc.

The data on which this paper is based stem from statistical reconstruction of information contained in personal files of 194 women who found themselves face-to-face with "marital crises," the majority of which involved battery and violence, and were housed between 1974 and 1976 in Women In Transition. Every woman, upon admission into the shelter, is requested to attend a brief interview session administered by a staff person, during which basic demographic data, such as years of education, history of employment, duration of marriage, age, mate's education and occupation, etc. are solicited.

A preliminary inspection of data pertaining to the 194 women seems to indicate some patterns and trends, which by and large are congruent with findings of United States studies on wife-battery.*

---

*The studies have been reviewed in another paper of mine, titled "Intrafamilial Violence: Myth-making vs Theory-building," which was presented to the 1977 Canadian Sociology and Anthropology Meetings in June at the University of New Brunswick, Fredericton, Canada. I have in mind three studies: Richard Gelles' *The*

The major objectives of this paper are:

1. To report some basic demographic data regarding the 194 battered women;
2. Given awareness of the gradual manifestation of some data "trends" and "patterns," and taking these demographic characteristics to be reported as the general data base, to discuss and assess the implications and connotations of the data. This is done in view of the stock of theoretical and empirical literature that we have accumulated in the area of intrafamily violence, wife-battery, and child-abuse included;*
3. To generate pertinent working hypotheses from the data that we presently have and the interpretations that we are to make for future research.

The potential value and importance of this bulk of data lie mainly in generating relevant research questions, which we hope to be able to answer in the long run. It is in this sense that our original contribution to sociological understanding of the phenomenon of violence in the family is intended to be understood. Moreover, with some seemingly scattered pieces of data in our hands, we feel more comfortable in theorizing, bearing in mind the need to impose some kind of control over our otherwise irresponsible "sociological imagination."

It is also important for us to be aware of the many methodological limitations of our data before we try to push our interpretations and conclusions too far. Ours is basically a convenience sample, i.e., women in our sample have chosen to solicit Women In Transition for institutional assistance, and, therefore, are by no means representative

---

Violent Home: A Study of Physical Aggression Between Husbands and Wives, 1972, Sage Publications, Inc.; John Flynn's *Spouse Assault: Its Dimensions and Characteristics in Kalamazoo County*, Michigan, 1975, unpublished manuscript of School of Social Work, Western Michigan University, Kalamazoo, Michigan; George Levinger's "Physical Abuse among Applicants for Divorce," in *Violence in the Family*, edited by S. K. Steinmetz and Murray A. Straus, pp. 85-91, 1974.
*For an intensive review of the pertinent literature, read my two papers: "Infrafamilial Violence: Myth-making vs. Theory-building," and "Symbolic Interactionism: Implications and Applications for Theory and Research in Family Conflicts and Violence," an unpublished working paper.

of the thousands (or, millions) of women who have also been "historically" subjected to humiliation and physical violence within the household, but who have never allowed themselves to become a public statistic. As to be evidenced by the latter parts of this paper, almost all of these women come from the lower socio-economic strata of our society and are largely a typical manifestation of the classic "working-class, housewife syndrome": trapped in marriage, under-educated, deficient in marketable work skills, and "successfully" divorced from social and occupational participation in various levels of community life outside of the household.

A lack of representativeness of our sample hampers generalizability to women from other walks of life, women who are experiencing different kinds of life conditions and encounters. However, if we are able to throw light on the predicaments, economic and socio-psychological, of battered women from the lower layer of Canadian society, the major aspiration of this paper is fulfilled.

The Data

Age, Citizenship Status, Ethnicity, and Migrancy

There is a slight overrepresentation of relatively young married women in the overall population sample: While 62 women fall into the 20-25 age group and 63 women belong to the 26-30 age group, more than half of them range between 20 and 30 years of age. Correspondingly, 49 women out of the total sample of 194 are between 31 and 40 years old, contrasting with the 11 women who fall into the 15-19 age category. The general trend of the age data seems to indicate the higher prevalence of wife-battery among marriages in which wives are between 20 and 40 years old.

Parallelling the age of abused women with that of the children, the indication is that more than half of the 338 children, who accompanied their mothers during their stay at the shelter, are between one and six years old. While 48 children belong to the 7-16 age category, it is also important to note that 43 of these children are less than one year old. Of the 194 women helped by Women In Transition, 179 women came to the shelter with 338 children, giving an average of 1.9 children per woman who spent some time there, excluding the 15 women applicants who had no children.

Superimposing the age data of abused women on data for accompanying children, it is our speculation that two sets of problems immediately come to the forefront: 1) the maintenance of children's medical and emotional health severely taps the coping capacity of the mothers who are currently in distress; and 2) the continuation of children's education, coupled with the dim prospect of obtaining adequate housing or simply temporary accommodation, further aggravates the severity of the concurrent crisis situation.

Out of the total sample population of 194 women, 58 are immigrants, 10 are naturalized citizens who first came to Canada years before with landed immigrant status, and 126 are Canadian citizens. Further investigation into the detailed breakdown by the country of origin of the 68 naturalized citizens and immigrants reveals some interesting patterns. Nineteen of these women (almost 30%) came from the West Indies, which include Jamaica, Dominica, and Guyana. Women from the European countries constitute another large category: 10 from Italy, 4 from Germany, 9 from the United Kingdom, and 5 from Yugoslavia. During the same period, 4 women originally came from India, and another 3 came from Southeast Asia, which includes the Philippines, Thailand, and Indonesia.

Data bearing on the distribution of racial composition and ethnicity among the 194 women provide additional information about their ethnic-racial origins. While about 80% of these women are whites, 13% are blacks from the West Indies. Sixty-nine out of the total population of 194 women speak languages other than English.

Table 12.1
Ethnicity

Ethnicity	Number of Cases
White	154 (79.3%)
Black	26 (13.4%)
Oriental	3 (1.6%)
Native Canadian Indian	3 (1.6%)
East Indian	6 (3.1%)
Métis	2 (1.0%)
Total	194 (100%)

Further breakdown by languages spoken other than English serves to identify 12 who speak French, 15 Italian, 5 German, 6 Yugoslavian languages, 4 Hungarian, and 7 other miscellaneous languages.

Thirty-two of the 68 women who are either naturalized citizens or landed immigrants have been in Canada from 4 to 10 years, with another 10 women whose Canadian residency period includes 16 cases of unknown length, 8 cases falling into the 1-3 year period, and 3 cases who have been in Canada for less than a year. Fifteen women stated that they came to Canada "in order to join mate," 10 women "came with mate," and 3 came with parents.

Metropolitan Toronto is not only a city of attraction for immigrants from abroad, it has also absorbed a substantial number of migrants from other Canadian provinces. The factor of migrancy parallels that of immigrant status and merits some immediate attention in our attempts to reveal the demographic characteristics of battered women who came to Women In Transition. Twenty-eight women came to Toronto as migrants from all over the country, while 16 of them came from towns and cities in Ontario. Immediately prior to admission into the shelter, 23 of them had been in Toronto for less than one week, and another three for less than one month. Seventy-nine percent of the 28 women migrants stated that their reason for migration to Toronto was "to escape mate or husband," while two women indicated that they came to Toronto "to flee home, due to a mate's or husband's desertion."

In view of the fact that the large majority of these women migrants had only been in the City of Toronto for less than one week prior to admission, an interesting question arises as to how they initiated and arranged contacts with local social service agencies and, as a consequence, how these contacts resulted in their being referred to Women In Transition for temporary accommodation. More than 90% of all women who came to the shelter were put into the network of social services by some local government or private social agencies making referrals. About 44% of the total referrals were made by well-established and reasonably publicized social service agencies such as Metro Children's Aid Society, Metro Social Services, Family Services, Catholic Children's Aid Society, etc. At present we do not have data regarding the nature of mediational processes between these "conventional" social service institutions and centres providing innovative services and assistance to transient women confronted with crisis situations.

Education, Occupation, and History of Employment
Our analysis becomes a lot more theoretically exciting when it comes to data pertaining to the educational and socio-economic characteristics of these women. The overall impression of our sample women is one of extreme, devastating poverty, and economic and socio-psychological dependency on some specific source of income, which, in most cases, is nothing other than their mates' own job income.

Less than half of the total population sample has attained any form of formal education beyond Grade 10; 11% have lower than Grade 8 education, while only 26% fall into the Grade 11-13 category. What is more noteworthy is the fact that less than 7% of these women have attained education and schooling beyond Grade 13. A total of 171 women (i.e., 88%) out of the 194 declared themselves as "not employed" on admission. When asked when they were last employed in view of present unemployment, almost half of them stated that they had been working on some kind of job over 5 years before. Another 20% indicated that their last employment had ended between 1 and 5 years before. Only 17 women had been actively employed in the labour force less than 6 months before.

Table 12.2
Usual Occupation

Occupation	Number of Cases
Housewife	117 (60.3%)
Labour	36 (18.6%)
Clerical	32 (16.5%)
Professional	8 (4.1%)
Student	1 (0.5%)
Total	194 (100%)

It will not be at all surprising when "being housewife" becomes the full-time occupation for more than half of the 194 women. A research question becomes prominent at this juncture: What exactly does it mean when women declare their occupation as "housewife?" How do they see the role of "homemaker" and "housewife" as an occupation, understood in the most commonly used sense of the word?

Thirty-six women were engaged in some kind of labouring job, while another 32 women took up the traditional low-paid clerical positions in commercial firms and factory offices. Then there is the fact of the underrepresentation of "professional" women in the total sample.

For more than half of the 194 women, mate's job income becomes the major source of financial support. About 23% rely solely on public support such as welfare, unemployment insurance, and student loans. Only 28 women altogether derive their source of livelihood support from their own job incomes or from combined incomes.

Table 12.3
Sources of Support

Source of Support	Number of Cases
Own Job Income	13 (6.7%)
Mate's Job Income	113 (58.5%)
Combined Income	15 (7.7%)
Welfare	28 (14.5%)
Mother's Allowance	2 (1.0%)
Unemployment Insurance	15 (7.7%)
Student Loan	2 (1.0%)
Income from Sale of House	1 (0.5%)
None	2 (1.0%)
Unknown	3 (1.6%)
Manpower Retraining	0 (0.0%)
Parents	0 (0.0%)
Total	194 (100%)

How much cash did these women bring along with them when they were seeking entry into the women's shelter? At least 82 women labelled themselves as "plain broke" or "penniless," and another 25 women had less than three dollars on hand. Another group of 43 women declared their cash possessions amounting to less that 25 dollars, leaving 14 women possessing 14 dollars, and only 26 women having more than 50 dollars. At this juncture, one should entertain the idea that most of these women decided to flee their homes on the spur of the moment and had only limited time to get all possible financial resources together. The limited amount of cash in immediate possession would also hamper any desire for long-distance travelling to places where some kind of help was deemed accessible.

The In-Take Form,* which was used during each admission interview, was not purposely constructed to solicit data about the various background characteristics of women's mates. This becomes a definite deficiency in information input in view of the fact that the researcher has very little data about the men's own interpretation of the situation, and their ordinary means of livelihood. Only two items of information were recorded about men: their current employment status and their "usual occupation." At the time when these women sought admission into Women In Transition, slightly over 25% of their mates were unemployed, and the other 75% were actively employed in the labour force. More than half of these men declared and identified themselves as "labourers," 13% were in trade, and another 13% participated in some kind of clerical job. The very low representation of number of men in professional careers (only 5%) is not surprising.

Table 12.4
Mate's Usual Occupation

Occupation	Number of Cases
Labour	114 (58.7%)
Trade	25 (12.9%)
Clerical	24 (12.4%)
Professional	11 (5.7%)
Student	2 (1.0%)
Unknown	18 (9.3%)
Total	194 (100%)

*This In-Take Form has been subjected to a few substantial revisions, which have been deemed necessary as incoming information is becoming more complex, and, as a result of this, immediate attempts have been made to standardize and systematize this vast volume of data.

Marital Status, Duration of Marriage, and Separations

Quantitative information extracted from the files of the 194 women furnishes us with only very meagre knowledge of their marital history, let alone the nature and modes of intrafamilial interactional dynamics, and the incidence and prevalence of disputes and confrontations among the couples, which have historically culminated in the women deciding to seek help from community social agencies.

Regarding the then-current marital status of these women, 147 of them were married, while the remaining 47 women were in "common-law" relationships. An immediate research question arises: Does "common-law" marriage have anything to do with the nature and incidence of wife-battery, and, if the hypothesized relationship does exist, how does it operate and under what kinds of circumstances?

The most astonishing piece of data manifested itself when women were asked about the duration of marriage prior to admission. Half of these women had remained in the marital relationship for four to ten years. Thirty-three women had chosen to sustain the marital relationship for more than ten years!

Table 12.5
Number of Years with Mate

Number of Years	Number of Cases
Less than 1 Year	14 (7.2%)
1-3 years	40 (20.6%)
4-6 years	49 (25.3%)
7-10 years	48 (24.8%)
Over 10 years	33 (17.0%)
Unknown	10 (5.2%)
Total	194 (100%)

Roughly half of the 194 women had had previous separations from current husbands or mates on admission to Women In Transition. What kinds of economic or socio-psychological forces and processes are responsible for the continuation of the marital relationship despite at least one incident of separation? Exactly what kinds of factors had triggered these previous separations? How does the motivation behind this initial separation relate to the women's ultimate determination to flee the home and to seek outside, institutional help? These questions seem to promise exciting prospects for future empirical studies.

Battery, Drug Use, and Seeking Help

"Battery" is defined by staff at Women In Transition as "physical cruelty of any severity inflicted by the husband on the wife." When an arbitrary distinction is made by the staff between "severe" and "mild," 100 women were reported to have suffered severe battery, and 42 women mild battery. Fifty of these women named alcohol consumed by the husband as an implicating or precipitating factor in battery. We do not have parallel data regarding the extent of the wife's implication in alcohol consumption and the contribution of this factor to the incidence of wife-battery.

The staff at Women In Transition made no attempts to construct a psychiatric or clinical assessment of women upon admission. However, it was found that 47 women had a history of use of "psychotropic drugs," i.e., prescription drugs such as Valium, Vivol, and Librium, which are taken mainly for the relief of anxiety. Forty-six women were at least at one time under some kind of psychiatric care.

Although a large majority of these women was able to cite a close relative, a friend, a family doctor, or a lawyer, when they were asked to do so, one begins to wonder if the women have actually consulted with any or all of these individuals outside the family situation for information, resources, and financial and socio-emotional help. Only 25 women arrived at the shelter from a stay at a domestic home other than their own, and another 8 came directly from an institution, e.g., prison, hospital, and other residences including Nellie's Interval House, Dundas Family Shelters, etc. How these women in distress make contacts with the environment outside the household, especially in terms of both informal and institutional sources of assistance and counselling, is a critical area for future research.

Activities During Stay at the Shelter

During their brief stay at Women In Transition, a majority of these women did make contacts with various social service agencies in Metro Toronto, contacts which were initiated by the staff members who were making referrals. Services provided by public health centres were most frequently sought, followed by Ontario Housing Corporation, Day Care Services, and Children's Aid Societies. It was found that five women had voluntarily chosen to place their children with the Children's Aid Society for care and supervision.

A casual examination of the kind of agencies contacted and consulted and the specific type of service sought by these women indicates that medical care, housing, and the welfare of children seem to be the top priority concerns.

Although 23 women did obtain a lawyer and another 53 had instituted legal or family court proceedings, only 16 of them (8%) had actually followed through the larger part of the prosecution process and laid assault charges. This exceedingly low incidence of attempts to undertake legal steps necessitates immediate explanation. The research question becomes: What kinds of economic and socio-psychological forces and conditions have deterred these women from implicating their abusive mates in the criminal justic process? The data itself thus apparently suggest the need for future investigations into the rationale behind their unwillingness to prosecute and to lay charges.

Activities after Departure from the Shelter

The 194 files also contain information about the various situations that women have entered into, especially in the areas of housing, employment, daycare of children, and probability of receiving welfare. Only 3 women reported having found employment, and 7 women were able to place children in daycare. Housing must have presented a very serious problem to almost every one of the women because only 5 of them obtained apartments in Ontario Housing Corporation buildings. Without conducting structured follow-up interviews with women who have left the shelter, we have virtually no knowledge of how they worked out or coped with problems in these areas. Our most educated guess is that these problems will remain difficult, if not insurmountable. It is indeed frightening to entertain the idea of an almost instant relapse into yet another crisis situation saturated with economic desperation, poverty, and socio-psychological dependency. Our data seems to bear out this prediction: 30% of them returned to the former apartment with former mates and children, and another 3% found a new apartment with mate and children. Only 60% of these women were able to find either new or old apartments alone with children, or were admitted into other hostels, psychiatric institutions, or hospitals.

This grim and stunning set of statistics brings up the distressing question as to why these women, after the sojourn at a women's shelter, have eventually chosen to return to their apparently abusive husbands. Just as one wonders why a woman has been able to put up with 25 years of marital life that is saturated with violence and aggression, one also is forced to speculate on the kinds of socio-structural and psychological factors which in one way or another are responsible for women's seemingly absurd decision to return to abusive husbands.*

It will be theoretically interesting to ask if women who have been able to make out on their own with children after departure from the shelter differ from those who have eventually returned to their mates. If these differences do exist, the next research task becomes one of probing into the implications and dimensions of these differences for community social service agencies in offering assistance to women currently in distress.

Interpretation and Discussion

Class, Stress, and Violence

An overwhelming majority of the women in our sample have attained a very low level of education, possess little or no marketable working skills, and have not been actively participating in the labour force for an extended period of time. Although their husbands seem to be a little better-off, low occupational prestige and socio-economic status, which are endemic to menial jobs, and the constantly threatening prospect of unemployment are still there and will always be there.

On first thought, the foregoing analysis of socio-economic and demographic data pertaining to the 194 women housed at the women's shelter between 1974 and 1976 seems to have carried with itself a momentum driving home a *premature conclusion*: that the high incidence and frequency of wife-battery is essentially a working-class

---

*In a paper titled "Abused Wives: Why Do They Stay?" Richard Gelles touches on a few of the determinants of abused women deciding to stay: severity and frequency of violence administered by mates, past experiences with violence during childhood, and amount of resources and power possessed by wives. This paper appears in *Journal of Marriage and the Family* Vol. 38 (November 1976), pp. 659-668.

phenomenon, the dramatic manifestation of which takes place in poverty-stricken, multi-problem families which are constantly at the mercy of seasonal waves of under-employment and unemployment, and other socio-structural forces. Findings reported by investigators of recent studies in the United States* in the area of intrafamilial violence, unfortunately, have argued otherwise, indicating that violence in the family does not respect variables such as class, ethnicity, or religion.

Existing empirical data regarding the class-wife-battery relationship is at best equivocal, the clarification of which awaits findings generated from a large, nation-wide survey with a much larger sample size and, therefore, a more general data base.**

The many merits of large-scale, survey-type research, however, do not negate the value of intensive, in-depth interview studies of a select sample of subjects. Given that our subjects are of working-class background, the major question confronting the family researchers can be construed as follows: Exactly what kinds of stress, distress, and other frustration factors are operating in these working-class families, and how are these factors instrumental in the repeated eruptions of physical violence between husband and wife? Armed with an explicit recognition of a "systematic" bias which is inherent in a study concerned only with battered women from working-class families, we would like to explore the hurdles and predicaments of working-class family life and to relate them to the probability of marital discords, conflicts, and violence.

---

*At least four studies can be cited at this juncture: John Flynn's *Spouse Assault: Its Dimensions and Characteristics in Kalamazoo County, Michigan*, 1975, unpublished manuscript of School of Social Work, Western Michigan University, Kalamazoo, Michigan; John O'Brien's "Violence in Divorce-prone Families," in *Violence in the Family*, edited by S.K. Steinmetz and M.S. Straus, 1974, Dodd, Mead and Co., N.Y.; Rodney Stark and James McEvoy's "Middle-class Violence," in *Psychology Today* Vol. IV (Nov. 1970), p. 52; and George Levinger's "Physical Abuse Among Applicants for Divorce," in *Violence in the Family*, edited by S.K. Steinmetz and Murray A. Straus, 1974, pp. 85-91.

**Murray Straus, Richard Gelles, and Suzanne Steinmetz are presently engaged in a survey study of this kind, using a national and, therefore, more representive sample of American families. The title of this project is "Physical Violence in American Families," which is funded and supported by the National Institute of Mental Health.

A study by McKinley[15] indicates the association between a person's degree of occupational self-direction and amount of aggressiveness manifested in father-son relationships. McKinley's data also indicate that a man who derives little satisfaction from his job is more liable to resort to harsh punishment, an observation cutting across all class units. If McKinley is correct, one begins to wonder if his observations regarding the relationship between occupational self-direction and physical punishment can also be applied to husband-wife relationships, thus giving the multitude of working-class males the charter to wreak violence on their spouses as a result of deriving little or no occupational satisfaction from menial jobs.

In his attempt to identify the strategic causal variables pertinent to the incidence of child abuse, Gil (see Reference 8, page 352) argues that "one major source of stress and frustration for adults in our society is the multi-faceted deprivations of poverty and its correlates: high density in overcrowded, dilapidated, inadequately served neighbourhoods; large numbers of children, especially in one-parent, mainly female-headed households; and the absence of child-care alternatives." Gil continues to argue that the alienating circumstances in most work places, especially the high degree of competitiveness, occupational pressures and interpersonal exploitation, and the hierarchical impersonality and authoritarianism inherent in most bureaucratic structures, constitute a major source of psychological stress and frustration for most working persons.* A recent report by a task force of the United States Department of Health, Education, and Welfare[20] has pointed to the all-encompassing and pervasive phenomenon of working alienation in American society's economic and productive system. The attempt to link alienation to the various indices of crime and delinquency, and mental disorders and illness is deeply rooted in the tradition of studies in the area of deviance.

What merits immediate attention is that alienation is such an endemic feature and systematic product of our existing socio-economic structure that it defies individual intelligence and capacity to cope. "The home as the last resort" or "the home as haven" metaphor

---

*For an excellent discussion of the alienating circumstances that working-class people find themselves in, read Richard Sennet and J. Cobb's *The Hidden Injuries of Class*, Vintage Books, 1972.

reminds us that one can only expect a man overburdened with feelings of frustration gathered from the work place to unload and discharge them upon coming home, an environment which had long been considered the place in which to do so. Moreover, for many modern males, it is only within the home setting that he can feel a minimal sense of potency, power, and control, and there he sees the chance of exercising some authority to get what he wants. To the extent that this male yearning for control over the home environment is challenged or thwarted, especially in situations in which there is active female participation in the work force, conflicts between spouses and child-abuse in the form of violent physical outbursts begin to make their respective appearances.

Family frustrations are best understood when viewed as a total of the frustrations brought into the family from the outside, and perceived and assessed as such by husband, wife, and children individually, coupled with frustrations generated from intrafamilial interactional dynamics.[4] Regarding the kinds of frustrations confronting housewives. Steinmetz and Straus[19] have made an interesting observation:

> But since the main avenue of achievement for women had been in family rather than in occupational roles, we must look within the family for the circumstances that are frustrating to women. An obvious one is the presence of a large number of children. Another is a high degree of residential crowding ... lower-class wives are less likely to have the material means to carry out family functions—few home appliances, little money for food, etc. Their absence, together with many children, and overcrowding, makes the lower-class wife's family role more frustrating.

It will not be too difficult to add to the above list of wife-encountered frustrations and strains when we start to divert our attention from mere physical and materialistic household conditions to the numerous demanding, often times unrewarding duties and responsibilities assigned to housewives by cultural tradition. Childrearing is one. It is indeed a paradox that parents are taught childrearing practices by their first-born child.[3] Not knowing exactly how to nurture children, but left with no alternatives because life goes on and juvenile needs have to be continually met and satisfied, parenthood indeed constitutes a crisis for many individuals.[11] This observation is repeatedly borne out and stressed in child-abuse literature.[10]

The tedium and monotony of routine housework, plus its failure in generating intrinsic motivation and gratification, as long pointed out by women liberationists, is another potential source of stress and frustration for many homemakers. One would venture to speculate that work within the home provides minimal opportunity for achievement of occupational satisfaction; neither does it contribute to self-awareness of potentialities and deep-seated needs, nor to self-actualization. It would be foolhardy to regard housework as a "job" in its conventional, socio-economic sense. Social and sometimes physical isolation is another source of frustration for housewives; without a job to link the individual to the outside world, housewives are often besieged by a desperate sense of futility, alienation, and boredom, which in appropriate triggering contexts could result in frustration and, in turn, lead to aggressive behaviour.*

It is clear that the concepts of frustration and stress are convenient research aids in directing our attention to the structural sources of tensions and strains within the family, which have the potential of gradual accumulation to such an extent that, given other appropriate conditions (e.g., alcohol intoxication), physical violence becomes at least one of the many probable resultant courses of action. Perhaps we need to construct a typology or a number of typologies of frustrative events, and to explain individual differences in reactions to each of these frustrating situations. We might want to start asking questions as to how conditions like social comparison, i. e. , the acute awareness that one is socio-economically deprived and inferior to his or her neighbours and, more critically, that one sees no hope in improving his or her lot in the immediate future, can be conceptualized as a mode of structural frustration? Another recurrent source of frustration is chronic unemployment or seasonal employment, a highly prevalent condition among the working class.[7] Familial frustration is a highly diffuse and complex phenomenon; the mere attempt to construct

---

*Burgess's "Clockwork Orange" theory, linking boredom and deprivation to frustration and aggression, is most interesting reading, especially when we connect his premises to the many situations of "bored desperation but inaction" that contemporary youth find themselves in.

typologies can only facilitate conceptual thinking. Then the foremost problem for researchers in intrafamilial aggression and violence is to analyse and assess the linkage between broader social processes and forces that operate on the family, and the various patterns of intra-personal and interpersonal conflicts and discords observed within the family.

Normalization and Routinization of Violence

Interpolating from our own data, we are tempted to suggest that quite a substantial number of violent marital relationships probably do have a long history, and have been sustained and put up with over an extended period of time. Fifty-eight women out of our total population sample of 194 (almost 30%) are between 30 and 50 years old; 97 women have been married for four to ten years, and 10 women have been cohabiting with their current mates for more than ten years. Half of our women have had previous separation experiences with their current mates prior to admission to the shelter. Thirty-three percent of these women, after spending some time in the shelter, eventually returned to new or former apartments with current mates and children.

At this juncture, two very critical questions emerge: First, why have they stayed for so long with their abusive mates? Second, why have they returned to former violent marital relationships, knowing that "tomorrow will not be any better than today or yesterday?" These two questions open exciting avenues of future reseach, the directions of which might have more fruitful and rewarding payoffs if they concentrate on the economic and socio-psychological predicaments of today's working-class housewives.

It is Lofland's idea[13] that various modes of deviant behaviour, including violence and aggression are subject to normalization which is characterized by complex socio-psychological processes such as "social identification as pivotally normal" and "escalation to normal identity." The same idea has led Ball-Rokeach[1] to enumerate three modes of justification of violence: violence as a means to desired ends; violence as duty and obedience; and violence in the context of extenuating circumstances, such as fear, exhaustion, temporary insanity, or the influence of drugs or alcohol.

Lincoln[13] proposes that justifications of violence may be based upon any (or indeed a combination) of five critical factors: 1) behaviour of the victim, 2) characteristics of the victim, 3) behaviour of the attacker, 4) characteristics of the attacker, and 5) other utilitarian factors. In an attempt to elaborate on the meaning of "utilitarian factors," Lincoln (see Reference 73, page 56) continues to argue:

> The use of violence also may be justified because violence is seen as the most advantageous way of accomplishing a highly desired goal. Violence could be viewed as "necessary" to either accomplish a desired goal or perhaps to prevent an undesirable end state. In these cases the utility of violence transcends the immediate situation.

In a recent speech delivered to a conference titled "Domestic Violence Between Mates: Couples in Conflict" that was held in March, 1977 at Ontario Institute for Studies in Education, Toronto, Ontario, Gelles, interpreting data gathered from a United States nationwide study of a representative sample of American households, made two crucial observations: 1) almost any incident of husband-wife or parents-children violence can be and is indeed eventually justified by some techniques or measures; and 2), perhaps, a major causal factor of the high incidence and prevalence of violence within American families has a lot to do with the propensity of American citizens, be they abusers or victims, to view violence as an *accepted, valued,* and *normative* way to deal with frustrating situations and relationships.

Given this slice of literature bearing upon the notion of "normalization of violence," it is to be hypothesized that the historical maintenance and stabilization of a certain level of violence and aggression within the household is contingent upon the readiness and inclination of both the victimizer and the victim to perceive and define a specific level of violence as normal, necessary, and acceptable. To the extent that violence in marital relationships is defined by both parties as acceptable, it thus gradually becomes amenable to routinization and ritualization. Rituals implicate routine, regularity, and predictability having a scene of initiation, a building-up transitional period, and an ending point. Every time a violent episode is in camera within the household, both husband and wife know within themselves that it is somehow going to end in due course. To the extent that violence as a mode of behaviour is normalized and routinized within the household, it ceases to be defined by both the abusing and abused parties to be deviant or problematic; violence has then become a systematic and inherent feature of family life.

Initial acts of marital violence in young families might have surprised and stunned a few innocent wives and, to some extent, the husbands too; therefore, these acts could be psychically costly in terms of creating tensions and apprehensions in the marital relationship. The same tensions and apprehensions might be diffused or rationalized away once violence has begun to take on a specific pattern of regularity and a predestined course of action. Once violence assumes a regularized pattern of behavioural routine, to a certain extent, the abused wife begins to look forward to its occurrence because it seems to offer the only solution, however temporary, in spite of its grave, long-term consequences to the accelerating and accumulating tensions and anxieties of family life. Once violence becomes regularized, provided that it does not become severe enough to take the life of a family member, it is accepted by both marital partners as a problem-solving strategy. In a sense, violence begins to take on instrumental roles.

If it is indeed true that violence, like many other modes of human behaviour, is eventually subjected to normalization and routinization, it is here suggested that the extent of routinization of violence is a function of the duration of marriage. It then follows that marriages in the early stages of the family life cycle are less likely than those in the later stages to exhibit routinized patterns of violent interaction.

Having entertained the concepts of normalization and routinization of marital violence, we might also want to enumerate their implications and dimensions in the immediate family context:

1. Violence becomes the most immediate, direct, simple, and effective means of control. In a sense, violence as a weapon is always physically available and accessible.
2. Husbands begin to realize that when all other means of control fail, they can always resort to some degree of violence. To their minds, no marital situations can really get out of control.
3. Husbands will be more likely and probable to resort to violence as a means of mate control when they know that their wives will not resist, jump back, or get out of the home situation to appropriate community help or intervention.
4. Wives have begun to accept some degree of intrafamilial violence as

"normal and acceptable," provided that it will not degenerate into severe physical injuries or homicide.

5. Having seen and understood that marital violence is routinized and regularized, wives have begun to tell themselves that violence is indeed a process having a beginning and an end. Some of them might even rationalize that they are responsible for the episode of violence being triggered. Once the "show" is started, the wife is left with no alternatives other than sustaining the process of violence to an end or secretly hoping that no major physical injuries or death will occur.

6. Perhaps, most distressingly, the abused wife's high threshold of tolerance of intrafamilial violence, coupled with her own readiness to contribute to and activate mechanisms underlying the routinization and normalization of violence, renders her unlikely to define husband-wife violence as problematic enough to prompt her to sever the relationship permanently.

What is most important is our contention that the continuation of violent marital interaction is impossible without the propensity of both parties to define this specific mode of behaviour as normal in the family context. Historical routinization of violence thus derives its impetus from a definition of the "violent" situations as "normal." Consequently, a seemingly erratic behaviour has gradually over time become a regularity, a routine, a predictable and, perhaps most importantly, an inherent part of family life in a lot of households in our society!

Economic and Socio-psychological Dependency

Our data denote that more than half of the 194 women have identified themselves as "housewives" when asked when they were last employed. Fifty percent stated that they participated in the labour or work force more than five years before, while another 20% had ended their last employment between 1 and 5 years before. Low educational achievement, and lack of vocational, marketable skills and talents, have severely affected these women's chances in actively participating in the work force. Consequently, they, either voluntarily or involuntarily, have opted to stay within the home as "housewives" or "home-makers."

Upon admission to the women's shelter, 82 women declared that they were plain broke and "penniless," and 25 women had less than 3 dollars, 48 had less than 25 dollars, 14 women had 14 dollars, and only 26 had more than 5 dollars. Without a job or an independent source of income, these women were forced to enter into a once-in-and-no-exit predicament of extreme economic dependency. Our conjecture, which is not altogether unreasonable, is that to many of these women physical separation from their mates meant instant poverty and material deprivation; housing, medical care, boarding, and child care immediately become serious problems. Detached from husbands, however abusive, women, with the acute awareness of a very grim prospect of obtaining employment and accommodation, become incapacitated and disabled.

Our contention is that any attempt to get at the reasons that women staying with or returning to apparently abusive husbands has to come to grips with the economic dependency underlying the "housewife syndrome." Just as a woman has to depend on her mate's source of income for livelihood, she, having been emotionally committed to the romantic idea of a family and "entrapped" in the marital situation, is also dependent on her mate for socio-psychological and affective support. Economic dependency breeds socio-psychological dependency. In this connection, two working hypotheses are constructed for future research: 1) the more that the wife is economically dependent on her husband for the support of herself and children and, at the same time, is cut off from economic resources of social and kinship networks, the more likely she will be to stay with or return to her abusive husband, and put up with repeated violence; 2) the more the wife is socio-psychologically dependent on her husband (e.g., in the forms of extreme familism or emotional entrapment in the institution of marriage), the more likely she will be to stay with or return to her abusive husband, and put up with repeated violence.

While it is suggested that women's economic and socio-psychological dependency seem to be the major determinants in the historical maintenance of violent marital relationships over an extended period, the same kind of dependency also explains why women return to their abusive husbands with their children after their stay at the women's shelter. On departure from the shelter, only three women found employment, five obtained apartments through Ontario Housing Corporation, and two women were able to place children in daycare. Once completely on their own, housing, employment, child care, and health become paramount problems which are more often than not beyond their capacity to cope with. Homelessness, economic and emotional insecurity, and a painful sense of loneliness, have functioned to reawaken their once-dormant dependency on their husbands. "Returning home," in view of all these objective deprivations and hard realities, is not a very insensible and unwise choice after all!

Migrancy, Failure to Prosecute, and Isolation

Our further inspection into the data reported in the above description suggest three other crucial areas of study, our knowledge of which, even aided by all kinds of existing literature on intrafamilial violence, is at best deficient and ambiguous: 1) the relationship between migrancy and immigrant status and wife-battery; 2) the problem of the victim's failure to initiate legal proceedings against an abusive mate; and 3) the nature of mediation and transaction between women in general, and full-time housewives in particular, and their external environment. Our data indicate that 35% of the total sample are immigrant women, which perhaps might be a result of sampling artifact. Two questions arise: 1) whether stressful life events confronting immigrant, working-class families, e.g., various forms of racial discrimination and prejudice, differ from those confronting their non-immigrant counterparts; and 3) whether these stressful life events, provided that they are unique and different, predispose these families to a high incidence of wife-battery. Our impression is that the saliency of immigrant and working-class status does matter in Canadian society, although we do not know exactly how and why it matters, as far as the etiology of intrafamilial violence is concerned.

A majority of these women have chosen not to initiate legal proceedings against their mates. As a matter of fact, only 8% of the total 194 women had actually initiated the criminal justice process and had laid assault charges. What precisely is the rationale behind this unwillingness and unreadiness, on the part of the victims, to lay criminal charges? Perhaps light will be thrown on this dark area when we go back to the long historical process of normalization and ritualization of family violence prior to these women seeking institutional help, and the economic and socio-psychological dependency into which they have cast themselves. Coupled with this tinge of dependency may perhaps be the unreadiness of these women to involve the criminal justice system outside of the family to effect some kind of punitive measures such that the husband-wife relationship will be improved. It may be their secret wish to have brutality ended, but not necessarily through initiation and mobilization of legal proceedings. If change is the ultimate goal, punishment of the abusers by the criminal justice machinery *may not* be *the means* that these women would choose.

Women hesitate to prosecute because they still have difficulty in perceiving and defining "wife-battery" as criminal behaviour that violates the ultimate rights and dignity of the individual; it is also because they are too dependent on their husbands in a wide variety of ways to implicate them in the criminal justice mechanism. To many of them, laying charges and getting their husbands convicted spell permanent severance of a long relationship, which might not be exactly the thing that they desire!

In order to locate at least one referent person in times of emergencies or accidents, women were asked during the admission interview to cite a close relative or a friend. Most women can cite names of a relative or a friend. A lot more can name a family doctor or a lawyer for medical or legal advice. However, the same data does not enable us to evaluate the nature of mediation and transaction between these violent families and their immediate networks of kin, friends, and other community social service agencies. Flynn[6] suggests that families fraught with conflicts and interpersonal violence have maintained, at best, meagre and precarious relationship with their immediate social environment, resulting in a state of familial isolation such that forthcoming patterns of help from the outside are either inaccessible or simply discouraged.

Gelles (see Reference 7, page 133) has come up with similar observations regarding the relationship between social isolation and conjugal violence:

> The interview with members of the 80 families gave the impression that the violent families were almost completely cut off from their neighbours. They did not know them, they had few friends in the neighbourhood, they almost never visited their neighbours, and, in short, had few social resources in the community who they could turn to for help when they encountered family problems. While violent families did not know their

neighbours, their non-violent neighbours were knowledgeable about their neighbours and had many friends in the neighbourhood.

According to Gelles, there are at least two possible contending explanations to bear on the social isolation-conjugal violence relationship: 1) that marital conflict and violence lead to, and, therefore, precede isolation, and 2) that social isolation happens temporarily prior to family violence, and is thus one of the causal factors contributing to a family becoming violence-prone. Gelles (see Reference 7, pages 134-135) seems to be more sympathetic toward the second position:

> There are indications in the interview data that the second causal sequence is the one which applies in most cases of isolation and violence. . . . It is an empirical question why these families become isolated in the first place, but it does seem that social alienation could be an important factor involved in conjugal violence. Social isolation of a family can mean "no one to turn to" for help or advice in times of crisis and, thus, the crisis may escalate into conflict and violence. Isolation also may deprive the spouses of a "neutral zone" to escape to in case of escalating conflict.

Theoretically speaking, therefore, familial isolation from immediate environment has several detrimental and far-reaching consequences:

1. Familial isolation deprives a family unit of an integral component of resources, both of which severely affect the family's overall ability in coping with life stresses and troubles.
2. Familial isolation, by virtue of making transactions between family and environment problematic, if not impossible, deprives the family of adequate exposure to alternatives of coping with stress other than resorting to severe marital discords and violence.
3. Physical isolation of a family, as a result of infrequent contacts with the outside, leads to socio-psychological isolation which lays the ground of breeding negative and fatalistic attitudes on the part of family members toward the socio-psychological environment in the immediate vicinity, and the society at large.

Trapped in a state of socio-psychological and physical isolation, the family is unlikely to seek help from external sources, even in times of severe stress and frustration. The underlying realization may be that help will not be forthcoming even upon request, or the offer of help is perceived to be impotent and ineffective to furnish any viable solution to the problem.

It is important to realize that severe familial isolation from other significant and helpful people is extremely costly for the female victims, and is much more so than for the male victimizers. We suggest that many battered women have, by and large, failed to recognize and identify the criminality and illegality of wife-battery because of their prolonged, almost total, physical confinement to the home. Consequently, they have few chances of being exposed to the alternative lifestyles of other married couples, their definitions of the problem of wife-battery, and their choice of strategies in coping with various crisis situations. Isolation breeds premature enclosure-to-exploration into chances and fulfilment of aspirations, and prevents the possibility of perceiving an old problem from a different perspective. Our conjecture is that most of our sample women have scarcely talked with anyone, whether he or she is a social worker or simply a close friend or relative, in their daily life about their own feelings, wishes, motivations, or desires. Neither do we expect them to discuss regularly their perception of the problem of wife-battery with close friends and relatives.

Conclusion

We have suggested in the beginning of this paper that our contribution to the ever-increasing literature in the area of intrafamilial violence in general, and wife-battery in particular, lies in our attempts to generate important research questions from the data that we have been able to compile, which in turn are amenable to formulation of pertinent working hypotheses for future research endeavours.

Four areas of concern have been identified: 1) the relationship between socio-economic status and wife-battery, which seems to be mediated by a multitude of yet unclearly identified *"stressful life-events and deprivations,"* which are generated from diffuse and all-encompassing conditions of life endemic to each class position; 2) the socio-psychological mechanisms and processes underlying the *normalization and routinization of violence* within the family, which, as we have suggested, are associated with individual propensity *to perceive and define* a specific mode of behaviour as normal or deviant, criminal or legal; 3) the *economic and socio-psychological dependency* in which housewives, especially those recruited from the lower stratum of our society, have unfortunately and tragically cast themselves; 4) the *physical and structural isolation* of problematic and violent families.

It is hoped that our evaluation of pertinent concepts and notions which are identified in the above discussion will provide some theoretical insights and throw light on the complexity and intricacy of the problem of wife-battery. At present, deficiencies in theoretical and empirical knowledge do not enable us to construct a viable theory of intrafamilial violence. However, it is our belief that the several hypotheses formulated in this paper will at least promise an immediate head start in the right direction.

References

1. Ball-Rokeach, Sandra J. "The Legitimation of Violence," in James F. Short, Jr., Marvin E. Wolgang, and Aldine Atherton, eds. *Collective Violence, 1972.* Annals of American Academy of Political and Social Science, p. 391.
2. Burgess, Anthony. *A Clockwork Orange,* N.Y.: Ballantine Books Inc., 1962.
3. Campbell, James S. "The Family and Violence," in S.K. Steinmetz and M.A. Straus, eds. *Violence in the Family.* New York: Dodd, Mead, and Co., 1974.
4. Chan, Kwok B. "Intra-familial Violence: Myth-Making vs. Theory-Building." A paper presented to the 1977 Canadian Sociology and Anthropology Meetings in June at the University of New Brunswick, Fredericton, Canada, 1977.
5. "Symbolic Interactionism: Implications and Applications for Theory and Research in Family Conflicts and Violence." Unpublished working paper, 1976.
6. Flynn, John et al. "Spouse Assault: Its Dimensions and Characteristics in Kalamazoo County, Michigan." Unpublished manuscript of School of Social Work, Western Michigan University, Kalamazoo, Michigan, 1975.
7. Gelles, Richard. *The Violent Home: A Study of Physical Aggression Between Husbands And Wives.* Sage Library of Social Research, 13. Sage Publ. Inc., 1972.
8. Gil, David G. *Violence Against Children: Physical Abuse in the United States.* Cambridge, Mass.: Harvard University Press, 1970.
9. "Unravelling Child Abuse." *American Journal of Orthopsychiatry* 45, No. 3 (April 1975), pp. 346-356.
10. Helfer, Ray E. and Kempe, Henry. *The Battered Child,* 2nd ed. Chicago: The University of Chicago Press, 1974.
11. LeMasters, E.E. "Parenthood as Crisis." *Marriage and Family Living,* (November 1957), pp. 352-355.
12. Levinger, George. "Physical Abuse among Applicants for Divorce," in S.K.

Steinmetz and M.S. Straus, eds. *Violence in the Family.* New York: Dodd, Mead and Co., 1974.

13. Lincoln, Alan Jay. "Justifications and Condemnations of Violence: A Typology of Responses and A Research Review." *Sociological Symposium*, No. 9, 1973, pp. 51-67.

14. Lofland, John. *Deviance and Identity.* Englewood Cliffs, N.J.: Prentice Hall, Inc., 1969.

15. McKinley, Donald G. *Social Class and Family Life.* New York: The Free Press, 1964.

16. O'Brien, John. "Violence in Divorce-prone Families," in S.K. Steinmetz and M.S. Straus, eds. *Violence in the Family.* New York: Dodd, Mead and Co., 1974.

17. Sennet, Richard, and Cobb, Jonathan. *Hidden Injuries of Class.* New York: Vintage Books, 1972.

18. Stark, Rodney, and McEvoy, James. "Middle-class Violence," in *Psychology Today* 4 (November 1970), p. 52.

19. Steinmetz, Suzanne K., and Straus, Murray A. "The Family as Cradle of Violence," in *Society*, formerly *Transaction* 10 (Sept.-Oct. 1973), p. 50.

20. Task Force to the Secretary of The Department of Health, Education and Welfare. *Work in America.* Cambridge, Mass.: MIT Press, 1973.

13/The Initial Effect of Divorce Upon Children*

Sally Palmer

Much of the work done by social workers and social agencies centres on the family. In particular, social workers find themselves concerned with broken families in various stages, that is, families in a separation crisis, others in post-separation adjustment, and individuals who are the products of broken families. These problems have become more significant with the increase in divorce since the change in Canadian divorce laws in 1968.

In working with families going through divorce, considerable attention tends to be centred on the implications for dependent children. There is the question of custody, the problem of redistributing financial resources, and the issue of continuing contact between the children and the departing parent. Social workers, as well as parents, need objective information on which to base their thinking about these arrangements. Ideally, they should know the possible implications of separation for dependent children and the effect of various arrangements. Such questions have been asked by those writing about divorce (see Reference 2. Bohannan, page 55 and Reference 4, Despert, page 117), but few objective answers are available.

There has been almost no research done in Canada on children of separated or divorced parents. Some of the legal writers have touched on the social aspects of divorce, making the point that maintenance and custody are often decided prior to court application by divorcing parents in their own interests rather than those of the child (see Reference 10. McRuer, page 596 and Reference 20. Wuenster, page 397). Two Canadian studies of remarriage have referred to the aspect of child adjustment,[15/11] but research in Canada is generally lacking.

The American literature on children of divorce also fails to answer the above questions. It was possible to find only one study of

*This study was financed by the Welfare Grants Division, Department of National Health and Welfare, Canada.

the actual arrangements made for custody and parent visitation and this was basically descriptive.[7] Another article pointed out that custody may be used as a weapon by a rejected spouse (see Reference 8. Harris, page 13).

The findings that compare children of broken and intact homes show a slight disadvantage for the former. A comparison of juvenile delinquents with non-delinquents concluded that slightly more delinquents came from divorced homes (see Reference 6. Glueck, page 91). A much earlier study of 13 000 American school children showed children from broken homes with slightly lower scores on personality adjustment tests and on teachers' ratings for obedience. On other characteristics there was little difference: teachers' ratings on social aggressiveness and emotional stability showed a slight advantage for girls from unbroken homes but none for boys.[18]

A more recent study reached the conclusion that children of unhappy marriages had some problems: 4% were delinquent and 10% were identified at school as needing treatment, but this was not viewed as much different from children in general (see Reference 9. LeMasters, page 88). Another study used personality tests to measure stability, dominance/submission, and self-sufficiency in children of remarriage. The results were comparable to children from first marriages on the first two characteristics, but were lower than average in self-sufficiency (see Reference 1. Bernard, pages 307-9).

These findings suggest that children of broken homes may have adjustment problems but the difference between them and other children is not great. One writer attempted to explain this by the inherent "resiliency" of human beings, particularly children. She indicated that children generally undergo a variety of traumatic experiences throughout their development, most of them less obvious to others than the experience of divorce (see Reference 1. Bernard, page 322).

Another writer supported this view from his clinical experience with broken families (see Reference 8. Harris, pages 15-16). He noted that children use restorative manoeuvres in an attempt to regain the security that they have lost, such as manipulating parents in order to control them.

The personal characteristics of the individual child affect his or her adjustment to family breakdown. It has been found, for example, that boys tended to be less self-reliant than girls when their mothers worked (see Reference 12. Nye and Hoffman, page 271). Boys have also been found to have distorted relationships with their mothers when they lived with them alone, the sons apparently becoming substitutes for the absent husbands (see Reference 17. Strean, page 331). The birth position of the child in the family is another consideration. There is some evidence that the oldest child reacts somewhat differently from the others (see Reference 3. Christensen, page 764). There is also evidence that the addition of an infant may be a cause of separation (see Reference 14. Palmer, page 261).

There has been some exploration in the literature of visiting between parents and children after separation. The two Canadian studies of remarriage mentioned earlier found that contact between visiting parent and child terminated in about 40% of cases. Some of the reasons for this have been suggested by other writers: parents tend to use visits to bargain about their own conflicts (see Reference 5. Egleson, page 210 and Reference 8. Harris, page 15); the parent with custody is often opposed to the visiting (see Reference 7. Goode, page 208); visiting can be awkward for parents and children alike (see Reference 11. Messinger, page 8); the departing parent often moves some distance from the family (see Reference 15. Schlesinger, page 23). Visiting patterns and their effects have not been given much attention in the literature, although the importance of predictability has been stressed (see Reference 3. Christensen, page 753).

It seems evident from the foregoing that there are gaps in our knowledge about children of divorce. There is little information from North America on the kinds of arrangements made for children after a separation, and the findings are inconclusive about the effect of family breakdown on children. The continuation of relationships with the non-custodial parent have not been studied except as a by-product of other research. Given the concern of social workers and parents about the effect of divorce on children and the lack of adequate research, it is important to discover more about what actually happens to these children.

The following is a study of such families, with emphasis on the effect of divorce on children.

Method of Research

The data were obtained by interviewing 291 families (with 566 children) that had commenced divorce proceedings. These were all the families with children under age 16, who were seeking divorce in one county of Southwestern Ontario over a 2.5 year period in the mid-1960's. Access was gained to the families through the divorce court process which required information about the plans made for dependent children.

The interviewing took place just prior to the change in the Canadian divorce law in 1968. Ideally a study of Canadian children in divorce should include a similar group of families who divorced under the new law. This is not possible, because the mandatory interviewing of divorcing families was altered by the government shortly after the Divorce Act 1968. Presently, only those who cannot agree on custody are interviewed by an agent of the Court.

The interviews centred on the arrangements made for the ongoing care of children, the continuation of a relationship with the absent parent, and the reactions of children to separation, primarily in their functioning at school. A questionnaire was used to gather the information. It included demographic data on custody, support, visiting, personal characteristics of the child, and Juvenile Court records. In addition, evaluative data were sought concerning the child's functioning at school. To obtain this, the author interviewed the child's teacher, except for a few reports completed during the long vacation, when the school report had to suffice. The teacher was questioned about the child's behaviour, academic performance as related to potential, and observed reactions to the separation if this were recent. These data were combined in a measure called the child's "school functioning." This was felt to be an important measure of the child's adjustment to family breakdown for the following reasons: 1) school is the major area where demands are made on children, thus the effects of stress at home are likely to show up in their performance. Their ability to work effectively and behave appropriately is an indicator of emotional stability; 2) the teacher can provide a fairly objective assessment of the child based on long-term observation and comparison with a group of peers.

"School functioning" became the independent variable in the data analysis. The relationship of school functioning to dependent variables such as living arrangements, support, and contact with absent parents was found by applying the p test for statistical significance. The other part of the analysis was a frequency distribution to obtain a descriptive picture of children in divorce, and the arrangements made for their care.

In summary, this is a study of 566 children from 291 divorcing families, the homes and care provided for them, as well as their functioning outside the home, especially in school. The purposes are to identify patterns of custody, support, and visiting, and to discover relationships between these variables and the child's functioning in school.

The Findings

Custody

As stated earlier, the Court is concerned about the arrangements for dependent children when families divorce. In decisions of custody, the Court's prime consideration is said to be the child's best interest. Yet the findings in this study cast some doubt on whether the children's best interest is met by the arrangements made.

Although the families had not yet been to court at the time they were interviewed, they had usually reached agreement about custody;

Table 13.1
Placement of Children at Commencement
of Divorce Proceedings

Placement	No. of children	% of Total children
Mother	361	63.8%
Father	96	17.0%
Mother and relatives	42	7.4%
Father and relatives	11	2.0%
Maternal relatives only	13	2.3%
Paternal relatives only	18	3.2%
Other private homes	21	3.6%
Institution	4	.7%
Totals	566	100.0%

often the children had been living for some time with one or the other parent. A few who disagreed with the arrangements admitted that they had given up custody in order to obtain the divorce.

The custody arrangements did not necessarily follow accepted principles for childrearing. For instance, it is generally accepted that children need their mothers during their developing years, and that girls cannot be reared by a father alone as easily as can boys. Yet a sizable minority of children did not live with their mothers: 29% lived with their fathers, relatives, or in other homes. The distribution of children is shown in Table 13.1.

Children Separated from Mothers

Two questions might be asked about the placement of so many children away from their mothers: 1) Were these particular mothers less adequate to care for their children? Or did they give up custody for some other reason? 2) Did those children who lived apart from their mothers suffer emotional damage? The associations between variables provide some answers to these questions.

l. First, let us examine reasons for giving up custody. As mentioned earlier, custody may be part of a bargain between parents in which one gives up the children in return for the other's co-operation in obtaining a divorce. Thus a mother who has found a new partner and wants to remarry might agree to give up custody, as the following finding suggests: Almost 40% of the wives were defendants in their divorce actions and a much smaller percentage of these kept their children than did the plaintiffs (51% of defendants compared to 91% of plaintiffs: $p < .001$). This tendency for custody to be associated with the presence or absence of extramarital relationships suggests that custody decisions were not necessarily related to the welfare of the child. They may have been related to the feelings of the mothers about their own behaviour. Some of the mothers interviewed expressed feelings of guilt which inhibited them from seeking custody. They found it difficult to reconcile a self-image as an unfaithful wife with that of a good mother. The following is a case in point:

> Mrs. N. was a defendant wife who had left home, allowing her
> husband to keep the children. She was in tears during the

interview about the prospect of losing her children permanently. She expressed the feeling, however, that she had no right to her children because she had become involved with a man other than her husband.

In effect, Mrs. N. felt that she was not an adequate mother to her children because of her extramarital behaviour. In such a case, a child might lose the parent who could best meet his or her needs because of an issue which was not central to his or her welfare.

Other mothers may have felt as Mrs. C. below that they were willing to give up custody in order to obtain a divorce and be free to remarry.

As mentioned above, the adequacy of the mother should have a bearing on custody. Two characteristics related to adequacy were the mother's age at marriage and admitted personality problems. It was found that mothers who had been under 18 at marriage kept their children as often as those who had been older; thus age was not a significant variable. As for personality, 10% of the mothers in the study admitted to having personality problems or that they had suffered from mental illness. This percentage was the same for those who gave up their children, as for those who kept them. This further suggests that custody was not decided according to the child's best interest; otherwise, mothers who were better prepared for motherhood (i.e., older at marriage and with no identified personality problems) would have been more likely to have custody.

2. The second question asked about children living apart from their mothers was whether they seemed to suffer emotional damage. As mentioned, the measure which was chosen as indicative of adjustment was school functioning. In the analysis, it was found that children of school age who lived with their mothers alone did better than those who lived with fathers alone; 66% of the former had no problems at school compared to 49% of the latter ($p < .01$). Thus, there is some support for the notion that children from separated families will do better if they live with their mothers.

As mentioned, the sex of the child is expected to have some bearing on custody. Fathers might be viewed as more important to older than to younger children, and to boys than to girls. It was expected that there would be some tendency to arrange custody with this in mind, indicating that parents had tried to meet the needs of the individual child despite their own personal preferences. Such a tendency was not found. The percentage of boys living with their fathers (60%) was not significantly different from the percentage of boys in the total group (55%, p<.17). Likewise, the percentage of children ten years and over living with their fathers (35%) was not significantly different from the percentage of children ten years and over in the total group (29%, p<.16).

Again, it would appear that influences other than the child's needs were affecting the parents' decisions regarding custody. The extramarital involvements of the mother have already been mentioned. Another related issue is the use of custody as a bargaining point, as illustrated in the following case:

> Mrs. C. left her son Robert, age one, with her husband's parents when the marriage broke up. She was pregnant at the time and her lawyer suggested that she leave Robert with his grandparents until the baby was born.

The following year, Mrs. C. tried once to get Robert back, but the grandparents resisted. A year later, at the time of the divorce, she said that she wanted custody but decided not to seek it because she wanted the co-operation of her husband in obtaining the divorce. Mr. C. told his wife that he would only provide the evidence of adultery she needed if she left Robert with his grandparents.

The foregoing illustrates the problems created by the divorce law prior to 1968, when adultery was the main ground for divorce. With the additional grounds for divorce in the present law, bargaining for children may not be as prevalent.

In summary, a sizable minority of children lived apart from their mothers, although there was some evidence to support the notion that placement with the mother was preferable. The above analysis suggests that many custody decisions are not based on the child's welfare but rather on the parent's own circumstances. The main influence seems to be the existence of a new partner and the probable desire for a divorce, even if this means losing custody.

Living with Relatives

Another pattern noted in the custody plans of the families studied was the frequency with which support was sought from relatives. As shown in Table 13.1, many separated parents with custody went back to live with their own parents. This reflects on the personal capacities of the parents to bring up their children independently. A parent who moves in with relatives is asking for help and willing to assume a somewhat dependent role.

Such an arrangement also has implications for the child's experience. In our society, which is based on a nuclear-family system, it can be difficult for a child to live with his parent in the home of relatives, who are usually the grandparents. A parent who moves in with relatives has to give up some of his or her autonomy. As a result, the parent's authority with the child may be undermined. Such a situation is frustrating for a child who must respond to two distinct authorities from different generations.

An even less supportive arrangement for children is one in which they are living with neither parent. As shown on Table 13.1, a number of children were left with relatives, in other private homes, or in institutions. This suggests that neither parent had the personal resources or the desire to care for the child, a condition which may have existed prior to the divorce or separation. Here the incapacity of the parents is indicated more strongly than in the previous arrangement. The possible effects on the child can be expected to be more traumatic than if he or she continued to live with one parent.

Disagreement about Custody

Another cause of disruption for children was parental disagreement on which of them should have custody. In 8% of families, the parents could not come to an agreement and both were applying for custody. There were indications that some of them had personal problems which interfered with their ability to be parents, and they may have been seeking custody to meet their own needs.

> Mrs. D. spent some time in psychiatric hospital after her separation, leaving 3-year-old Catherine with Mr. D. After her discharge she wanted Catherine back and a custody struggle ensued.

The prognosis given by Mrs. D.'s doctor was that her mental health was uncertain. Her suitability as a mother was also thrown into question by her attitude toward an out-of-wedlock child that she had conceived. Although she expressed a strong desire to have Catherine, she was planning to give up the out-of-wedlock child. In effect, the mother's needs for her daughter may have been greater than daughter Catherine's need for her.

In other cases where custody was an issue between the parents, a "tug of war" developed in which the child was subjected to a great deal of trauma. There were instances of one parent taking the child from the other's home without warning. This would tend to intensify the conflicting loyalties experienced by the child, as well as creating insecurity for her about the possibility of another imminent move.

In the families described above, it might be said that the parents' possessiveness led to situations potentially damaging to the child. This adds to the picture of parental inadequacy and decisions which centred on their needs rather than those of the child.

Children Living in New Unions

A percentage of children listed as living with "mother" or "father" were in fact living with a quasi-stepfather or stepmother as well (28% of those with fathers, and 14% of those with mothers lived in this type of home).

The advantage of a new union is that it brings in another adult to share in child care and it may alleviate financial strain by providing another income. The main problems are the adjustment of children to a step-parent and the uncertain social status of such a family until there is an opportunity for divorce and remarriage. From the point of view of child adjustment, it is likely that children will be pleased that their parent has found a partner, but they will also experience some ambivalence because of loyalty to the other parent. Older children, who are aware of the general social disapproval of common-law unions may be uncomfortable about this.

In an attempt to assess the adjustment of children to new unions, their school functioning was compared to children living alone with their parents. The findings suggest that there might be an advantage to children living in new unions with their fathers, but no such advantage was indicated for those living with the mother. For those children living with fathers, 76% of those in new unions were reported to have no problems, compared with 49% of those living with fathers aloe (p<.01). Children living with mothers showed no significant difference; 61% of those in new unions were said to have no problems compared to 66% of those living with mothers alone (p<.29).

The difference between mothers and fathers in this respect may reflect the double standard for sexual behaviour. A mother may feel uncomfortable toward her children about living with a man to whom she is not married, as this appears to be condoning sexual behaviour outside marriage. A father, on the other hand, may not experience the same discomfort. Many fathers presented their new partners to the children as a housekeeper; in effect, they had a socially acceptable rationalization for their living arrangements.

As a group, the children living with their parents in new unions had no more school problems than those living with parents alone. In fact, children living with their fathers seemed to do better when the father had a partner. This limited information suggests that the advantages of new unions to children may outweigh the disadvantages.

In summary, the findings about custody are not inconsistent with society's image of the broken family as a separated mother living alone with her children. In the group studied, the majority of children lived with their mothers, but their mothers did not always live alone—they were often living with relatives or a new partner. A significant minority of children lived with their fathers, again often with relatives or with the father's new partner. A few children had lost both parents when the marriage broke down and were living with relatives or foster parents.

Some of the associations found between the parents' personal circumstances and the custody plans suggest that the child's best interest tends to be given less priority than the parents' needs at the time of custody decisions. Mothers who were involved with other men were more likely to give up custody. There was no evidence of younger children or girls being more likely to stay with their mothers; nor did the mothers who seemed to be more suitable tend to keep their children. The benefits of staying with mother alone as opposed to father alone were suggested by variations in children's school functioning, as was the advantage to a child living with his or her father in a new union, rather than alone. The evidence suggests, in general, that custody arrangements were based on considerations other than the children's needs, and tends to support the importance of a mother figure in the home.

Financial Arrangements

Financial arrangements are an important contributor to the child's welfare. First, there is the amount of support paid by the absent parent; second, the element of coercion of the parent to pay; and third, the effect of financial support on the continuing parent-child relationship.

Amount of Support. The average amount of financial support paid by absent parents was found to be less than would be expected to meet the needs of the child. Even allowing for inflation since the mid-1960's, it is noteworthy that only 25% of the absent fathers paid more than $10 per week for each child. As for the remainder, 11% were in arrears over $100 on Family Court orders, 36% paid no support, and the other 28% paid $10 per week or less per child.

This low level of support was probably a reflection of the fathers' low incomes. The group of fathers had an average income about 20% lower than that of all male family heads in the same community. Contributions did not bear any relation to the income of the mother if the child lived with her. For example, it would be expected that children who lived with their mothers in new unions would receive less support from their fathers. This did not occur. Forty-nine percent of fathers paid support regularly when their wives lived in new unions, and 51% of those whose wives were living alone (2-sided $p = .82$). Thus, children who lived with their mothers alone tended to be economically disadvantaged. Children also suffered if their absent fathers had found new partners; only 58% of fathers who were in new unions paid support to their wives who had the children, compared to 69% of fathers living alone ($p < .04$). In effect, support seemed much more related to the father's circumstances than to those of the child.

Coercion to Pay Support. The second point mentioned above was that of coercion on the parent to pay support. The financial arrangements may be made privately or by the parent with custody seeking a court order for maintenance. It would seem to be in the best interests of children for a parent to pay voluntarily, indicating a sense of responsibility or a feeling of good will toward the child. In this study it was found that 41% of absent fathers contributed voluntarily to the support of their children, while no mothers did so. Thus concrete evidence of interest from the absent parent was lacking for the majority of children in the study.

When voluntary support was not forthcoming, the parent with custody had the right to take the other parent to Court, where an order could be made for regular support payments. This was only partially successful. Twelve percent of the men paid support regularly by court order, but another 11% were in arrears of at least $100 (approximately 10 weeks' payments) on their court orders. One reason for payments being in arrears is the system under which the Family Court operates. It is left to the parent with custody to locate the other parent and to initiate court action if payments are not kept up. If the initiative is not taken by the custodial parent, very often nothing is done, as the following case illustrates.

Mr. H. was over $6000 in arrears on a Family Court order after 10 years' separation. His wife and two children had been on public assistance since the first year of the separation. The younger child had health problems which prevented Mrs. H. from seeking employment. They lived under financial strain; for example, John, 9, wanted to join Cubs, but they could not afford the uniform.

Mr. H., who lived only a few blocks away from the family and wanted visiting privileges with the divorce, said he could have paid more maintenance. He projected the blame for the arrears on the Court and welfare officials saying that they made him angry. It seemed that the Court had been completely ineffective in enforcing its order.

It might be asked why Mrs. H. did not take her husband back to court and press for the arrears to be paid. Many of the mothers interviewed were reluctant to do this. The general feeling was that it was humiliating to have to take their husbands to court; thus, they preferred to manage on their own incomes. A similar feeling was expressed by the wives who received no maintenance from their husbands and did not taken even an initial court action (36% of those with custody); their feelings about the marriage made them want to avoid any further conflict.

The difficulty in obtaining support for children in separated families suggests that their best interests are not being served by the present system. It would be better for the custodial parent if the Court took the initiative in pursuing those who were delinquent with their payments. Under the present system, mothers with custody are often inhibited from seeking support by negative feelings about their ex-husbands. The child's right to support, however, should not depend on his or her parents' personal feelings. As will be seen, the issue of support has implications for the father-child relationship.

Effect on Father-Child Relationship

In this study, it was found that 88% of fathers who supported their children voluntarily also visited them regularly, compared to 27% of those who did not provide support (p<.001). The most interesting group was the one that paid under a Family Court order. Forty-eight percent of them visited their children compared to 27% of the non-supporters (p<.02), even though they were apparently contributing under coercion.

Fathers who visited, even when their wives had taken them to court for non-support, may have had a stronger emotional investment in their children because they were taking some responsibility for them. On the other hand, fathers who did not contribute might also refrain from visiting because they felt guilty about not supporting their children. Certainly the feeling was expressed by some mothers that support and visiting were interrelated. A number of them said they preferred their husbands not to contribute because they did not want them to visit the children.

The finding that visiting was associated with support suggests that a court order might help to preserve the parent-child relationship. Fathers who had been ordered to pay were more likely to visit, thus their children received both financial and emotional support.

In examining the various arrangements made for financial support after separation, it could be said that the welfare of the child was not always given priority. Firstly, the amount of support was inadequate. Fewer than half the children were supported voluntarily by their absent parents. Even when payments were regular and voluntary they tended to be minimal, and it seemed that the total financial resources of the separated family were not adequate to meet the needs of the children. When the coercion of court had been invoked to seek support, it was found that almost half the fathers were substantially in arrears.

Secondly, it appeared that the support was dependent to some extent on the relationship which existed between the estranged parents. In turn, the father-child relationship was associated with the payment of support. This suggests that, even with the coercion of a court order, payment of support should be encouraged in the interests of the father-child relationship in general.

Children's Reactions to Separation

The effect of separation on children is very difficult to measure. First, it would be exceedingly difficult to distinguish the problems created by an unhappy home from those arising from the separation itself. Second, it is difficult to obtain objective information about children's reactions. Parents are too subjective to assess their own children, yet there are few other people in a position to observe them. As discussed under Method of Research it was decided to use "school functioning" as a measure of the child's adjustment. Another source of objective information was the Juvenile and Family Court which had records on all children charged with offences. The findings reported below were obtained by telephone interviews with the teachers of the 340 school-age children and from the Juvenile Court records which were checked for children ten years of age and over.

School and Community Performance

School Functioning. Most children (63%) were reported by their teachers to have no problems in school. Their behaviour was said to be satisfactory and their academic performance appeared to be consistent with their ability. This suggests that these children were quite resilient in reaction to the family problems. In effect, they continued to function well in the main area in which demands were made upon them, despite the trauma of the separation.

Those children who did exhibit problems in school (37%) could be categorized as follows: the greatest number (25%) was described as unable to concentrate, apathetic, withdrawn, or not working up to ability. A smaller group (9%) was described as attention-seeking, resentful of authority, disruptive, or aggressive. Others were said to be "immature," "nervous" (2%), while a few talked or cried about their home situations (1%).

Let us consider how the above problems might relate to the parents' divorce. Children who were unable to concentrate, etc., may have been distracted by something more important to them than school; or they may have been withdrawn at school because they lacked the confidence to cope with the world outside their homes. These states could have been reactions to insecure home situations or pervasive anxiety related to the insecurities of the past. The following case illustrates the association between children's difficulties at home and lack of effort in school:

> There were four children in the G family and they were shifted back and forth by their parents after the separation. Mrs. G. took the children from her husband two months after the separation, without warning him. When she became ill 2.5 years later, she returned them to him "temporarily." Her ambivalence about custody was shown when she then suggested to her husband that this be a permanent placement. The school reports indicated that the oldest child in the G family was doing well but that three younger boys were all failing, although they were of average intelligence.

The children who presented behaviour problems in class were probably seeking attention or testing the authority of the teacher. It is understandable for a child from a broken family to seek attention or test the other significant adults in his or her environment. His or her basic relationship with adults has been disrupted so that he or she will seek substitute relationships. Also confidence in adults has been undermined by the parents' failure to succeed in marriage so that the child needs to test other adults. The following case is an example of behaviour problems in a child who has not adjusted to separation:

> Bobby, age 6, was living with his paternal grandmother after the separation and was visited by his mother. He showed unhappiness very directly when his mother came to visit. He cried when she left and pleaded with her to take him with her. In his mother's absence he was a behaviour problem both at home and at school. His grandmother did not really want to care for him because he was very aggressive with his five-year-old brother. Also his behaviour

in school was disruptive and led to his being separated from the entire class of kindergarten children.

Children who were described as "immature" or "nervous" were probably demonstrating reactions similar to those who were said to be disruptive or withdrawn. On further questioning it was usually found that the term "immature" related to attention-getting behaviour, while the "nervous" child tended to be quiet and easily upset. A few teachers, however, were unable to be more specific, thus the children were categorized simply as "immature" or "nervous."

The last category of children was for those who talked or cried at school about the separation, a surprisingly small percentage. Part of this could be attributed to the passage of time, as only 25% of families had separated within the previous year. For children of the recently separated, however, it would be natural, at a time of stress, for them to seek comfort from a teacher whom they saw daily and who was interested in them. Yet these children tended to keep their feelings hidden or to express them indirectly through their behaviour.

The fact that most children did not discuss the separation at school may be an indication of how completely dependent they were on their parents. At a time when their parents were in a crisis and probably less able to respond to their needs, the children should have been able to seek support from other adults. Yet they did not turn to their teachers as an obvious source of support, and the teachers apparently did not reach out to them. This suggests that outside support is unlikely to be requested by, or offered to children undergoing divorce; this may be a weakness created by our system of isolated nuclear families.

In summary, the reports from teachers indicate that many of the children seemed well adjusted. For those who did not, poor concentration and withdrawal were the most common problems noted, while aggressive behaviour was evident in a smaller group. There was very little direct expression of feeling by children to their teachers, suggesting that the children were left to resolve their feelings by themselves.

Delinquency. In addition to teachers' reports, the Juvenile Court records indicate if a child had been charged with delinquent behaviour. The percentage of children age 10 and over who had been charged was

1.3% per annum over a four-year period (1964–8) compared to 1% for the general population of London and Middlesex, not a significant difference (2-sided p = .70).

This delinquent behaviour on the part of a few children is similar in nature to aggressive and disruptive behaviour in school. Although antisocial behaviour in the community is a more serious problem, both kinds of behaviour could be described as the "acting-out" of disturbed inner feelings.

In general, delinquency could not be said to be a particular problem of children in the divorcing families studied. A substantial number of children had trouble controlling their behaviour in school and, for a few, this extended to delinquent behaviour in the community, but the rate of delinquency was similar to that for the general population.

Parental Response to Problem Behaviour. In some of the families interviewed it was found that the parent who had been most effective in disciplining the child was the one who had left the home. Often the remaining parent showed a tendency to be very permissive, which may have been an indirect expression of parental guilt about depriving the child of a normal home. Sometimes a child used the conflict between parents to play one against the other, as illustrated below.

> Billy G., age 5, was reported by his teacher to be difficult to handle, and there were indications that his mother had a similar experience with him. During the interview in the home, he constantly demanded food from his mother. When Mrs. G. tried to put limits on this, Billy threatened to report her to his father, which seemed to immoblize her. Eventually she gave him what he wanted.

In many separated homes it seemed that there was insufficient time and energy available for the care and guidance of children. In general it appeared that behaviour problems, noted outside the home, may have been created by the lack of parental guidance when one parent had to provide this virtually alone. There were indications that children took advantage of the rift between the parents and that the parent left with custody had depended upon the other parent to provide the discipline during the intact marriage. After the separation, the resources available for the care of the child were inadequate.

To summarize, the parental responses to the reactions of child to separation often seemed to be inadequate. Children were able to use the parental conflict to their own advantage, and personal resources available for child care often seemed to be insufficient.

Vulnerability of Children According to Age, Sex, and Position in the Family

Separation is undoubtedly painful for all children, but there are individual differences which affect their adjustment. According to ego psychology, a child's response is determined by his or her ego strengths which enable him or her to deal with crises and adapt to change. A child's response also depends upon age, sex, and birth position in the family.

In the following analysis the children's school functioning is compared according to their age, sex, and position in the family.

Age. The study of child development had identified two age periods when children tend to be in particular conflict with their parents over issues of dependence/independence. This first happens around age two and again in adolescence. If a child's parents separate during one of these periods, it may be expected that the child's normal resolution of dependence/independence will be interrupted by the family crisis. The emancipation process will also be jeopardized by the absence of one parent subsequent to the separation. The consequent interruption of developmental tasks will probably create difficulties for the child in meeting social expectations.

In this study there was no objective information about social functioning for very young children. For adolescents, however, school functioning was a good indicator of adjustment, as the major social expectation for the older child is for success at school. As adolescence is a vulnerable age, we might expect the school functioning of this age group to be affected.

This expectation was partially supported by the findings in the present study. There was a greter incidence of school problems reported by teachers when children were over ten years of age at the time of their parents' separation. Fifty-one percent were reported as having problems compared with 34% of those who were ten or under at the time of the separation ($p < .02$). The possibility was ruled out that this finding simply reflected greater problems with teenagers generally. It was found that the older group (11-15 years) did not have significantly more problems at the time they were interviewed than the others (40% had problems compared to 35% of the others, $p < .20$). Thus, the influential variable seemed to be the age at which separation occurred.

This finding probably relates to the interruption of developmental tasks of adolescence when a separation occurs. Adolescents in intact families tend to question their parents' attitudes and behaviour. They test out their parents in the process of forming their own value systems and asserting their individuality. On the other hand, adolescents whose family is in crisis cannot afford to put too much pressure on their parents by constantly testing them. As the family is in a vulnerable state, their own security is endangered if they create stress for their parents. In the absence of opportunities to resolve their inner conflicts within the family, they are likely to internalize conflicts or to express them outside the home. In this way the interruption of normal adolescent development may lead to problems in school and community functioning.

Another influence on older children is their sensitivity to social norms. They generally do not want to be different from their peers. They are likely to be acutely uncomfortable about the public aspect of the family's separation, as it sets them apart from their peers. This feeling was expressed very directly by a thirteen-year-old boy, who refused to attend Scouts after his mother left the family. He expressed a fear that everyone would be talking about him.

Apart from the adolescent group, there was no evidence that the age of a child at separation was associated with subsequent problems in school functioning. Reports of satisfactory performance were almost equal for those who 0-5 years of age and those who were 6-10 years of age at the time of the separation (65% and 66% respectively, 2-sided $p = .84$). It was mentioned above that the children are especially vulnerable in relation to their family around age two. Yet the findings do not support the notion that the early resolution of dependence/independence drives would be interrupted by the separation. Upon reflection, it becomes evident that the conflict at age two is usually centred on the mother/child relationship, as the mother is usually the main caretaker. Thus the emancipation process will not necessarily be interrupted by separation. The majority of children stay with their mothers and can continue to resolve this relationship.

To conclude, the findings suggest that adolescence is the most vulnerable age for a child to experience family breakdown. It is probable that the separation interrupts the essential developmental tasks and that the social implications of family breakdown are especially difficult for the adolescent.

Boys vs. Girls. The different adaptations made by boys and girls to society's expectations have been discussed in the Introduction. In general, more problems were identified for boys than for girls. The findings in this study tend to confirm the greater vulnerability of boys. There was a higher incidence of problems reported for them (40% compared to 31% for girls, $p < .04$).

One reason that boys may have more difficulties is related to the parent of the same sex. Throughout the developing years, children tend to see less of their fathers than their mothers. The separation adds to this imbalance, as it is usually the father who leaves, thus removing the role model for masculine behaviour. Even frequent contacts do not compensate for daily observation of the father in the home. It is also difficult for a boy to integrate his father's absence with his image of an ideal man. He may have a sense that his father has deserted the family, which creates ambivalence for him and his own masculinity.

In addition to the absence of a role model, boys who live with their mothers alone may develop an overly close relationship to make up for the absent father. A case in point is the following:

> Bob S., age 11, was an only child who lived alone with his mother after his parents separated. Mrs. S. provided him with a great deal of stimulation through reference books and interesting trips. Yet Bob was lacking in other ways: he did not have friends his own age, he was overweight, and had no physical activities other than swimming and bowling with his mother. The school principal reported that Mrs. S. often called the school to say that Bob was not well enough to attend.

The same could occur with girls but it was infrequent for girls to live alone with their fathers.

In general, girls showed fewer problems in school than boys. It is likely that they respond better to the trauma and insecurity of family breakdown, because most of them did not lose their role model nor were they placed in the position of filling in for the absent partner.

Sibling Position. It is generally conceded that the position that children occupy in a family has some bearing on how they are treated by parents and how they perceive themselves. As mentioned earlier, first-born children tend to have a unique relationship with their parents, thus they may be affected differently by a separation.

In this study it was found that first-born children were less likely to have problems in school (68% were reported to be functioning well compared to 57% of later-born children, $p<.03$). The same association was not found for children who had no siblings. They tended to be like later-born children (59% were reported satisfactory and 57% of later-born children, 2-sided; $p = .70$).

There were some examples in the study of favouritism to first-born children, especially with an absent parent wanting to see the first child but showing no interest in younger ones. One father telephoned his thirteen-year-old son regularly but never asked to speak to his younger son who was 11. Another always remembered his older daughter's birthday but not that of her younger sister.

The special position of first-born children tends to create closer ties with their parents. They are the first embodiment of their parents' hopes for offspring and the recipients of all parental attention for a time. As a result, they are likely to be more sensitive to their parents' needs, so that they may be used by parents as a source of comfort during the crisis of separation. Younger children on the other hand may be perceived as a burden by parents during a separation. In some cases the separation may even have been precipitated by the arrival of the youngest child, as discussed in the Introduction.

We might expect an "only" child to have some of the same advantages as the first-born child in enjoying a special relationship with his parents. "Only" children, however, have some disadvantages. They have no siblings to lend support through the transition to becoming a single-parent family. They may be more aware of conflicting loyalties to their two parents as they are conscious of being the only child to each of them.

The above findings tend to support the comparative advantage of first-born children when a family breaks up, adding to the other research on sibling position in the family. "Only" children did not seem to share this advantage, possibly because there were offsetting disadvantages. Generally, the characteristics associated with the best school performance among children from these divorcing families were those of being first-born, female, and younger than age 11 when the separation occurred.

Visiting
The question of visits to children when parents divorce creates problems which may persist long after custody has been settled and maintenance payments have settled into a predictable pattern. The Court usually makes a ruling about access to the children for the absent parent, but it is the willingness of parents to co-operate that determines whether visiting becomes a source of support to the child, a battleground for the parents, or whether it dwindles and lapses completely.

Lack of Visiting
The most significant finding in this study was the lack of visiting by absent parents as shown in Table 13.2.

Table 13.2
Visiting by Absent Parents

Frequency	Children visited by fathers		Children visited by mothers	
	Number	%	Number	%
Weekly	73	15.9	28	17.2
Regular (less than weekly, at least monthly)	51	11.1	24	14.7
Irregular (less than monthly)	57	12.4	40	24.5
None (absent parent lives less than 2 hrs. away)	140	30.5	29	17.8
None (absent parent lives more than 2 hrs. away)	138	30.1	42	25.8
Totals*	459	100.0	163	100.0

*These totals do not include children living with the parent whose visiting is being considered: 107 children living with fathers and 403 children living with mothers.

Over 60% of the children whose fathers were absent received no visits from them, while 44% of those whose mothers were absent received no visits from them.

One reason for not visiting expressed by some parents was a desire to avoid pain. As one father said, "If I don't see my children, it doesn't hurt so much." Another said that he avoided visits because his daughter, age 5, always cried when he left and that he was afraid of crying too.

Some parents indicated that contacts with their children intensified their feelings of guilt about having separated. For example, a mother said that she could not explain to her daughter why she had left home, so she preferred not to see her. A father said that he avoided visiting because his daughter had not been given an explanation for the separation. Although he had left ten months earlier, his wife had told his daughter that he was working out of town rather than admit that a separation had occurred.

There were other parents who were inhibited from visiting because of the relationship with their ex-partners. An example was a mother who said that she quarrelled so much with her husband during the marriage that she could not face the prospect of another quarrel if she initiated visiting. Another said that she stopped visiting because her husband always lectured her about her past and present shortcomings. This lack of visiting may have facilitated the parents' adjustment but did not take into account the needs of the children. The effect on them is illustrated by the K family.

> Mr. K. took out Bruce, age 11, regularly but did not ask to see Jane, age 8, or Kim, age 6. He was soon go be getting custody of Bruce, while Kim and Jane would be staying with their mother. The girls were upset about their father's apparent lack of interest in them. From Mr. K.'s point of view, he was reluctant to ask to see the girls because he was afraid of an argument with his wife.

These feelings of antipathy were often shared by the parent with custody. Many of them expressed negative views about visiting, based in part on signs of disturbance of the child after visits. As a social worker in a child care agency, the author often observed foster children after visits with their natural parents. It was common for them to return to the foster home either overtired or hyperactive. Parents and children alike tended to be anxious about the visits and to react in extreme ways, especially when visits were infrequent. If a visit were enjoyable, they wanted to prolong it to the point of fatigue; if it fell short of expectations, they came back feeling disappointed.

Antagonism to visiting on the part of the custodial parent is likely to create inner conflict for the child. Often this antagonism is not directly expressed. In the writer's experience, many foster parents showed their displeasure by facial expressions, body tension, and irritability at visiting times. Children tended to respond by an apparent loss of interest in the visits. Similarly, a parent with custody who is ambivalent or negative about contacts with the other parent may cause conflict within the child by his or her attitude.

As mentioned, the law attempts to protect the child-parent relationship against antagonism between parents. This is done by setting up rights to access by the absent parent. Prior to a divorce, access is often arranged in a separation agreement. It would seem, however, that feelings such as those described above have a much greater influence than formal agreements. It was found, for example, that fathers who had written agreements about access were less likely to visit their children than those who did not. (Only 37% of fathers who had written agreements visited compared to 54% of those who did not, $p < .05$). The numbers for mothers could not be compared statistically as there were too few. The pattern with fathers suggests that it is likely to be the emotional aspects of visiting that inhibit parents rather than formal limits on access.

Another aspect of visiting was the distance between children and their non-custodial parents. Table 13.2 shows that half the fathers and over half the mothers who did not visit their children had moved to at least a distance of two hours' travel by automobile from one another. It is unlikely that there were practical reasons for all these people to have moved. Many of them wanted to escape familiar surroundings that would remind them of the loss of their families. In such cases, the child's need for contact with the parent was secondary to the parent's personal concerns.

The priority given by parents to their own needs was also suggested by the visiting patterns of fathers when the mother was living in a new union with the children. Children might be expected to have less need for visiting when they had a substitute father living with them. Yet these fathers visited as often as those where the mother lived alone (61%, compared to 58% when the mother lived alone, 2-sided, p = .71). Thus many children had no apparent father figure in their lives while others had two.

Effects of Visits on the Children

In view of the different visiting patterns and the strong feelings of many parents on the subject, it seems important to find some objective indicators of the possible effects of visiting on children. One approach is to relate the children's functioning in school to the visiting they received.

It was found that there was an association between good school functioning and regular but not too frequent visits. Children who were visited regularly, at least monthly but less than once a week, were more likely to have no school problems (71%) than those who were visited irregularly (55%: p<.04) or those seen weekly (56%: p<.04). There was not a significant difference in the behaviour of children who were never seen or those whose absent parent lived far away.

Less frequent, but regular visits would be inclined to give the child the security of consistent visits without the disruption of constantly shifting back and forth between homes. In contrast to this, children who are visited irregularly have to live with uncertainty. Many of the parents who visited irregularly tended to make promises to visit more often, but did not follow through. This is likely to add to the child's uncertainty and disappointment, as shown in the following case:

> Tom, age 6, saw his father on an irregular basis. Tom did not express his feelings about his father to his mother, but he did so with his teacher. After an incident when his father had promised to take Tom out and had not appeared, he told his teacher that he didn't have a father.

It has been noted earlier that if the degree of predictability is not enough to allow the child to identify with his environment, some degree of personality disorganization will result. If visiting is very irregular, it may be more beneficial to a child to have no contacts with the absent parent. This leaves the child free to form an identification elsewhere.

As for weekly visiting, this may interrupt life in the primary home and create anxiety for a child. It usually means that the child spends one or two days of the weekend in the home of the absent parent. The latter home usually has different rules from his or her primary home, thus the child must re-adapt with every change. It is also difficult for a child to keep up relationships with school and neighbourhood friends if he or she is away every weekend. The anxiety connected with weekly visiting is illustrated by the following case.

> Jean, age 9, asked her teacher every day when Wednesday would be coming. The teacher discovered that Jean's mother visited every Wednesday. Jean's overconcern and apparent reluctance to ask this question of her father at home indicated that she was very anxious about the visits.

From the foregoing, it appears that both irregular and weekly visiting have disadvantages. The first may leave a child feeling insecure while the second may disrupt normal activities. On the other hand, regular but less frequent visiting reassures the child of his or her parent's interest without disturbing the continuity of day-to-day life.

To summarize the findings on visiting, there was a predominance of families where contact had ceased between the absent parent and the children; there was also a substantial minority where children were seen irregularly. Indications were that some parents felt the need to protect themselves from the pain of seeing their children. Contrary to expectation, written agreements were not associated with more visiting by fathers, nor was there more contact when the mother lived alone with the children.

It was found that regular, but not too frequent visits was associated with better functioning in school. This involved a minority of the children in the study. Generally the visiting patterns were not those that were likely to be most helpful to the child; rather the circumstances of the parents seemed to have precedence over the child's need to maintain a relationship.

Conclusions

The findings on custody indicated that only about 70% of children lived with their mothers; almost 20% were with their fathers, while 10% lived with neither parent. Reasons for a mother relinquishing custody did not seem to be related to her adequacy as a parent but more to her personal interests, such as extramarital relationships. Mothers who were or had been involved with another man were much less likely to have custody, yet children who were living with a parent in a new union were no more likely to have problems according to teachers' reports. These findings are in accord with statements by McRuer,[10] Harris,[8] and Wuenster[20] that custody is often decided according to the parents' own interests.

The financial arrangements made by most divorcing families were not usually adequate for the support of dependent children. No absent mothers contributed toward the support of children, and only 41% of fathers did so voluntarily. Another 12% paid regularly through the Family Court, but almost as many were in arrears on their payments. The amount paid also tended to be insufficient, probably because it was based on the limited incomes of most fathers.

Visiting showed a strong positive correlation with the payment of support. The relationship between these two variables was maintained, to a lesser degree, even when payments were made under duress.

The findings on the effect of marriage breakdown on children suggested that there was some maladjustment, but the children's behaviour did not differ greatly from those in the non-divorced population. The present results are fairly consistent with those from the 1930 White House Conference[18] and with those of LeMasters[9] and Bernard.[1] Contrary to the findings of the Gluecks,[6] delinquent behaviour was not significantly greater than in the normal population. About one-third of the children had problems at school according to their teachers. Usually this took the form of withdrawal, although some children tended to be aggressive and disruptive. Both withdrawal and aggression have been characterized as symptoms of anger by a psychologist studying children from broken homes (see Reference 8. Harris, page 11). As mentioned in the Introduction, such behaviour is probably an attempt by the child to regain the security that has been lost. Very few children talked to their teachers about their family problems, but tended to express their feelings indirectly.

There were indications from the individual families that some parents had difficulty controlling their children because the children used the conflict between the parents to their own advantage. This is consistent with Harris' finding[8] that children of divorce often try to control their parents.

Variables which seemed to affect adjustment were sex, age, and sibling position. The findings on sex agreed with those of Strean,[17] while findings on age accorded with general knowledge about child development. The findings on sibling position add to the ideas of Christensen[3] and to the earlier work of this writer.

Visiting of children by the non-custodial parent was generally in the parent's interest, not that of the child. Many parents avoided contact as noted in the other Canadian studies by Messinger[11] and Schlesinger.[15] There was frequent resistance to visiting by parents with custody as noted by Goode.[7] The right to access as part of a written separation agreement was negatively associated with visiting. Children who were living with their mothers were no more likely to see their fathers than those who had substitute fathers. Parents used visiting to meet their own needs, as a bargaining point with their spouse, a position consistent with the work of Harris[8] and Egleson.[5] The association of visiting patterns with child adjustment needs further study to test the suggestion that regular, less frequent visiting is best.

In general, the findings indicated that the children of divorcing families are often left with meagre resources in terms of financial and emotional support from absent parents. In addition, decisions made about custody do not seem to be based upon the child's needs. The courts are oriented to the interests of the children in divorce cases, but in matters of custody it is difficult for them to change arrangements made by parental agreement. From the above findings it would seem that the courts might do more for the child regarding financial contributions. In relation to visiting, it appears that the courts should be encouraging contact with the absent parent.

Despite the inadequacies identified in arrangements for children, the children as a group did not seem to be particularly maladjusted. The general impression left by the findings, in the context of the literature, is that divorcing families are particularly lacking in resources and responsiveness to children's needs, but that the children do relatively well despite these disadvantages.

References

1. Bernard, Jesse. *Remarriage*. New York: Dryden Press, 1956.
2. Bohannan, P. *Divorce and After*. New York: Doubleday and Co., 1970.
3. Christensen, H.T. *Handbook of Marriage and the Family*. Chicago: Rand McNally and Co., 1964.
4. Despert, L. *Children of Divorce*. New York: Doubleday and Co., 1962.
5. Egleson, Jim, and Egleson, Janet. *Parents without Partners*. New York: E.P. Dutton & Co., 1961.
6. Glueck, Sheldon, and Glueck, Eleanor, *Unravelling Juvenile Delinquency*. Cambridge: Harvard University Press, 1950.
7. Goode, William J. *Women in Divorce*. New York: The Free Press, 1956.
8. Harris, M.W., "The Child as Hostage," in Stuart and Abt, eds., *Children of Separation and Divorce*. New York: Grossman Publishers, 1972, pp. 7-17.
9. LeMasters, E.E. "Holy Deadlock: A Study of Unsuccessful Marriages." *The Midwest Sociologist* (July 1959), pp. 86-91.
10. McRuer, J.C. *Proceedings of the Special Joint Committee of the Senate and House of Commons on Divorce*. Ottawa: Queen's Printer, 1967.
11. Messinger, Lillian. "Remarriage between Divorced People with children from Previous Marriages." *Journal of Marriage and Family Counsellors*, 1976.
12. Nye and Hoffman. *The Employed Mother in America*. Chicago: Rand McNally and Co., 1963.
13. Palmer, S. "Children in Long-term Care: The Worker's Contribution." *Journal of Ontario Association of Children's Aid Societies* (April 1974), pp. 1-14.
14. Palmer, S. "Reasons for Marriage Breakdown." *Journal of Comparative Family Studies* (Autumn 1971), pp. 251-262.
15. Schlesinger, Benjamin. "Children of Divorced Parents in Second Marriages," in Stuart and Abt, eds. *Children of Separation and Divorce*. New York: Grossman Publishers, 1972.
16. Statistics Canada. *Vital Statistics*, Vol. 2, Marriage and Divorces Catalogue #84-205, 1974.
17. Strean, H. "Treatment of Mothers and Sons in the Absence of the Father." *Social Work* (July 1961), pp. 29-35.
18. White House Conference, 1972 (report on 1930 study), pp. 117-118.
19. White House Conference on Child Health and Protection, *The Adolescent in the Family*. New York: Arno Press, 1972.
20. Wuenster, T.J. "Canadian Law and Divorce," in S. Parvez Wakil, ed. *Marriage, Family and Society*. Scarborough: Butterworth and Company, 1975, pp. 295-316, 397.

14/Factors in Marital Break-up: Separation and Divorce Decision-Making

Robert N. Whitehurst,
Gerald Booth, and
Mohammad Hanif

A renewed interest in continuing high divorce rates is indicated in Canada and the United States by a recurrent emphasis in the popular press on the subject. As well, agencies in both countries have given more funds for research and have focalized some of the issues recently on divorce. This paper is a preliminary report of a small but unique study of factors entering into separation and divorce decisions by 369 Southwestern Ontario respondents who have experienced at least one separation of some duration.

There is a relative dearth of socio-psychologically related material on divorce in North America. On the one hand, we can find good demographic analyses and some estimates of the probable causes and background factors related to divorce decisions, but few studies can be found that investigate the interactions, feelings, and problems from a micro-sociological viewpoint. Waller,[5] in his early essay on marriage-alienation probably set the tone for some basic research, but the difficulty of doing good research in the area has made studies sparse. Goode's Detroit study[2] still stands as one of the few empirical orientations to the problems related to divorce decisions, because few have followed his lead. Popular sociology abounds with case histories; these have often proved insightful, but have limitations in furthering understanding (Kitson, 1976).* The purpose of this study is to provide some information on the impacts of changing sex roles, sexuality, careers, jobs, and children on the decision to separate. Also, some of the problematic areas of adjustment for those experiencing separations are investigated.

---

*Kitson notes that data are needed to test the points made in all of these monographs (six of which are reviewed briefly in the article). This study is an attempt to face some of the issues raised by Kitson in the review cited (see Reference 3, page 446).

Sample and Method

The sample is non-random and consists of 369 persons recently separated or divorced in Southwestern Ontario. The sample was interviewed by sociology students who were given training as part of the course in sociology. Students conducted from one to ten interviews personally, although the interview schedule was self-explanatory as an open-ended, focussed-interview format. Students were instructed to probe for details and for more information when respondents were willing to discuss in more detail the issues in their cases. The 369 cases were then coded on IBM format, translating the qualitative data into quantitative categories. Only one student in the graduate programme was responsible for this task, placing the entire onus for coder reliability and the problems of such coding in the hands of the student and his or her supervisor. Close supervision and reworking of several of the problematic categories was necessary: we are satisfied that we have eliminated all the possible biasses within the confines of this style of work.*

Sample Characteristics

For this sample, 134 males (36%) and 235 females (64%) were interviewed.** The mean age was about 30 years, the modal-age category being between ages 26 and 30. The mean duration of marriage was between five and six years.

Occupationally, the sample comprised about one-third service-connected persons, 19% professionals, and less than 10% either blue-collar or white-collar workers (self-defined).

The mean number of children of the marriages in the sample was 1.45, with 25% of the families having just one child. Of the 214 cases

---

*The authors would like to note that although this method of data collection does not warrant the title "scientific" in the most rigorous sense, we feel that the value of the data cannot be overlooked in terms of insights into the dynamics of separation and divorce. Thus, we make no claims beyond the purposes of the data but feel that the data warrant serious consideration on their own merit as important socio-psychological pieces of information which together are important clues for research.

**We feel that the proportion of the sample that is male is relatively high for such a study and makes the study important from the vantage point of data collected from males.

reporting on the child-custody relationship, 91% of the mothers retained the children, while nearly 5% of the respondents had an arrangement whereby the children were either "shared" regularly or the children in the family were split up among the parents.* An apparently non-permanent and somewhat illegal adaptation seems to be occurring in some cases, where the couple lives in the same house but does not have an intimate relationship. This adaptation has been called "distancing," in which former mates tend to treat each other as fellow roomers rather than as spouses.** It seems to have limited relevance now, but may be increasing as a form of temporary adaptation.

The mean number of separations (of more than a few days duration and interpreted as "serious" separations by respondents) was 1.9. Of the total, 86% had experienced three or fewer separations of this nature.

Among those husbands who perceived their wives to be in a struggle for liberation and equality, 46% said that their wives wanted equality of sex-roles, jobs, and a general decrease in double-standards, while 24% claimed that their wives were after sexual liberation, including the freedom to engage in sex with outsiders. However, 79% did not respond to this item, which leaves unclear the status of liberation-seeking for most in the sample. There were no significant differences for males and females on this item.

With respect to household division of labour, wives were about four times more likely to complain that husbands were inadequate in terms of expectations than vice-versa. Husbands did not generally see housekeeping as a large item in terms of separation or divorce-seeking.

Wives also tended to feel that husbands abuse them much more frequently than vice-versa. Wives' most frequent complaint about

---

*Unless otherwise specified in this paper, percentages reported will refer to the proportion of the sample answering that item on the interview schedule.

**This term is sometimes used by therapists to describe the phenomenon of sharing a house—but no longer sharing life together. It is often a temporary expedient, until one or other of the spouses is in a position to move out. It thus serves the double function of continued testing—in the event that the couple in some instances may recreate a viable relationship, and at the same time make it economically feasible to make the transition to another residence. Most couples who adopt this behaviour seem to finally split up in separation or divorce.

being dominated by husbands was that the men gave orders and used verbal abuse (77% claimed this, 49% said that the husband gave orders, 28% said that he used verbal abuse). Thirteen percent also claimed that their spouses used physical abuse that was instrumental in their deciding to seek a separation or divorce. By way of contrast, only 40% of the husbands in the sample claimed that their wives used verbal abuse; the only other response worth noting was that wives were seen as making one-sided decisions (27%). It is obvious that women's complaints are roughly twice as frequent or more in terms of feeling dominated or abused by the spouse. The ratio of male-female physical brutality or violence was 14/3. Three percent of the men in the sample admitted to being physically attacked by wives.

There was also a significant difference in the frequency of feelings registered by the sexes in terms of perceptions of failure of emotional support. Although both males and females claimed a high proportion of neglect of the emotionally supportive side of marriage, females more frequently complained, with 52% as compared with 48% of the husbands who responded to this item. They (both males and females) claimed that their feelings had been ignored. This may in fact be a crucial point at which the separation decision is often made, when this recognition occurs. Three times as many wives as husbands felt that there was too little talk of problems. On the other hand, husbands were about two and a half times more likely to claim that the problem was one of too little caressing and touching. One is led to the suspicion that males might have implied that lack of sexual caressing was the problem; it is also likely that the old scenario was involved wherein the husband failed at emotional supportiveness and talk, while still expecting sexual rewards. Later case excerpts will investigate the frequency of this occurrence in this study. Wives also registered feelings of being belittled or put-down twice as frequently as husbands.

Husbands disapproved of wives working in 52% of the cases reporting, while about 22% of the wives claimed that their husbands expected them to both work outside the home and to keep house.

About one-third of the reporting wives claimed that there was some disapproval of the liberation movement on the part of husbands, while nearly half reported arguments or disagreements on the nature of the women's movement. It should be noted, however, that only about 20% of the total respondents answered this item.

Educational problems seem to cut both ways, as 36% of the wives said that they wanted more education, but their husbands prevented them getting it. On the other hand, 29% said that the disagreement was in terms of the husband wanting the wife to go back to school and the wife not being interested. Of those answering, 53% of the wives wanted either a career or to return to educational activity, but their husbands disapproved. Of the husbands, 28% wanted their wives to seek a job or career and the wives were not interested. It is obvious that women more frequently want outside activity that husbands will not support, but it is often the reverse case in which women do not wish to pursue outside interests. This, of course, may be due in part to the institutionalization of a woman who has been trapped in a limiting housewife role for some time, and may in some cases simply reflect a woman's insecurity in making the initial step outward—and who becomes stopped by inertia.

Changing sexual values or patterns of behaviour were involved in the following ways: wife's low sex-drive, 15%, husband's low sex-drive, 23%. The incidence of adultery was seen as affecting the separation and divorce decision nearly four times as often for wives (whose husbands had committed adultery) than vice versa. Struggles and complexities of dealing with more open types of marriage was cited as a changing sexual problem for 21% of the cases.

With respect to other sexual problems, sexual non-co-operation was cited by 56% of those responding, while 20% said that they were turned off by the partner's alcohol abuse; another 10% simply cited sexual incompatibility.

In those cases, where children were present, 44% said that their presence was a deterrent to, or tended to delay, the separation and divorce decision. In 17% of these cases, the children were seen as causally linked to the sequence leading to separation. There was serious disagreement on childrearing in 15% of the cases, while 13% disagreed on whether or not to have children.

In rank order, the items cited as most crucial to the decision to get a separation were: 1) spouse no longer responded with feelings of love and/or communication, 2) adultery, 3) husband left, 4) failure of co-operation in household (and generally), 5) brutality, 6) sexual non-co-operation, 7) in-law problems. About 40% saw the problems involved in communications and chronic conflicts as crucial. In nearly 19% of the cases, the rationale was provided that the spouse was telling lies and making excuses for behaviour that was unacceptable.

The most frequent specific reason for the break-up was the involvement of another person (18%). Personality incompatibility was cited as the second most often direct cause. Other reasons given were drinking, brutality, or spouse wanting more sex.

In about half the cases, the wife was the person who left, while 37% of the husbands made the decision to leave. In 13% of the cases, the decision was mutual as to who should leave or how the actual separation should be handled. From this, it is apparent that separation is not often a mutual decision.

In terms of adapting to the new status of "separated," the following unanticipated problems were cited: loneliness and companionship-deprivation (29%) and social isolation (21%). Social deprivation and loneliness make up half those problems that are of a severity unanticipated. The third-ranked response, however, (15%) claimed that there were no unanticipated problems in separation. Economic problems were fourth-ranked.

The advice offered by the subjects who had gone through the separation and divorce process was as follows: In 39% of the cases, the advice simply was "do it." Many apparently felt it better to separate than to continue the struggle. About 26% said that the problem should be re-evaluated and to try for some kind of amicable settlement. About 21% said that professional help should be sought (even though their own experience with this was extremely limited, see below). Some fewer respondents suggested not delaying separation and divorce because of children, or to seek a trial separation. Women were twice as likely to recommend getting professional help as men.

Women were much more likely to say that their attempts at com-

---

*This may reflect in part what appears to be a fact from these data, that men are poor communicators in marriage and that they have, perhaps, a highly truncated sense of success or failure in communications. Of course, other interpretations are possible, but this one seems fairly obvious. In many of the cases, people had lost all desire to communicate with each other because of past chronic conflicts, and were either happy to stop trying to talk to the spouse or were just too weary and disgusted to try again. The responses, however, show a very large range of efforts at "communication" over the period of disruption and deterioration. It is likewise obvious from many responses that "communication" involved attempts at persuasion, threats, etc.

munications failed than men (63 versus 37% for men.)* Overall, 83% of the sample said that late efforts to communicate about their problems failed.

Of those who had some experience with counselling, 76% claimed that it was ineffective or that they received little or no help from it. Males were more likely to see counselling as helpful (39% versus 60% of females who said that it was of no avail). Less than 7% claimed that their late attempts at conciliation had any salutary effect. Many interpretations can be implied in this datum, but it is uncertain whether the crucial variable was the effort to salvage a relationship beyond repair, the unavailability of good counsel, or the fact that counselling is not really useful for persons nearing divorce.*

In any case, 61% claimed that they tried to get help and that it was not useful; 16% claimed that the counsel they used was simply ineffective; and less than 5% found counselling to be an effective means of helping them cope with their problems.

Some Male/Female Differences

Among the most striking of the findings of this study must be noted the differing responses of men and women to the same items. If any single and clear message is created by the data from this study, it is that men and women inhabit extremely different socio-psychological worlds and that their views vary tremendously. For example, the frequency of complaints about involvement in the household show a strict sex-role stereotyped response, with 79% of both males and females registering complaints about the opposite sex in this category. Wives claimed (at least 31% of them) that their husbands believed it was the sole duty of the wife to take care of the house. Some 55% also said that their husbands did not participate in any meaningful way in household chores.

---

*There are myriad reasons why counselling might "fail," including seeing counselling as a "failure" if it in fact frees up people to live less neurotic lives by themselves or with someone else. These interpretations obviously need much refinement to reflect the real reasons underlying the presumed failure of counsel. It is probable that most people have unrealistic expectations on going into counselling; failure is thus probably built into a great number of cases called to the attention of counsellors and agencies. Let us hope that, as professionals, we have gone beyond the image of counselling effectiveness as being involved only with reconciliation. Helping people obtain a reasonable divorce can be a most socially useful activity.

Only four respondents of the total said that their *own* low sex-drive was a problem in the relationship (two males and two females). Although the husband's low sex-drive is more often seen as a problem in the relationship, the husband's adultery is frequently seen as a problem. This is in part because female adultery simply occurs less frequently. The husband's low sex-drive was most often ranked as a problem, followed by problems in open marriages, adultery, and wife's low sex-drive. These problems, if they represent anything like the normal ones in contemporary divorces, do present some different aspects of sexuality. Nearly one-third of the females said that the husband's adultery was a serious problem, while few males cited the wife's adultery. Men more frequently, however, did complain about sexual non-co-operation (67% versus 49% for women).

A perhaps unexpected finding dealing with children was that men more frequently claimed the separation was delayed because of the presence of children (54% versus 39% for females).* Also, women were about three times as likely to say that children were implicated in a causal way with the separation and divorce than men. This can probably be explained because of the inordinate nearness of mothers, in terms of their lives, to children—even though it is not "moral" for mothers to express such negative feelings as these. There was no difference in the expression of males and females with respect to the proportions saying that they disagreed with spouses over childrearing.

Somewhat more men than women claimed their status-aspirations were a problem in the relationship. A somewhat larger proportion of men than women (27% versus 20%) wanted more money, status, and prestige. From comments, however, it is obvious that career- and job-problems can cut both ways in these days of high employment of both men and women.[1] Both can spend so much time, and develop such commitments to jobs and careers that there is little time to devote to maintenance of a meaningful relationship.** The usual problem appears to be the disparity of spouses' desires for levels of commitment

---

*This may, in part, reflect the very limited input of males into the lives of children. Men may have little desire to separate when children are present because they see little of them and often seem to like them.

**There is a great number of complications reported in our data with respect to work, careers, and relationships; many wives saw husbands as being lazy, chauvinistic,

to work and careers. It often seems that there is no real agreement on the importance of this in marriage. The most frequent complaint is that men place too much emphasis on their career-development. Of course the reward structure of our society precludes serious fatherhood and spousehood.

In terms of post-separation problems, 64% of the women and 36% of the men said that they suffered unanticipated loneliness and companionship-deprivation problems. Also, women mentioned economic problems as being severe four times as often as men did.

Women who had felt extremely dominated by their husbands were less likely to record unanticipated problems after separating. It may be that the sense of relief from the presence of a tyrannical husband may create an easier separation experience. Dominance by the husband, who tends to play boss and give lots of orders, was associated with the highest rate of wife's departing (52%), verbal abuse was the second most frequent reason (24%), while physical abuse was the third most frequent reason (18%) for the wife leaving.

The occasion of the wife leaving was also associated with having a husband who believed that housework was the sole duty of the wife (82% of wives who parted from husbands). Also, arguments and non-communications were often recorded by those wives who claimed that their husbands felt that housework was for women, those husbands having no regular household duties (75%).

In the case of husbands departing, 64% of these cases were associated with the husband either wanting extramarital sex or having in fact committed adultery. It can be seen from these data that there is a clear pattern of male-female disparity that helps to account for problems which become serious enough to lead to a separation or divorce.

---

two-faced, and simply irresponsible and negligent. Since we have a higher proportion of female responses in the data, one could easily be led to believe that men (at least those involved in separation and divorce experiences) are a sorry lot of immature boys who want to be taken care of and not have to face responsibility. Perhaps men come off more often as extremists with respect to careers—either experiencing what their wives term under-involvement or over-involvement—in either case the consequence can be detrimental to home and family life.

Some Observations from Qualitative Data

The following comments involve some observations discovered on rereading the original interview schedules, many of which escaped the coder's notes. Although it is obvious that this section of the reporting will suffer even more serious bias because of selective perception, it is an honest effort to summarize some of the recurrent themes and variations on the separation and divorce experience.

Although sexuality was not a major direct cause of marital breakdown in a large number of our cases, closer reading of the comments made by respondents gives the distinct impression that sexuality as a battleground for power, privilege, and identity was a powerful force in this sample. Indirectly or directly, sexuality was or tended to become an area of worry, deprivation, matter for loss of control over a spouse, or in other ways came to indicate lack of caring in a large number of instances. The problem of greatly differing expectations and "performance" in roles, including that of sexuality becomes more obvious on close observation of the case materials. In a very real measure, the sense of loss of credibility, trust, and simple courtesy to spouses as separation and divorce become more possible is nearly always reflected in changes in sexuality. One husband tended to sum up for many his feelings when he said (on finding someone who would listen to him), "I found somebody who'd listen to my problems." Without measures of interaction between spouses, we have no way of getting at the subtler shadings of meaning in statements like these. We know that spouses' definitions of the situation become changed when they do not find what they need within marriage.

Alcohol, other women (and men), careers (in both their failure to develop and their "overdevelopment"), the tendency to bicker, and the simple fact that husbands seem not to spend much time at home giving what seems necessary to the relationship, all seem crucial to development of the separation and divorce experience. Males simply seem to wander, to be away, and even on their own admission do not take much part in the lives of their children and wives.

When we recognize the male-absence pattern and match this with the frequent report (by women at least) that their men had extremely frail and large egos that needed constant bolstering, we can begin to see an emerging pattern as to why women seek something better. It is clear that with the trends toward continuing efforts of women to achieve equality and to discourage double standards, men are in for harder times in sustaining the kinds of relationships often reported in this study; that is, men will in the future probably have to either face more frequent separations or learn to give more to more closely meet female expectations. The impact and spirit of the women's movement is undoubtedly larger than recognized by the women subjects in the many and subtle ways that the new sentiments have affected their lives. Most are not declared liberationists, but the impact is there nonetheless. One wife, trying for a long period to salvage a marriage that ultimately disintegrated said it for many, "We lived for a long time in polite hostility." Women are now less willing to do this for quite so long as they once were.

Although we at times have felt that we are nearly past the time when divorce and separations were considered to be stigmatic, a large number of respondents (mostly female) reported that among their unanticipated problems was one of solidifying their social networks in their new status. Many said that even their own families seemed not to relate to them at all well and that old friends practically shunned them. The impression was that perhaps one who had become "contaminated" by separation and divorce might cause a chain reaction—or at least create some kind of unpleasantness by reminding others of the potential demise, or whatever, of their own relationships. People seemed singularly unable to relate openly to those who had separation and divorce experiences. This implies that separated or divorced persons often have to develop new networks of friends; these are often similar types who have been through the trials of separation and divorce (usually of the same sex). Sheresky and Mannes[4] point out that women with children, separated or divorced, are a drug on the matrimonial market. Our respondents verify this and add their affirmation to the old male belief system that all once-married females need sex regularly. One representative female said, "They all (men) want to know if you want 'your oil changed' and they are all anxious to help you on that score. Even more irritating is the fact they do not hesitate to use any language they choose to make clear their sexual objectives." Needless to add, the sense of frustration facing females in this situation is severe, chronic, and for most over 30 or so it is hopeless. It becomes easier to understand how women will put up with verbal and physical abuse, badgering and difficult situations in marriage when we see the alternatives open clearly to them: being rejected and treated coolly by friends, relatives, and peers; being seen as "fair-game" by any male on the prowl, facing double standards in which the freedom to move about in the world and to make a living freely are not realities, and being confined with children—in a status they never dreamed would befall them at the time of their marriages.[6]*

Summary and Conclusions

This study tends to support, at least by implication if not by direct replication, the conclusions cited by Goode.[2] Wives who seek divorce and separations see men as at fault in a number of crucial areas in terms of their expectations: lack of participation in the household, giving verbal and physical abuse, giving orders and not considering the feelings of wives, and in not talking about problems. Husbands at times disapprove of wives taking jobs or pursuing careers and education, and they often either disagree with the women's movement aims or disapprove of their wives being a part of it. Husbands are seen to fail in terms of being active enough sexually, but this is coupled with the failure of emotional supportiveness in some important ways. Husbands also tend to be involved more frequently in what must be construed as serious adultery that disrupts the marital relationship. Women are more often seen to view attempts at communication and problem-solving with husbands as troublesome and inadequate.

In turn, men's problems and complaints about women seem fewer but no less real. Neglect of the husband's feelings and the lack of caressing, including sexual co-operation, seem to be big complaints of husbands seeking separations. If Goode's analysis of the process of alienation and separation is correct, it is likely that for many of our cases the husband withdrew from communications (probably into work or other outside interests) with the wife, which in turn helped to

---

*Weiss claims that the tendency to either stay with, or return to, an unsatisfactory relationship is very strong. He calls this the "attachment" phenomenon. Obviously fear of the unknown and the institutionalization into the normal routines and roles of marriage do not prepare persons for the eventuality of separation. It is against these kinds of problems that those separating must work and no one claims the alternatives are easy in the short run—or even in the long run for a number of divorced people.

create an atmosphere of alienation. These dynamics are difficult to reverse once they are set in motion and no doubt account for a large proportion of separations. Sometimes husbands wanted wives to work and/or go to school, but the wives were unwilling. Of course, we know that in many cases husbands are unwilling to share the load equally or even nearly so, to create an atmosphere of support for such ventures on the part of wives. The encapsulation and institutionalization of the wife in traditional roles also may play a part in her unwillingness to go outside the home for educational or occupational purposes.

Such problems as "personal incompatibility" and the problem of communications are such that they reflect the popular folklore of marital disharmony rather than analysis. Whitehurst[7] has offered an analysis of the role of communications in marriage that differs from the popular notion. Modern marriage may place too heavy a burden of expectations in that we believe good communications can resolve nearly all problems. Extremely different expectations, values, and highly disparate socialization experiences of men and women make communications—of any variety—doubtful as a means to solving a number of marital problems. The problem of "personal incompatibility" may have some psychological relevance, but is not very useful as a tool in sociology. Rather, the structural aspects of marital supports (or the lack thereof) should be stressed as causal in most relationship break-ups. The loss of community—those watchful eyes that used to control behaviour adequately—are now all but gone, the family no longer exercises real pressures for conformity, and the church has all but lost its means to provide meaningful guidelines for behaviour that keeps people conventional. When this loss of structure is understood as combining with the disparate socialization experiences of men and women growing up in this culture, we can develop a powerful means of comprehending the separation and divorce experience of a great and expanding number of people today.

Separation and divorce are once more becoming popular as recurrent subjects in human affairs. This study should provide some further hypotheses about the changing problems and functions of this social phenomenon. It appears at this time that nothing short of an overhaul of the male/female socialization systems coupled with the development of marriage supports will create a climate of true marital stability. It seems too Utopian to hope for even minor changes at this moment, but we can become more aware of the implications of non-action and perhaps develop means to cope with high divorce rates.

One conclusion from all this is that marriage is very difficult to sustain—at least in terms of the expectations of women and men today. Men, at least in a large number of cases, seem poorly prepared for marriage. This is, in part, caused by their early socialization and preparation for adulthood, which create a sense of mastery and toughness in orienting men to the world. These are not attributes which make for success in marital relations, even though they help men achieve occupational success—the greatest source of rewards yet for men. This "success" is very likely frustrated at least in some measure for most men because of a number of factors, including high aspirations for nearly all men—which must be scaled to reality after maturity. The result is a sense of frustration, which is often vented against the nearest available emotional object, the wife.

For women, their very high expectations of emotional success in the family are often thwarted. There is little reality training for women to prepare them for the hardness of daily life with children and husbands. Husbands have their own problems—that they are often unwilling to share for a number of reasons. Men seem unable to give what is required of them by women in modern marriage—a sense of continuing love and support, including help with the household and the children. Thus, the consequences of these factors become obvious. The loss of structural supports for the maintenance of the web ensuring "conformity" to the community's standards, to religion's expectations, and to the family's demands is weakened significantly today. Unfortunately, as the marriage institution weakens, it becomes even more necessary for the personal survival of most, since there are few real and useful alternatives at present.

References

1. Butler, Peter M. "Single and Dual-Earning and Family Involvement in the World World," in K. Ishwaran, ed. *The Canadian Family*, 2nd ed. Toronto: Holt, Rinehart and Winston, 1976, pp. 310-324.

2. Goode, Wm. J. *After Divorce*. New York: The Free Press, 1956.

3. Kitson, Gay C. In review of Jos. Epstein, *Divorced in America*. New York: E.P. Dutton & Co., 1974. Review in *Contemporary Sociology 5*, no. 4, (July 1976), pp. 465-466.

4. Sheresky, Norman, and Mannes, Marya. *Uncoupling: A Guide to Sane Divorce*. New York: Viking Press, 1972, Ch. 3 "Affairs," pp. 31-35.

5. Waller, Willard, and Hill, Reuben. *The Family: A Dynamic Interpretation*. New York: Dryen Press, 1951.

6. Weiss, Robert S. "The Emotional Impact of Separation," in *Journal of Social Issues* 32, No. 1, (Winter 1976—issue on Divorce and Separation), pp. 135-146.

7. Whitehurst, Robert N. "Youth Views Marriage: Some Comparisons of Two Generation Attitudes of University Students," in Roger W. Libby and Robert N. Whitehurst, eds. *Renovating Marriage*. San Ramon, Calif.: Consensus Publishers, 1973, pp. 269-279.